W9-DGL-494

GODS OF SOCCER

Also by Men in Blazers

Encyclopedia Blazertannica

MEN IN BLAZERS
PRESENT

GODS OF SOCCER

THE PANTHEON OF THE
100 GREATEST SOCCER PLAYERS*

*According to Us

ROGER BENNETT, MICHAEL DAVIES
& MIRANDA DAVIS

CHRONICLE PRISM

Design by Paul Kepple, Headcase Design.

Typeset in Chromaletter Combo, Gza, Plantin, and Proxima Nova.

10 9 8 7 6 5 4 3 2

Chronicle books and gifts are available at special quantity discounts to corporations, professional associations, literacy programs, and other organizations. For details and discount information, please contact our premiums department at corporatesales@chroniclebooks.com or at 1-800-759-0190.

 CHRONICLE PRISM

Chronicle Prism is an imprint of Chronicle Books LLC, 680 Second Street, San Francisco, California 94107

chronicleprism.com

To our Great Friends of the Pod,
whose passion, joy, and creativity sustain us.
And to the memory of OG GFOP
Jason Kennedy (1970–2020) #YNWA

CONTENTS

INTRODUCTION

Can we be clear up front? To create a definitive list of the 100 greatest ever to have played football is an act of folly undertaken only by those who like to grab the third rail. One of the true joys of football is that no two fans' experience of it is the same. Everybody sees the game, the characters, and the key moments differently. That is what makes football the world's most compelling collective narrative. A shared text we all develop our own interpretations of, articulating and defending them with the heat of a thousand suns.

So, we present this book to you with a sense of joy and delight and an element of mischief. It is our hope you will revel in the depictions of players you adore, discover some stories you have never heard, then foam and fume at our idiocy, which can be the only plausible explanation as to why your favorite player is not included. That is the point of football. In the words of that great poet-philosopher Jürgen Klopp, it is "the most important least important thing," safely enabling us to experience every possible human emotion and walk away unscathed. It is the arguments and differences that make us feel alive.

So, to our 100, drawn up by the entire Men in Blazers staff. Many are players we have been blessed to watch perform the ineffable with our own eyes. Others are part of the lore we inherited from stories told by our parents and grandparents, who talked of their feats as if they were characters in ballads or woven into tapestries as in days of yore. Still more are legends in the ether, pioneers of the early game universally accepted as the giants on whose shoulders all who follow stand.

Everybody defines greatness differently. To be clear, greatness is not defined solely by glory. To us, football is about something more than winning trophies. The game is a mirror that reflects the politics, culture, and history of the societies surrounding it. In the individual moments of play, humanity itself is revealed. The great English commentator Martin Tyler once told us, "Football is a simple game in which a player has three decisions to make on the ball. Should I pass, run, or shoot? The greatest players just make better decisions more of the time than the merely good ones."

We believe that, absolutely.

So, this is a book of incredible humans who consistently made remarkable decisions in ways that either changed the game or, on occasion, the world around them. There are winners galore in here for sure. But there are also gutsy pathfinders who braved singular journeys, and in doing so, became radical changemakers. This is a book about football, yes. But it is also a book about much that is good in life: dreams, loyalty, self-confidence, tenacity, creativity, empathy, and collective commitment.

One last word. The football we watched in England in the 1980s was a gloomy, local affair played by huff-and-puff blokes, on muddy pitches, surrounded by fans who were there, as much as anything, for a pre- or post-match fight. The game has since changed and become a global spectacle. Every magical moment from every nation is now instantly shared around the world. As such, the game has become much more about superlatives, exclamation points, and the transcendent. And ever more about true greatness. No matter whom we are watching, be it Messi or Ronaldo, Sam Kerr or Vivianne Miedema, we strive hard never to take it for granted, and to revel in it, aware we are making collective memories together in the act of watching. This book is presented to you in that spirit. Of fandom built on love, respect, wonder, and gratitude. Our hope, dear reader, is that football continues to empower you to make great memories with those you love.

Now go and put together your 100 and email us at meninblazers@gmail.com.

Courage.

—THE MEN IN BLAZERS TEAM

MICHELLE AKERS

N 1991, WOMEN'S SOCCER WAS starting to gain a footing in Europe and Asia, and FIFA, ever on trend, organized an international women's tournament for that fall. It would retroactively be endowed with the title of inaugural FIFA Women's World Cup, but at the time, it was called the 1st FIFA World Championship for Women's Football for the M&M's Cup. The coveted Mars corporate sponsorship. All the boys were jealous.

At the time, the US had an embryonic women's team on their hands, having only established a national women's program seven years before. The United States Soccer Federation (US Soccer) sent the team to China for the M&M's Cup with a part-time coach and hand-me-down kits borrowed from the boys' youth team. Ten-dollar-a-day stipends in their pockets, the women subsisted mostly on peanut butter sandwiches and complimentary candy bars for the duration of the tournament. What they lacked in fitted garments and pocket money, however, they made up for in skill. Drawing from a generation of Title IX–backed women's college soccer players, the team was brimming with talent and experience.

Leading that team was a 5'10" 25-year-old with the most '80s mullet mop of curly hair you've ever seen. Her name was Michelle Akers. A four-time All-American and the University of Central Florida's all-time leading scorer, Akers can only be described as a one-woman phenomenon. Overflowing with confidence, strength, and precision, she was capable of steamrolling the opposition like they were sidewalk cracks. Akers found a way to reach every ball, every header. Combining control and pure physicality, she would dribble straight past defenders, brushing them to the side like gnats. And her shots—so powerful and accurate they often appeared to have smoke coming off of them. The other teams had no idea what to do with her. In the quarterfinals against Chinese Taipei, she scored five goals in a single match, making her the only person to have achieved the feat in a World Cup, men's or women's, until the Russian Oleg Salenko matched her against Cameroon in 1994.

It's difficult to overstate the extent to which the 1991 World Cup was a nonevent in the States. It had no media coverage, no broadcast deal for anything other than the final, which aired on a six-hour tape delay on SportsChannel America for those intrepid enough to find it in the cable backwoods of *TV Guide*. The tournament barely registered as a blip on the radar of the American public. Not just that no one in the country was watching. No one even knew it was happening, or that their team had made it all the way to the final. If the US had lost, US Soccer would have shrugged, patted the girls on the back, and returned to their lunches.

And the US were minutes away from losing, with the score tied up at 1–1 in the final against Norway. With two minutes to go, Shannon Higgins sends a long pass out of midfield. Michelle Akers charges forward, but the ball lands straight at the feet of Norway defender Tina Svensson. The play looks like it's over. Everyone is already moving on to penalties in their minds. Everyone except Akers. Instead of stopping, she barrels right into Svensson, shoves her aside, snags the ball, hops over the diving keeper, transfers the ball to her right foot, and taps it into goal.

The public wasn't watching. Even US Soccer officials didn't bother coming over until the semifinals. Nothing less than a win was going to convince the Federation that the women were worth investing in. Undaunted, Akers literally elbowed the US women into relevance. Suddenly, here was a team that was exciting and dominant and determined. Here was a team that could win. So they got more support for the 1995 World Cup. Then even more for the 1996 Olympics. By 1999, the US was hosting the tournament, and the US women were front-page news. All on the back of Michelle Akers's sheer unstoppability.

FULL NAME:	DATE OF BIRTH:	PLACE OF BIRTH:	NATIONAL TEAM:	CAPS / GOALS:
Michelle Anne Akers	*February 1, 1966*	*Santa Clara, California, United States*	*United States, 1985–2000*	*153 / 105*

JOSÉ ANDRADE

BORN IMPOVERISHED AND ILLE-gitimate in Uruguay's second city, Salto, at the turn of the 20th century, José Andrade's story is shrouded in exotic whispers. He was rumored to have been fathered by a 98-year-old escaped Brazilian slave, an expert in African magic. Andrade worked as a carnival musician as a teenager; people claimed that he had also moonlighted as a gigolo. To be an athlete in the 1920s already had a certain mythic quality attached to it. To be a poor Black South American athlete in the 1920s, stepping out onto the world stage, was akin to strolling in from Mars.

The Uruguayans were the first South American team ever to appear in a world football tournament when they qualified for the 1924 Olympic Games in Paris after winning the Sudamericano the previous year. They were an unfunded team, filled with meat packers, marble cutters, ice salesmen, shoe shiners. They traveled to Paris third class, sleeping on wooden benches and stopping for a brief exhibition tour in Spain beforehand to finance the trip. Ahead of their opening game against Yugoslavia, their opponents, curious as to what they were up against, sent spies over to watch them train. What they saw was a team that was confused, tired, and hard-traveled: misplaced passes, poor shots, players tripping over each other's feet. Before kickoff, they preemptively apologized to the Uruguayans for the merciless defeat they were about to inflict.

The Uruguayans accepted the apology graciously. Then they turned around and trounced Yugoslavia 7–0. With corporate espionage still a relatively unrefined art form at the time, the Uruguayans had gotten wind of the Yugoslavian spies and intentionally flubbed their performance in training to throw them off. When the local press asked how the team's movement was so good, Andrade quipped that they chased chickens in training.

The Uruguayans were above and away the best team at the tournament. They conceded just two goals in five games, clinching gold with a clinical 3–0 win against Switzerland in the final. Andrade was easily the most captivating player on the team—intelligent on the ball, athletic, graceful, exceptionally handsome. And Black. Most spectators had likely never seen a Black footballer before (Uruguay's racial integration was unusually progressive for the time). His renown and artistry quickly traveled throughout Parisian society, who embraced him with a quasi-fetishistic enthusiasm, dubbing him *la Merveille noire: the Black Marvel*. The paper *Le Matin* sent Colette, the famous French provocatrice, to report on a party thrown by the team. Taking an unabashed interest in Andrade, she wrote: "Uruguayans are a strange combination of civilization and barbarism. Dancing 'le tango' they are wonderful, sublime, better than the best gigolo. But they also dance African cannibal dances that make you shiver."

Andrade stayed in Paris for months after the Games, enjoying the perks of his new status. When he came back to Uruguay, he had expensive new clothes, a top hat and gloves, and an attitude of superiority. He was rumored to have had an affair with iconic entertainer Josephine Baker. He also had rapidly progressing syphilis. Incredibly, although he lost a step of pace (and the sympathy of his teammates, who were not particularly impressed with his new attitude), he would continue to play at the same level until the end of the decade, seeing Uruguay to gold yet again in 1928, and helping them to clinch the championship at the inaugural World Cup in 1930. By the 1930 World Cup, though, he was blind in one eye (some said the blindness was caused by a collision with the goalpost in the Uruguayans' semifinal against Italy in 1928, but odds are, yes, it was the syphilis), and his health was on the decline. He made a handful of appearances for various Uruguayan clubs in the early '30s, but by the middle of the decade he had all but disappeared, his celebrity expiring almost as suddenly as it had arisen. The first Black football star. The first real football star. Period. And the first in a long and distinguished line of football Icaruses.

FULL NAME:	DATE OF BIRTH:	PLACE OF BIRTH:	NATIONAL TEAM:	CAPS / GOALS:
José Leandro Andrade	*October 3, 1901*	*Salto, Uruguay*	*Uruguay, 1923–30*	*33 / 1*

NADINE ANGERER

Y THE AGE OF 28, NADINE ANGERER had won six major titles with the German national team. One World Cup, two Olympic bronze medals, and three European Championships. All without playing a single minute of a single game. She was the consummate reserve goalkeeper, lifting each trophy in her warmup kit, an entire decade spent on the bench behind exceptionally competent first-choice keeper Silke Rottenberg. And then on the last day of July 2007, one month before kickoff for the 2007 World Cup in China, it was announced that Rottenberg, who had torn a cruciate ligament back in January and had been battling to recover in time for the tournament, was tapping out. For the first time since 1997, Angerer, the perennial understudy, was up.

Angerer was not a nobody going into China. She played for Turbine Potsdam and was a well-regarded goalkeeper in her own right, with two Bundesliga titles, one UEFA Cup, and three German Cups to her name. But she was untested on the world stage, stepping into a lineup of grizzled veterans looking to win a second consecutive World Cup—a feat yet to be accomplished on the women's side of the sport—with only a couple dozen appearances in just over 10 years on the national team.

It's almost inconceivable, in retrospect, to think of Angerer as the unproven replacement. Within four weeks, she was the gold standard for goalkeeping in women's football, logging a masterclass performance so calm, so collected, so expert, that you entirely forgot that she hadn't been in goal for any of those previous tournaments (as did the Germans themselves—without any discussion, Angerer slid into the starting goalkeeper slot and stayed there until her retirement in 2015). Broad shouldered, stolid, steely eyed: rarely has any athlete transformed themselves faster into an immovable monument.

The Germans were a road-roller of a force in 2007. They had individual talent, collective understanding, and the wizened experience of champions. They battering-rammed into the tournament, beating Argentina 11–0 in their opening game and then—in large part thanks to Angerer—comfortably rolling their way through the draw. They scored at will and, crucially, refused to concede even a single goal in their first five games, Angerer fully locked down in front of the German net.

If you were a betting neutral going into the final against Brazil, you would have confidently put your money on that streak coming to an abrupt end on the back of a couple of good-looking Brazilian goals. There was no way that Angerer could pull out a final clean sheet against Marta, who was ripping through the tournament with seven goals in five games. The game got underway, Marta and the Brazilian forwards whipping the ball dangerously close to net. Angerer denied Marta once, twice. Birgit Prinz put Germany up at the beginning of the second half. In the 63rd minute, we watched Angerer stare down the barrel at a Marta penalty, the understudy goalkeeper against the global superstar, denying it emphatically to keep Brazil from leveling things up at 1–1. Thirty minutes and one German goal later, and Angerer was the first keeper, man or woman, to shut out an entire World Cup. After years of waiting at the back, politely lifting the trophy after all the starting players had their turn, Angerer stepped right up.

FULL NAME:	DATE OF BIRTH:	PLACE OF BIRTH:	NATIONAL TEAM:	CAPS / GOALS:
Nadine Marejke Angerer	*November 10, 1978*	*Lohr a. Main, West Germany*	*Germany, 1996–2015*	*146 / –*

ROBERTO BAGGIO

VERYONE'S FAVORITE BAGGIO GOAL comes in the 78th minute of Italy's group stage matchup against Czechoslovakia at the 1990 World Cup. Picking up the ball on the halfway line, he veritably skates up the field, sliding over, around, and straight through every member of the Czech defense to send the ball flying assuredly past the Czechoslovakian goalie and into the bottom corner. It's a riveting, hallucinatory goal, the way he just keeps going and going, propelled past the Czechs by nothing more than the slightest of feints and imperceptible drops of the shoulder. There was something almost transcendent about Baggio when he played like this, as if he were floating just above the grasp of the mere mortals with whom he was sharing the field.

This transcendence, plus a teenage conversion to Buddhism and a hairstyle that can only be described as "party in the front, rattail in the back," earned him his permanent moniker: *Il Divin Codino. The Divine Ponytail.* It would flap behind him as he moved around the field, dribbling and finishing with a smoothness that went beyond pure skill or vision. Watching him handle the ball, he seemed to be primarily powered by an almost otherworldly appreciation of beauty.

We came very close to a world without that ponytail. At 18, two days before Baggio was set to transfer to Fiorentina, he tore the ACL and meniscus of his right knee, forcing him to sit out the entire 1985–86 season. An injury sustained in his first appearance for Fiorentina the following fall put him out for another seven months. Doctors weren't sure that Baggio would make it back onto the field. During this time, Baggio converted to Buddhism. Not that we're keeping score or anything, but Buddha 1–0 everyone else; Baggio recovered and returned at the end of April '87. His first league goal for Fiorentina, scored two weeks later, was an example of the perfectly curving free kick that

Baggio proved so adept at over the course of his career. On this particular occasion, it saved Fiorentina from relegation to the second division. Only five appearances into his Fiorentina career, his legacy was secure.

After retirement, Baggio, who suffered from knee problems throughout his career, speculated that he was only ever fully fit two or three games a season. He was, in his own words, "playing on one-and-a-half legs." One can only imagine what a full-legged Baggio would have looked like. As it is, 50 people were injured when Fiorentina fans rioted in the streets of Florence to protest Baggio's sale to Juventus in 1990. "The angels sing in his legs," Fiorentina manager Aldo Agroppi once mused.

In the run-up to the 1994 World Cup Final, Baggio scored five goals for Italy in the knockout rounds, personally shepherding Italy into the final against Argentina. Following a relatively uneventful 90 minutes, that final became the first in World Cup history to end in a penalty shoot-out. After two misses from his teammates, Baggio stepped up and sent his penalty sailing three feet clear over the crossbar to seal Italy's defeat. In his career, Baggio took 116 penalties. He only missed 18. Tragically, it is Baggio bent over in exhaustion, hands on his knees, his eyes lowered in private mourning, that came to represent Baggio's presence at that tournament and became the default image of Baggio's career. "Only those who have the courage to take a penalty miss them," Baggio reflected later.

It is, in some ways, cruelly ironic that Baggio, the Divine Ponytail, a player who spent his career rising above the limits of what seemed humanly possible, should be so closely associated with this one moment of mortality. Yet, if that image represents Baggio at his lowest moment, it also reminds us of the heights he reached at his highest. Ask anyone who was around to watch Baggio play: Their eyes invariably light up at the memory.

FULL NAME:	DATE OF BIRTH:	PLACE OF BIRTH:	NATIONAL TEAM:	CAPS / GOALS:
Roberto Baggio	*February 18, 1967*	*Caldogno, Italy*	*Italy, 1988–2004*	*56 / 27*

GORDON BANKS

ORDON BANKS CONCEDED JUST three goals when he won the World Cup with England in 1966. He was a 29-year-old Yorkshire goalkeeper with jowly cheeks, sunken eyes, and an incurably bad haircut, who had built up his strength as a teenager by hauling bags of coal for a living. In England, where most keepers still belonged to the safe and stalwart school of goalkeeping, Banks was seen as a bit of an odd duck: He was obsessive and meticulous, studying angles and bounces, constantly working on his athleticism, insisting on barreling out of goal to stop shots before they were taken. Chronically mid-table Leicester City viewed Banks warily; in '67, they dropped him in favor of teenage reserve Peter Shilton, selling him to even more chronically mid-table Stoke City. But in the summer of '66, Banks was out on the global stage, and was widely agreed to be the best goalkeeper there. By all expectation, this should have been the apex of his career.

And then they started broadcasting the World Cup in color.

The 1966 World Cup had seen the first intercontinental broadcast. Crowds on the other side of the world, previously forced to glean together the day's action from highlights in newsreels and newspaper photographs, could finally watch games live. Mexico 1970 was the first tournament seen in full, vibrant color. The green of the grass, the canary yellow of the Brazilian kits, the rainbows of flags waving in the stands. Football, in many ways, is a game of colors. To viewers at home, the introduction of color gave the whole tournament a visual intensity that it had never had before.

Enter Gordon Banks, again. England is playing their second group stage match, against Brazil. Jairzinho sends an arching cross into the box, straight to a vaulting Pelé, who heads the ball so forcefully into the bottom-left corner, he actually shouts "Gol!" as he makes contact. It is as close to inevitable as any strike that tournament will be. But, somehow, Gordon Banks has launched himself all the way to his right, twisting his body in midair and perfectly judging the bounce of the ball to deflect it just in time, up and over the crossbar. Like a "salmon leaping up a waterfall," Pelé mused later, claiming that he still couldn't understand how Banks had done it. On the field, none of Banks's teammates react to the save. Perhaps because they are English and prefer to repress emotion. Partially because they are already busy setting up for the resulting corner. Bobby Moore, the England captain, quips, "You're getting old, Banksy. You used to hold on to them," as he walks past. The game continues. Brazil win 1–0 with a strike from Jairzinho in the second half. Banks is struck down with food poisoning ahead of the knockout stage, and England, amongst the bookies' favorites to win a second consecutive trophy, is sent home empty-handed in the quarters, conceding three goals to West Germany.

But in homes across the world, sitting enraptured in front of their TV screens, the impact of Banks's save was felt immediately. Pelé was the best player in the world, but Banks was the best goalkeeper, and he had just upstaged him. It was a vivid, riveting, impossible moment between two giants, instantly tattooed in bright pigments onto the minds of those who witnessed it. There had been great saves before; there were certainly great saves after. But this was the one relived and replayed and re-lauded until it became the most famous save of the century, inspiring generations of goalkeepers to attempt the unattemptable. The first global Technicolor save, permanently elevating goalkeeping to high art.

FULL NAME:	DATE OF BIRTH:	PLACE OF BIRTH:	NATIONAL TEAM:	CAPS / GOALS:
Gordon Banks	December 30, 1937	Sheffield, England	England, 1963–72	73 / –

FRANCO BARESI

IT IS OFTEN SAID THAT FRANCO Baresi read the game like he had written it. Like he knew where you were going to put the ball before you did. Most great athletes eschew limits; Baresi lived to create them, snuffing out any possibility before it even had a chance to peek its little head around the corner. Of all the expert defenders that Italy has produced over the years, he was not the most elegant, the most aggressive, or the most prescient; but he was somehow the perfect combination of all three, ideal quantities of each trait mixing to create a defender who seemed to overwhelm opponents with sheer solidity.

A one-club man, Baresi played 719 games for AC Milan, weathering two relegations to Serie B early in his career after Milan was implicated in the same 1980 Totonero match-fixing scandal that saw Paolo Rossi suspended for two years over at Perugia. The last true libero (a creative, free-roaming sweeper; see Franz Beckenbauer, who pioneered the role), Baresi won six Serie A titles with Milan, captaining the team to five of them, plus four Supercoppas and three European Cups, sporting tiny shorts always half covered by an obstinately untucked shirt as he shaped Milan's backline into one of the most impenetrable forces ever known to man, on par with Kevlar or the security of an under-the-table Swiss bank account.

Baresi won a World Cup with Italy in 1982 as an unused substitute. Owing to a fundamental disagreement with Italy manager Enzo Bearzot, who wanted to use Baresi as a central midfielder rather than a center back (his usual position), Baresi missed out on Mexico 1986. (Bearzot handed his spot in the midfield to Baresi's brother, Giuseppe, instead.) He didn't actually make his first World Cup appearance until 1990, at age 30, when Italy made a run to the semifinals before falling to Argentina on penalties.

Captaining the Italian team at the following World Cup in 1994, Baresi hobbled off the field in Italy's second match with a torn meniscus, and his World Cup career looked to be over—tragically, without the kind of headline-making performance worthy of a player of his stature. The rest of the Italian team chugged along through the tournament without him, slowly gaining momentum as they went, while Baresi was shuttled to New York for surgery.

Three short weeks later at the Rose Bowl in Pasadena, Italy faced Brazil in the final with their captain miraculously returned, having pushed back to match fitness from an injury that traditionally takes anywhere from six to eight weeks to recover from.

Each time Baresi went to ground during that final he grimaced, telegraphing the pain of his newly reconstructed knee to everyone watching. But he did not make a single mistake, defending and redirecting heroically to keep Brazil's Romário-led attack at bay for 120 minutes, sending the 0–0 game into penalties—the first time the tournament would be won on penalties—before collapsing onto the grass in agony and being stretchered off the field.

Minutes later, Baresi was back on his feet once more. Still shaking out his knee, he stepped up to take Italy's first penalty. He sent it rising over the head of the goalie, soaring well above the crossbar. Daniele Massaro missed his too. So did Roberto Baggio, taking a penalty almost identical to Baresi's, all of Italy's hard work flying into the crowd behind the net. Baggio's despair was the image that all the newspapers used to dramatize Italy's defeat. But just behind him was Baresi, nothing left in him, leathery, grizzled, hair thinning, always impenetrable, sobbing like a small child in the arms of his manager.

FULL NAME:	DATE OF BIRTH:	PLACE OF BIRTH:	NATIONAL TEAM:	CAPS / GOALS:
Franchino Baresi	*May 8, 1960*	*Travagliato, Italy*	*Italy, 1982–94*	*81 / 1*

GABRIEL
BATISTUTA

TALL, STURDY, WITH A JUTTING square jaw, big gray eyes, and long, stringy blond hair, Gabriel Batistuta looked a lot like Jesus, if Jesus had been known to moonlight as a barback in a backwoods Argentine dive bar. There are some players who play exactly the way you'd think they would, and Batistuta is their permanent poster child. The son of a slaughterhouse worker from the Argentine agricultural province of Santa Fe, he had this specifically rural, almost gaucho-like combination of violence and low-key joviality about him; one glance in his direction as he trotted onto the pitch conjured visions of a forceful, aggressive player, strong, hardworking, and good-natured, ferociously attacking and whooping all the while. Which was, in fact, exactly how he was.

Batistuta turned up in the global imagination in 1991, when he joined Fiorentina from Boca Juniors. Roughly speaking, Serie A was to the early '90s what the Premier League became in the 2010s: a league flush with big, global audiences and even bigger money, teams teeming with the best players in the world, each more exotic and exciting than the next. None more so than Batistuta, whose name itself sounded like an exclamation. He had this incredibly distinctive style of charging in on goal, accelerating at the last moment—a flash of controlled brutality—to strike the ball with such force that you could see the air being displaced around it as it cannoned past helpless keepers. He was Fiorentina's top scorer for nine seasons, his entire tenure at the club, blasting in a total of 167 goals for the Tuscan side. Fiorentina never managed any particular success during Batistuta's time there—that decade they won just two domestic cups and one Serie B title (having been relegated after Batistuta's second season)—but Batistuta, despite being on the radar of every top club on the continent, was not interested in greener pastures. His enjoyment of football seemed to be founded in impulses more basic than titles or hardware: a sense of loyalty, a pursuit of personal glory, and a profound love for the physical act of scoring. Plus, the Firenze violet brought out his eyes so perfectly. Batistuta did not win a Serie A title until he moved to Roma in 2000 in the last years of his career, but this did not diminish his stature. The Fiorentina fans erected a bronze likeness in front of the stands as commentators the world over joyously shouted "Batigol!" each time he murdered another ball into the back of the net.

Batistuta's international career followed a similar trajectory to his club career, with individual achievements vastly outstripping collective wins for the Argentine international. He was the country's all-time top scorer for 18 years until Messi finally surpassed him in 2016. He had a particular relish for doing what he did best on the global stage. Only seven men in the history of the sport have scored more goals than Batistuta at World Cups, and he is the only person ever to record hat tricks in two different tournaments. The Argentina team as a whole, struggling to bounce back after Maradona's doping suspension and subsequent retirement, fell short of expectations at all three of Batistuta's World Cups, losing in the round of 16 in '94 and the quarterfinals in '98. When Argentina lost in the group stage in 2002—their worst result in over 30 years—Batistuta, who had been subbed off during the second half, did not go out to commiserate with his teammates. Instead, he stood alone on the side of the pitch and shed private tears. He had only scored one goal that tournament and, at 33, with no cartilage left in his knees, was keenly aware that he would never score again at a World Cup.

It goes almost without saying that Batistuta is in the slightly unfortunate position of being sandwiched in Argentina's football history between the two most devoutly worshipped gods of modern football, Maradona and Messi. Even at his height, Batistuta was never a god. With his raw power, his straightforwardness, and his noble greatness in the midst of collective underachievement, like all good gauchos, it was his humanity that compelled.

FULL NAME:	DATE OF BIRTH:	PLACE OF BIRTH:	NATIONAL TEAM:	CAPS / GOALS:
Gabriel Omar Batistuta	February 1, 1969	Reconquista, Santa Fe, Argentina	Argentina, 1991–2002	78 / 56

FRANZ BECKENBAUER

RANZ BECKENBAUER EMBODIED just about every negative stereotype ever tossed derisively in the general direction of the German people. The defender was more logical, aloof, arrogant, conservative, consistent, and efficient than Angela Merkel, Augustus Gloop, and the Scorpions combined. Beckenbauer's persona was so utterly Teutonic that his nickname was simply *Der Kaiser*. So, it is perhaps the greatest testament to the extent to which he reengineered the modern game that it is impossible to hold any of this against him.

In five World Cup finals as a player and a coach, Beckenbauer never finished below third place, and he remains one of only two men to lift the trophy as both captain and manager. (The other being Didier Deschamps, who lifted the trophy with France as captain in 1998 and as manager 20 years later.) Technical yet graceful, elegant yet rugged yet elegant, and physical enough to channel Willis Reed and battle on with his arm strapped to his side after dislocating a shoulder in a semifinal against Italy at the 1970 World Cup. But his greatest attribute was his ability to use his mind to control the game. A midfielder-turned-defender, he reinvented attack as the best form of defense in a new role—a libero, a creative force who would carry the ball from the back, pushing up to fuse the midfield with the forward line.

Before the libero, defenders were large, crude, and awkward on the ball. They were about as likely to leave their own half as the agoraphobe you just invited to your birthday party. Beckenbauer changed the categories of the game, taking advantage of the fact that he was rarely closely marked to storm out of defense with trademark runs that were as revolutionary as defenseman Bobby Orr's rink-length rushes with the NHL's Boston Bruins.

Beckenbauer was the pop star of German football—first symbolically, then literally, as he leveraged his fame by entering the studio to record a hit single in 1966. Philosophically entitled "Gute Freunde kann niemand trennen" ("True Friends Can't Be Separated"), it is a hurdy-gurdy track, part Donovan, part Hasselhoff, with lyrics that summed up the team-first ethos of the West German teams he marshaled:

Good friends—no one can tear apart
Good friends are never alone
Because in life one can
Be there for one another

History has not recorded whether the 1974 World Cup squad Beckenbauer captained listened to the track on the locker room boombox before matches, but their cohesive spirit and organization were evident as they undid a flamboyant Dutch team captained by Cruyff in a battle royale of a final. Beckenbauer combined with prolific goalscorer Gerd Müller, shocking the world as they upset the widely favored Dutch team—a team so slick they had managed to score a goal before West Germany had even touched the ball. Beckenbauer's total control of the German team during that campaign was as evident off the field as on: He picked the roster, shaped their tactics, handled the media in his coaches' stead, and even negotiated their win bonus.

All of this was ideal preparation for 1990, when Beckenbauer successfully managed the German team to victory in Italy. By way of a coda, he returned to the World Cup to chair the organizing of the tournament in Germany in 2006. Ever the control freak, he used a helicopter to crisscross the country and attend 48 of the 64 games, even managing to squeeze in his third marriage between matches. The tournament, predictably, ran like clockwork.

FULL NAME:	DATE OF BIRTH:	PLACE OF BIRTH:	NATIONAL TEAM:	CAPS / GOALS:
Franz Anton Beckenbauer	*September 11, 1945*	*Munich, West Germany*	*West Germany, 1965–77*	*103 / 14*

KYLE BECKERMAN

IF, AT THE END OF 2019, THERE HAD been an award given out for the decade's most successful attempt to pull off white dreads, the finalists would have been Rachel Dolezal, Post Malone, and former US Men's National Team midfielder Kyle Beckerman. And Kyle Beckerman would have won, hands down. He combined the three most admirable qualities in football: tenacity, vision, and extraordinary commitment to a widely derided hairstyle.

As a kid in Crofton, Maryland, Beckerman would leave notes for his parents to let them know he was out playing soccer. He would sign them with his full name, followed by "USA #15." This was a boy with a dream. A dream that for a while there seemed to be nothing more than wishful thinking. Beckerman was an MLS flag-bearer, joining the league in its fourth season and helping to build soccer markets from the ground up in Colorado and Salt Lake. He was an aggressive, grinding defensive midfielder known for clean passing and artful tackles, but, for whatever reason, he had fallen out of favor with USMNT manager Bob Bradley and was left for years wandering the international wilderness, watching from home in 2010 as the US reached the round of 16, going out to Ghana in extra time.

In normal life, Beckerman is a chill, affable, all-calm-on-the-Western-Front kind of guy. His football, however, was predicated on single-minded persistence. He beat opponents by working harder, dogging them until they made a mistake; if they didn't make a mistake, he would make one for them. He was an absolute pest of a player, impossible to shake off, coming back again and again until he got what he wanted.

At 32 years old, Beckerman finally got what he wanted. After years off the national team radar, he mounted an indefatigable late-career, *Revenant*-esque return, clomping in from the cold to become a centerpiece of Jürgen Klinsmann's revamped USMNT side. In October 2013, with the US already qualified for the next World Cup, Beckerman took the field in Panama. It was a meaningless game for the US, but a win would knock Panama out of qualifying and hand their World Cup ticket to Mexico. One expected Klinsmann's team to take it easy, but Beckerman seemed to have missed the memo—he played the entire 90 minutes like he was already at the World Cup. From the press box, you could see the Panamanian midfielders jawing at him. With two unapologetic stoppage-time goals, the Americans quashed Panama's World Cup dreams. After the final whistle, Beckerman confided that the Panamanian midfielders had been begging him to take it easy. "They kept saying, 'Take it easy, bro, you have already qualified for the World Cup,' and I just said to them, 'My team may have qualified, but I ain't booked my place on that team yet . . . bro.'"

His place booked, Beckerman arrived at his first (and last) World Cup that summer. The team shocked everyone, emerging unscathed from the group of death, edging out Portugal and Ghana to proceed to the knockout rounds. Beckerman, despite his conspicuous hairstyle, never played conspicuously good football. With a style that was all grind, no glitz, it was often easier to notice his contributions in absentia, by what was missing when he was not there. Disastrously, Klinsmann elected to bench Beckerman in their round of 16 match against Belgium, wanting players who were better in the air to defend them against Belgium's Marouane Fellaini–shaped aerial threat. The Americans allowed 38 shots, 18 shots on goal, lost 2–1, and were eliminated from the competition. But Beckerman had made it to the World Cup. Kyle Beckerman, USA #15. And, if it's any consolation, *Vogue* did name him one of the 12 most attractive players at the tournament, dreads and all.

FULL NAME:	DATE OF BIRTH:	PLACE OF BIRTH:	NATIONAL TEAM:	CAPS / GOALS:
Kyle Robert Beckerman	*April 23, 1982*	*Crofton, Maryland, United States*	*United States, 2007–16*	*58 / 1*

DAVID BECKHAM

HE STORY OF HOW DAVID BECKHAM became the most recognizable footballer of all time is really a tale about the advent of the Premier League and the global commercialization of football. It is a story about ostentatious celebrity, the leveraging of fame, and the emergence of modern tabloid paparazzi. It is a story about the confluence of time and space and people that occurred to create one of the best teams in the history of the English game. It is a story about a media-savvy Spice Girl and the benefits of marrying a woman much smarter than you.

More than anything, though, it is a story about beauty.

The Abercrombie-mall-model muscles. The always meticulously coiffed hair (there are only six standard Premier League footballer haircuts, and David Beckham arguably invented all of them). Those unmistakable hazel eyes and the crinkles around them. The Michelangelo jawline paired with that soft, forgiving smile. In pubs around the country, big burly men with beer dabbled down the front of their shirts—the kind of men who you know mostly frequented pubs in order to bond over their mutual heterosexuality—could be found eyeing Manchester United's number 7 hungrily and debating the different merits of his rotating hairstyles. It wasn't any individual piece but rather the transcendent magnetism of the sum of his parts that made our stomachs drop a little with the knowledge that we had just peeked behind the curtain into a world infinitely prettier than our own. This knowledge was not without consequence. Men who had previously appeared attractive to us—husbands, children, David Ginola—were suddenly repugnant trolls in our eyes. But this was a price we were willing to pay.

Beckham wasn't the best footballer—he was arguably third best out of the six members of the famous Manchester United Class of '92. Cynics would describe him as a bit of a one-trick pony, practicing his free kick with the single-minded obsession of David Fincher on the set of *Zodiac*. God, though, was that trick magnificent to behold. Teasingly, tantalizingly slow, flirting with the wind and the crowd and geometric perfection as it spun towards the top corner. Opposing goalkeepers and defenders would just stand and watch as the ball flew by, their faces colored not by shame, but by the secondhand glow of the divinity in their midst.

When Beckham got himself sent off with a red card against Argentina in the round of 16 at the 1998 World Cup, dragging England out of the competition with him, we jeered and spat. We cursed his name, mocked his accent and fashion choices, and hung effigies outside our pubs. The *Daily Mirror* went as far as to print a tear-out dartboard cover of Beckham's face for a nation to vent its anger upon. Three years later, when Beckham spanked one of his signature free kicks in the last minute of a crucial qualifier against Greece to secure England's entrance into the next World Cup, we breathed a sigh of relief and quickly dug our Beckham Armani posters out of the closet. There is nothing more futile in this world than trying to hold on to old grudges in the face of a really, really, really ridiculously good-looking ball played by a really, really, really ridiculously good-looking man.

We had entered the 21st century. We didn't just want to win anymore. We wanted aesthetic revelation. Beckham gifted us that. In return, we gifted Beckham our raw lust, our fantasies, our wonder, and our petty jealousy, all of which he absorbed without judgment or complaint. He was trying to be a good husband and a good father and a good footballer, but, first and foremost, he seemed to understand as well as we did that his most important job was to be our favorite objet d'art.

FULL NAME:	DATE OF BIRTH:	PLACE OF BIRTH:	NATIONAL TEAM:	CAPS / GOALS:
David Robert Joseph Beckham	*May 2, 1975*	*Leytonstone, London, England*	*England, 1996–2009*	*115 / 17*

GEORGE BEST

MANCHESTER UNITED SCOUT named Bob Bishop once spent an afternoon in Northern Ireland watching a 15-year-old George Best play at a local Belfast park. Before returning home that evening, he sent a telegram to the club's manager, Matt Busby. It read simply, "I think I've found you a genius."

Every so often in a sport—maybe once in a generation, if you're lucky—you get an athlete who appears to be operating on an entirely different physical plane than everyone around them. Think Federer. Think Messi. Think LeBron. Players who create not just space, but time, moving frictionlessly through the ether, seeing passes before they happen, reacting to things the rest of us haven't even had time to register yet. This was George Best. Playing through the mud and brutality of 1960s English football, he was, in a word, a revelation. More dancer than athlete, he'd glide over tackles and bend himself around defenders, moving as if his feet weren't tethered to the ground by gravity in the way that everyone else's were. If he didn't get the ball to you, it wasn't because he had missed; it was because you hadn't yet realized where you were supposed to be. Likewise, if he got the ball past you, you weren't doing anything wrong. Like watching a live stream with an almost imperceptible lag, you were just existing in a world that was ever so slightly behind the one happening out on the pitch.

Best started his first game for Manchester United in 1963 at the ripe old age of 17; within three years, he was one of the most famous footballers in the world. His entrance onto the stage of global celebrity was the 1966 European Cup quarterfinals against Lisbon's Benfica. Before the match, Busby instructed his team to keep it tight for the first 15 minutes and see how things went. By the 13th minute, Best had already scored twice—once with a perfectly placed header, once with a freewheeling, cheeky run that evaded three defenders and then the keeper before Best gently tapped the ball into goal. Busby turned to Best after the match and quipped that perhaps the Irishman hadn't been listening in the locker room. The Portuguese press, eager to title the man who had so thoroughly shown them up, dubbed him *O Quinto Beatle* (*the Fifth Beatle*), on account of his disheveled good looks and mop of dark hair. The nickname stuck. Football's first rock star was born.

With modeling appearances, his own fan club, and late-night antics that were perpetually pouring out of the tabloids, Best lived up to his moniker, doing exactly what the Beatles did—fusing genius with outrageous celebrity. He lived a titillating life filled with excess, which ultimately overshadowed the true poetry of Best the footballer. It should not, however. Despite leaving Manchester United at 28, at what was arguably the peak of his career, moonlighting for a cascade of more and more random clubs (highlights include four years in the North American Soccer League and a stint in Asia), Best's on-field legacy is scrawled decisively in dark red ink on the ledger of English football. All in all, he played 470 games for Manchester United, scoring 179 goals, winning two league titles, and piloting the club in 1968 to the first European Cup ever won by an English team—claiming the Ballon d'Or and becoming the youngest-ever Football Writers' Association Footballer of the Year winner in the process.

Off the field, Best's legacy is no less permanent. He took the mischief and showboating that had always been part of football and transformed it into high art, becoming as iconic a symbol of '60s youth counterculture in England as the Stones or DayGlo, an entirely new kind of football star.

FULL NAME:	DATE OF BIRTH:	PLACE OF BIRTH:	NATIONAL TEAM:	CAPS / GOALS:
George Best	*May 22, 1946*	*Belfast, Northern Ireland*	*Northern Ireland, 1964–77*	*37 / 9*

OLEG BLOKHIN

IN KEEPING WITH THE ETHOS OF communism, rarely did Soviet football teams feature standout performers. They were very much the sum of their parts, imposing, collective armies of interchangeable Eastern European men trotting out onto the pitch with the Cyrillic CCCP emblazoned on their shirts. The first wave of Soviet football had come out of Russia, with stocky dark-haired Muscovites making up the majority of those early teams. By the 1970s, however, the power center of Soviet football had migrated 500 miles southwest to Kiev, the Russians replaced by lean, blond Ukrainian specimens. In the basement offices of Dynamo Kiev the Soviet footballing ethos was officially codified, transformed into a science by legendary Dynamo Kiev and USSR manager Valeriy Lobanovskyi.

A trained engineer and amateur statistician in addition to being a former Dynamo Kiev forward, Lobanovskyi determined early in his management career that a team that committed errors no more than 18 percent of the time would win any given football match. So he went about reducing those errors, testing players for their athletic prowess and tactical acumen, selecting them based on results, and molding them according to his own specifications by working on fitness, reaction time, and strategic movement, asking them to memorize books of plays like American football players. The approach was entirely antithetical to the way the rest of the world wanted to view the sport: as a creative pursuit motivated by the inventive playmaking of the individual footballer. However much the purists moaned about the spiritual implications of Lobanovskyi's method, though, it proved effective. Under his command, Dynamo Kiev dominated the Soviet Top League for two decades. Nearly all the core members of the Soviet national team from 1975 until the Fall of Communism were chosen from Lobanovskyi's machine. They were a sight to behold: fluid, exact, in sync, and indefatigable, like a well-rehearsed ballet company. Not the best team in the world, but easily one of the most satisfying to see in action.

If Lobanovskyi set out to build the ideal Soviet footballer, he achieved his goal in Oleg Blokhin. Long-legged, stone-faced, and made entirely of muscle, Blokhin exuded pure Slavic athleticism. He had the pace of an Olympic runner, graceful footwork, exceptional spatial awareness, and smooth, quick reflexes. He would stride up the pitch with the ball at his feet, his clean, clinical precision sending slight shivers up your spine, almost uncanny in its perfection. Ironically enough, Blokhin's ability to perfectly execute Lobanovskyi's vision of collective, personality-less football actually drew attention to his own exceptionality, and he became the first real Soviet football star since the early '60s.

Blokhin's renown had been increasing gradually over the course of the early 1970s, slowly making its way beyond the Iron Curtain to the rest of the continent. It was assured during the 1975 Super Cup against Bayern Munich. Gaining the ball in the 66th minute of the first leg, Blokhin races up the length of the left flank. When he gets into the Bayern penalty area, he slows down and looks for support, but he is alone with the Bayern backline, the rest of the Dynamo players left trailing behind with the German offense. Without missing a beat, Blokhin speedily maneuvers the ball in quick succession around 1974 World Cup winners Hans-Georg Schwarzenbeck and Franz Beckenbauer, launching it over goalkeeper Sepp Maier and across the line. All the stunned German commentator can think to exclaim is "World class!" But that misses the point somehow. Because, as will be remarked when Blokhin wins the Ballon d'Or that year, beating out the likes of Beckenbauer and Cruyff by a landslide 80 points, Beckenbauer *was* world class. The rest of the Dynamo Kiev roster was world class. Blokhin at his peak was somehow operating beyond that.

FULL NAME:	DATE OF BIRTH:	PLACE OF BIRTH:	NATIONAL TEAM:	CAPS / GOALS:
Oleg Vladimirovich Blokhin	*November 5, 1952*	*Kiev, Ukraine*	*Soviet Union, 1972–88*	*112 / 42*

ZBIGNIEW BONIEK

 NCHORED BY ONE OF THE WEIGHT-iest, most memorable mustaches in football history, Zbigniew Boniek was formally introduced to the world at the 1982 World Cup. He was a wiry 26-year-old from Bydgoszcz, Poland, that many-consonanted city sometimes known as Bromberg, built at the meeting of the Brda and Vistula rivers, the proverbial rope in the millennium-long territorial tug-of-war between Germany and Poland. Boniek played as a forward for Widzew Łódź, a team that no one outside of Poland would have been expected to know anything about, except that with Boniek helming their attack, they had knocked Manchester United and Juventus out of the 1980–81 UEFA Cup before losing in the third round to the eventual champions, the once-mighty Ipswich Town. (Football is not the animal it once was.) He had momentarily turned heads at the 1978 World Cup in Argentina as a clean-shaven 22-year-old when he scored a brace against Mexico in the group stage, but Poland was grouped with Argentina and Brazil in the second round, and, thoroughly outmatched, they were summarily dismissed before Boniek could manage to repeat the feat and garner any real attention.

Four years later, he was back. He looked like he had popped by from a day job as head counselor at Soviet Pioneer Camp, with tousled strawberry blond hair, the matching mustache (which somehow, his entire career, always looked like he had just grown it from the losing end of a bet), and a puka shell necklace around his neck. He was charismatic and impetuous and lightly sunburnt and had returned to the world stage, this time as an integral part of the Polish front line. Boniek's game was predicated on blistering pace; incising straight through vulnerable defensive lines, he would deconstruct opposing sides on the counterattack. He wasn't much of a personal goalscorer, preferring to hand the ball off once he had gotten it as far downfield as he could, but he grabbed the limelight with both hands when he scored a hat trick against Belgium in the opening game of Poland's second round.

It is a near perfect hat trick, of the kind that comes around very rarely, with each goal as superb as the one that precedes it. Four minutes in, he begins with a thundering 18-yard shot off a cross from winger Grzegorz Lato. He follows that with a shrewd header, rushing in at the last minute to pop the ball over Theo Custers, the Belgian goalkeeper. And for the pièce de résistance, he gains possession on the edge of the box after a superb passing sequence and, one-on-one with Custers, blithely accelerates around him to tap the ball in and slam the door on the Belgians in the 53rd minute. The expression on Boniek's face in celebration can only be described as bemused.

Poland drew with the Soviet Union in their second game of the second round, and Boniek's hat trick was enough to see them through to the semifinals on goal difference. Unfortunately, a yellow card in the 88th minute against the Soviet Union—his second of the tournament—meant that Boniek had to sit out Poland's semifinal against Italy, and without their main counterattacking force, they fell without too much resistance.

After the tournament, Boniek was snapped up by Juventus for about $2 million, making him by far the highest paid Polish player in the world at the time. Juventus president Gianni Agnelli nicknamed him *Bello di notte—Beautiful by night*—because he seemed to perform best in European tournament matches, which were usually played in the midweek evenings, partnering with Frenchman Michel Platini to slice straight through the continent's top teams, who tended to be less defense-minded than Juventus's fellow Serie A sides. Observing him from the other end of Italy, Maradona was said to have admiringly declared Boniek the greatest counterattacking player in the world, marveling at the sight of the Polish genius wheeling away after scoring a crucial goal on a great European Cup night, the floodlights and the world's attention soaked up by Boniek and his magnificent mustache.

FULL NAME:	DATE OF BIRTH:	PLACE OF BIRTH:	NATIONAL TEAM:	CAPS / GOALS:
Zbigniew Kazimierz Boniek	*March 3, 1956*	*Bydgoszcz, Poland*	*Poland, 1976–88*	*80 / 24*

VERO BOQUETE

HEN VERO BOQUETE SCORES A goal, she covers her face with her right hand, fingers outstretched like the tentacles of an octopus, a staple food in her hometown of Santiago de Compostela. The capital of Galicia, Spain's northwesternmost autonomous community, Santiago de Compostela is a legendary landmark: the final stop on the Camino de Santiago pilgrimage route that stretches from the French Pyrenees all the way to the city's cathedral. Each year, hundreds of thousands of pilgrims make the 800-kilometer trek to see the shrine of St. James, where relics of the apostle are said to be buried.

Now, if a pilgrim, tiring momentarily of holy bones, were to pop out of the cathedral and stroll about 3 kilometers due west, they would find a shrine of a different sort: Just down the road is the Estadio Vero Boquete de San Lazaro.

Vero Boquete has played in Spain, the US, Russia, Sweden, Germany, China, France, and Italy. One year older than the Spanish women's league (which was not fully professionalized until 2020), she has been hopping the continents since the early 2000s, influentially plying her trade in almost every major women's football league in the world. Galician through and through, Boquete plays pure now-you-see-it-now-you-don't football, ferrying the ball through the opposition with labyrinthine drag backs, direction changes, and abrupt chips. Often landing in leagues that, like the US, historically have tended to emphasize results over technique, Boquete can sometimes feel as if the sport she's playing has slightly different rules than everyone else's. She is a nimble, scene-stealing number 10, playing organic football of the kind that can neither be fully learned nor taught, an emissary of Spain in foreign lands. "I have always held that at the moment of my birth I heard a whistle blow," Boquete insists.

Despite being the pathfinder for Spanish women's football—or perhaps because of it—you will not find her in the ranks of the Spanish national team these days. In the early part of the last decade, Boquete drove a young up-and-coming Spanish side at long last into major tournaments, scoring a 122nd-minute goal against Scotland to send Spain to the 2013 Euros, and captaining them through qualification for the 2015 World Cup. But after a disappointing World Cup performance, which she felt unfairly reflected the quality of the team, Boquete led a team-wide revolt to oust the team's longtime coach, Ignacio Quereda. The revolt worked: Quereda, who had been in charge of the women's national team for 27 years—27 stagnant years, in Boquete's blunt appraisal—was sacked just weeks after Spain's group stage elimination. But so was Boquete, who had stirred up a little too much dust for the Spanish Football Federation's taste. Spain's recent progress in international competition built on the back of Boquete's work, rather than with it.

Likewise, you will not find Boquete on the cover of *FIFA*, although she is the reason there are women in the series at all, having circulated a petition in 2013 to get the game to include women footballers in their digital ranks. She is neither as loud nor as belligerent as her activism would make her seem. But she is strong-willed and sure-footed. In Santiago de Compostela they adore her. There are maybe six women in the world with football stadia named after them. Three are literal queens. One is Vero Boquete.

FULL NAME:	DATE OF BIRTH:	PLACE OF BIRTH:	NATIONAL TEAM:	CAPS / GOALS:
Verónica Boquete Giadans	*April 9, 1987*	*Santiago de Compostela, Galicia, Spain*	*Spain, 2005–17*	*62 / 38*

LUCY BRONZE

HEN LUCY BRONZE RETURNED to Manchester City in the fall of 2020, it felt significant. Most footballers represent a single era. Bronze spans two. She was born in October of 1991, 19 days before the inaugural Women's World Cup. Bronze grew up in Alnwick in North East England, an old market town of 8,000 residents, replete with castle and formal gardens on the north Northumberland coastline. She grew into a story familiar to generations of female footballers in Northumberland and beyond. She aged out of the Alnwick Town AFC boys' team when she was 12, as per the Football Association (FA) regulation that teams be segregated at puberty, and she spent the next seven years driving an hour south each day, first to Blyth, then to Sunderland, in search of a women's team she could play on. At 17, she moved to the United States to play for the University of North Carolina at Chapel Hill. But, told she needed to be in England to have a chance at playing with the national team, she moved back after her freshman year—despite the fact that in 2009, with the inaugural season of Women's Professional Soccer underway, the US was a very good place to be a professional footballer. England less so. Bronze enrolled in a sports science course at Leeds Beckett University, got a job at a Domino's, and returned to Sunderland.

Sometime in the next couple of years, as Bronze hopped around the newly formed Football Association Women's Super League, two things happened. First, Lucy Bronze—whose full name, incidentally, is Lucia Roberta Tough Bronze—became one of the most visible female footballers in England. Right back is not a traditionally glamorous position, but Bronze made it persuasive, playing with gusto, driving attacks out the back, eyes on goal, hand on the gear shift. She did not personally score goals with any regularity, but she picked her moments with zest, netting game-winners in the round of 16 and the quarterfinals of the 2015 World Cup to propel England into the semifinals for the first time in the team's history.

The second thing that happened was the simultaneous rise of Olympique Lyonnais Féminin in France, which saw the club skyrocket into the stratosphere as the most successful women's team in history. Bronze, playing at Manchester City, encountered them in the semifinals of the 2016–17 Champions League. OL beat City 3–2 on aggregate, going on to win the final against PSG in a tense penalty shoot-out. Four months later, Bronze was off to Lyon. When Bronze moved away, it felt right: England's greatest defender plying her trade for the best team in the world. When she moved back three years later, the exclamation point on a wave of world-class players migrating to an English league growing increasingly in stature and talent, it felt equally right. The Women's Super League, for years an ironic name for a league with a massive inferiority complex, had finally materialized. Lucy Bronze was back.

FULL NAME:	DATE OF BIRTH:	PLACE OF BIRTH:	NATIONAL TEAM:	CAPS / GOALS:
Lucia Roberta Tough Bronze	*October 28, 1991*	*Berwick-upon-Tweed, England*	*England, 2013–*	*82 / 9 *as of August 2, 2021*

GIANLUIGI BUFFON

HEN GIANLUIGI BUFFON MADE his first senior team appearance at Parma, the year was 1995, OJ Simpson had just been acquitted, and "Gangsta's Paradise" by Coolio was at the top of the charts. Buffon, a gangly 17, all limbs and nose, stepped into goal against the season's eventual Serie A champions, AC Milan. Goalkeepers tend to take longer than other players to find their feet. Some take years. Buffon took everyone by surprise, walking out with his sea legs already under him, denying shots by Ballon d'Or winners Roberto Baggio and George Weah to keep a clean sheet. It was a widely feted debut. But you couldn't have known, watching Buffon in goal that day, that 26 years later he'd still be in goal—for Parma, no less, returning to the club in 2021 after 20 years away—entire decades after most of the players on the field in 1995 had retired from the sport, playing with the children of his former teammates.

Buffon (Gigi to his friends, and at this point, aren't we all his friends?) has played many roles over the course of his extensive career. At 17, he was a cocky teen wunderkind, saying to Parma manager Nevio Scala, "Listen, boss, in a normal month I train really well for 29 days. But one day a month you need to accept that I'm not going to be myself, because I'll be having a bad day. And you need not to get angry about that." At 20, he was coining his own nickname (a greater indication of the man's courage than any goal-front scrum he has ever thrown himself into), ripping off his jersey to reveal a Superman shirt underneath. At 23, he was Juve's new star, the most expensive goalkeeper in the world—a record he held, even in the era of exorbitant transfer fees, until 2018.

In quick succession in 2006, Buffon was disgraced—embroiled in the 2006 Calciopoli match-fixing scandal, staying with Juve as they were stripped of their previous two titles and relegated to Serie B—and then heroized, scraping Italy through a penalty shoot-out against France just two months later to win them the 2006 World Cup. We thought he was peaking then, but if anything, he got better in his 30s, improving his footwork and morphing into the wise elder statesman of Italian football. He has been goofy, eccentric, arrogant, vulnerable, imperious. Like all the best Italian players, he has worn fascist iconography on more than one occasion (allegedly unwittingly). There is almost nothing in the football world that Buffon has yet to do, other than win the Champions League, an unresolved quest that has given him a bit of a deranged, ragged look behind the eyes in recent years.

If Buffon is not the best goalkeeper of all time, then he is certainly the best loved. This is helped by the fact that he has a funny name, which looks a lot like buffoon. And that, despite going through a severe depression in his early 20s, he has always seemed to be haunted by slightly fewer raging demons than some of his counterparts. But he is mostly beloved for his longevity itself, which has provided a comforting constant in a world of perpetual motion. If he ever retires, and that point is honestly debatable, he will always be remembered, in the moments before kick-off in a massive game for Italy, booming out "Il Canto degli Italiani," the Italian national anthem, with eyes closed and chin up, proudly, fearlessly ready for all that is to come.

FULL NAME:	DATE OF BIRTH:	PLACE OF BIRTH:	NATIONAL TEAM:	CAPS / GOALS:
Gianluigi Buffon	*January 28, 1978*	*Carrara, Italy*	*Italy, 1997–2018*	*176 / –*

ERIC CANTONA

"HEN THE SEAGULLS..." CANTONA started in his heavy French accent, pausing as he took a long sip of water, "... follow the trawler, it's because they think sardines will be thrown into the sea. Thank you very much." There was a flicker of a twinkle in his eye, hiding between the prominent Roman nose and the unforgettable unibrow, but mostly he just seemed pensive in a blasé sort of way, like a college professor explaining something that should be entirely obvious to a lecture hall filled with students he knows will never get it. Then he stood up and walked out. The press shifted uncomfortably in their seats. Some Parisian journalists in the back grumbled at the prospect of having to translate the thing into French (*seagull*, it turns out, is *mouette*, should you yourselves ever need it). Some people giggled. Were they the seagulls? Was he allowed to do that? Was that free verse or iambic pentameter?

Eric Cantona. Poet, actor, beach soccer manager, artist, social revolutionary, football god.

Back in the fall of 1992, things were looking a bit iffy for Cantona. He had retired from football a year earlier after a disagreement with the French Football Federation (and by disagreement, we mean he threw a ball at a referee, received a one-month ban, called the Federation idiots at his hearing, received two more months, and quit the sport in protest). On the joint advice of his psychoanalyst and Michel Platini, Cantona decamped to England to restart his career, signing with Leeds United. He quickly made an impact with Leeds, helping them secure a surprise title win, but Cantona wasn't getting along with grim manager Howard Wilkinson, who didn't quite know what to do with him. So, in November of 1992, Leeds offloaded Cantona onto Manchester United for a meager £1.2 million. When Man United's left winger, Lee Sharpe, who was down in Leeds doing some autograph signing, heard the news, he responded simply: "Yeah, right."

Sometimes things just click. Cantona—commanding, intimidating, confident to the point of arrogance—was in need of a club where he could conduct the orchestra. Manchester United, filled with fresh-faced academy graduates (that famous class of '92) and still reeling from the previous year's late-season collapse, was in need of a leader. The fans just wanted to win for the first time in 26 years. It is an immense credit to the vision and management skills of Sir Alex Ferguson that everyone got what they wanted.

Cantona brought presence and imagination to Manchester United. The pitch had a certain feel when he was on it, like he was stretching and sculpting it to fit his own purposes and everyone else was just along for the ride. His vision was sublime—his best goals, like the two-touch volley against Wimbledon in 1994 or the exquisitely judged chip over the Sunderland keeper in '96—are creative, breathtakingly unexpected pieces of artistic flair. He would celebrate by furrowing his brow, slowly raising both arms, puffing out his chest, and squinting indifferently, as if to say, "Yes, of course I just did that." As if the feat he had just executed was not only easy, but also somehow guaranteed. Fans loved him; his teammates stayed later and practiced harder in an effort to impress him. United won the league in Cantona's first season with the club. Then they won it again in his second. Everyone called him *the King*.

United was probably on track to win it in his third year, too, but in January of 1995, Cantona launched himself right-foot first into the face of a particularly obnoxious Crystal Palace fan who'd been taunting him from the other side of the fence after he was sent off with a red card. Cantona was charged with criminal assault and banned from football for nine months. As was his wont, he took personal offense at the severity of the ban—leaving the English to mull over his seagulls quote, Cantona announced his intention to retire and returned to France. Fergie, man-managing his heart out, followed Cantona to Paris and coaxed him into coming back; with their King reinstated, United won the league again in '96 and '97, officially solidifying their dominance in the Premier League era. In the summer of 1997, eight days short of his 31st birthday, Cantona retired, explaining that he had gotten all he could out of the sport and wanted to pursue other careers that allowed more time for drinking and going out with friends.

FULL NAME:	DATE OF BIRTH:	PLACE OF BIRTH:	NATIONAL TEAM:	CAPS / GOALS:
Eric Daniel Pierre Cantona	*May 24, 1966*	*Marseille, France*	*France, 1987–95*	*45 / 20*

JOHN CHARLES

TO UNDERSTAND HOW WALES ENDED up at the 1958 World Cup, you have to remove your socks and shoes and wade into the farcical inner workings of mid-century international football. In the wake of World Cup 1954, FIFA decreed that the world would be divided into continental football associations. For most countries, this didn't mean very much, as World Cup qualification groups were already drawn geographically by FIFA.

But the Middle East, which had previously been haphazardly included in the European group, suddenly found itself in the newly established Asian Football Confederation. Together with the Confederation of African Football, they were collectively awarded a single spot at World Cup 1958, with 10 teams vying. Turkey withdrew in the first round of qualifying in protest of their placement in the Asian confederation rather than the European group, sending Israel through on a walkover. Indonesia and Egypt dropped out in the second round, refusing to play Israel in solidarity with the Arab League's boycott, which sent Israel and Sudan through automatically to the final round where—you guessed it—Sudan refused to play Israel, who was suddenly into the finals for the first time in their existence: all without having set foot on a football pitch.

This didn't sit well with FIFA. They whipped up a playoff between Israel and the runner-up in one of the eight UEFA groups to make sure Israel would play at least one game before qualifying. The lucky country was to be drawn, purportedly, out of the Jules Rimet cup itself. Wales—who had lost out in their group by two points to Czechoslovakia—was not picked. Belgium was. After a little reflection, however, Belgium politely declined out of embarrassment at the situation. Third time's the charm: Wales was picked on the second try, and had none of the Belgians' prideful compunctions. They summarily beat Israel, who, had they been a better team, probably would have been allowed in without the playoff fuss in the first place.

Wales was a middling team, with more than half the roster playing their club football in lower leagues. But, as has become something of a Welsh tradition, they had one star upon whom to pin their dreams. More recently, it's been Ryan Giggs or Gareth Bale. In 1958, it was John Charles.

John Charles is football's great renaissance man. He began his career at Leeds United as a well-respected center back. Two years later, with Leeds desperately in need of goals, he was switched to center forward. Having scored just four times in his 109 club appearances, Charles took to the new responsibility with aplomb. His 29 goals in the 1955–56 season saw Leeds promoted back into the top division. The following season, Charles was the league's top goalscorer with a casual 38 goals that ballooned Leeds into the table's top 10. It's a relatively unheard-of position switch—imagine Virgil van Dijk hopping up front and winning the Golden Boot. Famously, in the space of one week, Bobby Moore was asked to name the best striker he had ever faced, and Nat Lofthouse the best defender. Both responded: "John Charles."

Charles is a veritable Leeds United deity. If you ever find yourself in the neighborhood, you will be forced to conclude that he built it himself. There is John Charles Way and John Charles Approach, the John Charles Centre for Sport, and the John Charles stand. Despite being there for only six years, moving to Juventus in 1957 on a then-unheard-of transfer fee. Charles was equally beloved in Turin, leading them to the top of the league that first season.

Wales rolled into Sweden in the summer of 1958 with an air of unlikely possibility. They emerged unscathed from their first three World Cup matches, drawing 1–1 with Hungary and Mexico and 0–0 with Sweden. With no goal difference rule in those days, Hungary and Wales went to a playoff match. The Hungarians, no longer the Mighty Magyars, having lost much of their roster during the 1956 revolution, resorted to hacking their way through the Welsh team, cutting Charles down on every occasion. Wales won the match, but Charles limped impotently through most of the second half and was forced to sit out the quarterfinal against Brazil. Wales defended well and went down to a single goal, scored by a 17-year-old Pelé—his first-ever World Cup goal. This is one of football's favorite sliding doors moments: What would have happened if John Charles had been healthy, if Wales had beaten Brazil, if Pelé had not scored? But Wales wasn't even supposed to be in the tournament at all.

FULL NAME:	DATE OF BIRTH:	PLACE OF BIRTH:	NATIONAL TEAM:	CAPS / GOALS:
William John Charles	*December 27, 1931*	*Swansea, Wales*	*Wales, 1950–65*	*38 / 15*

BOBBY CHARLTON

OBBY CHARLTON'S STORY BEGINS in tragedy. In 1958, just two years into his senior career at Manchester United, Charlton and the team were on their way back from a European Cup game in Belgrade. Halfway home, they stopped in Munich to refuel. It was early February in Germany and the ground was covered in melting gray slush. During takeoff, the plane began to skid down the runway, and it became clear that the plane wasn't going to be able to accelerate enough to lift into the air. Tragically, it was also too late to slow down. The team said their prayers as the plane veered off the runway and crashed into a nearby house, splitting in half and depositing passengers every which way. When Charlton's teammate, Harry Gregg, dragged him out of the fiery wreckage by the seat of his pants, he assumed that Charlton was dead. Astonishingly, two minutes later, there was Charlton—the shy 20-year-old kid from the mining town of Ashington, Northumberland—standing on the edge of the blaze, surveying the wreckage.

That Charlton lived to play 22 more years is a miracle. That he managed to accomplish what he did in that time is a miracle on top of that. The numbers speak for themselves: 17 years and 758 games played for Manchester United, 249 goals, one European Cup, three League titles, one FA Cup, 106 caps for England, one World Cup championship in 1966 (the first and only in English history), one Ballon d'Or, one side of the stadium named in his honor at Old Trafford, one knighthood. When you add all this up, you get one of the most impactful careers in English football.

Yet perhaps the most indicative number of all is just *two*. Two yellow cards in the entirety of Bobby Charlton's 24-year career. That's almost unheard of. Wayne Rooney, the man who eventually broke Charlton's goalscoring records for both England and Man United, logged 145.

Out of the ashes of the Munich Air Disaster rose one of the best teams the English game had ever seen, flanked by George Best on the right and Bobby Charlton on the left. Best was the rascal; Charlton, the gentleman. Best, unscathed by Munich—he was only 11 at the time of the accident—restored a sense of mirthful youth and optimism to the club. Charlton did not have Best's natural talent or his sense of revelry. But what he brought back with him from Munich was arguably more remarkable.

Watch Charlton's goal against Mexico in the group stage of the 1966 World Cup. It is a powerful, commanding strike, hit from 30 yards out with almost no spin on the ball. Deft, clean, precise. Everyone else is running around getting their feet dirty. Charlton, with his dinner jacket combover—the envy of pipe-smoking, prematurely balding men across the continent—is playing an elegant, refined sport.

FULL NAME:	DATE OF BIRTH:	PLACE OF BIRTH:	NATIONAL TEAM:	CAPS / GOALS:
Sir Robert Charlton	*October 11, 1937*	*Ashington, Northumberland, England*	*England, 1958–70*	*106 / 49*

BRANDI CHASTAIN

HEN YOU THINK OF THE '99ERS, that iconic, World Cup–winning US Women's National Team that brought women's soccer into the view of the American public, you immediately think of the team's star player, Mia Hamm. When you picture them, however, it is not an image of Hamm that comes to mind. It is instead the image of a comparatively unknown defender named Brandi Chastain.

Despite the nickname *Hollywood*, coined by Julie Foudy in reference to Chastain's Cali roots and penchant for showmanship, Brandi Chastain was by no means a headliner on the US team that turned up that summer for the third edition of the Women's World Cup. Chastain was coming into 1999 as an experienced veteran, with a World Cup and an Olympic gold already under her belt; unlike striker, though, defender is not a flashy position. Weeks away from her 31st birthday, she had neither the name recognition nor the quantifiable accomplishments of teammates like Michelle Akers or Hamm. When the team sent Chastain instead of the spotlight-shy Hamm to appear on *Letterman* three days before the World Cup kickoff, he couldn't even remember her name, settling for "the woman we talked to about soccer" when referencing her in a later segment.

Like the tall kids in elementary school, defenders are lined up in the very back of every photo. We primarily pay attention to them when they make mistakes. Chastain made one such mistake that tournament during the quarterfinal against Germany. In the fifth minute, she regains possession on a German press and sends an innocuous enough back pass to keeper Briana Scurry. As soon as she looks up and sees that Scurry is standing about two feet to the right of where Chastain thought she was, however, her face falls with the realization that she has just made a potentially career-defining error. Without a German in sight, the ball rolls right past Scurry and into goal. Tiffeny Milbrett evens things up in the 16th minute, but a stoppage-time goal at the end of the first half launches Germany back out in front. Then, in the fourth minute of the second half, Chastain hits a beautiful right-footed volley off a corner kick—her only goal of the tournament—and brings the US back into the match. She falls to the ground with her arms splayed, snow angel–style, radiating relief that her legacy will not be defined by getting her team knocked out of the 1999 World Cup in the quarterfinals.

Nine days later, in the sweltering Pasadena summer afternoon heat, Chastain sends the US' final penalty careening into the top right corner of China's net, winning the tournament on her left foot. She rips off her shirt and drops to the ground for the second time in two weeks, sinking to her knees with eyes closed, mouth wide open in a roar of triumph, arms out in front of her, fingers wrapped tightly around the shirt in her right hand. The image will be used as the cover of *Sports Illustrated* and *Newsweek*, plastered onto newsstands across the country for weeks. It will be voted the second-most iconic cover in *Sports Illustrated*'s history. Unlike Chastain's first celebration, it is not an image of relief. It is an image of pride, of strength, of achievement, and of pure, unadulterated ecstasy. Because society is the way it is, much of the discussion of this photograph tends to center around Chastain's bared bra and the musculature of her arms and abs. But what sticks with you about the photo is the exuberance. This is Chastain's legacy.

FULL NAME:	DATE OF BIRTH:	PLACE OF BIRTH:	NATIONAL TEAM:	CAPS / GOALS:
Brandi Denise Chastain	*July 21, 1968*	*San Jose, California, United States*	*United States, 1988–2004*	*192 / 30*

JOHAN CRUYFF

OHAN CRUYFF WAS SO INDISPENS-able to the great Dutch "Clockwork Orange" side of the 1970s that he had his own customized uniform. Because Cruyff was sponsored by Puma and the Dutch jerseys were made by Adidas, the team provided him with a tailor-made shirt featuring Puma's logo instead of the three stripes worn by the other players. Gifted with balletic grace and a Jedi-like ability to switch direction and leave everyone behind, this gaunt, long-nosed, rakish Amsterdamer was one of the greatest players never to win the World Cup.

It took only seven games during his one and only tournament in 1974 to establish his legend. His enormously gifted Dutch team pioneered *Total Football*, the versatile system in which all 10 outfield players could play in any position, confusing their opponents by consistently switching roles to take advantage of open space. Cruyff, nominally the striker, was almost always the fulcrum, finding a way to drop off to the flanks and attack from the wings. All 15 of the Dutch goals seemed to start or end with him and his flowing style and revolutionary thinking. The fact that his team fell short in the final against West Germany made him even more compelling and beloved.

By the next World Cup, he was gone. His controversial retirement from international soccer at his peak, on the eve of the 1978 Argentina World Cup, has never fully been understood or explained. It was suspected at the time that Cruyff declined to participate in the tournament so as not to be used for propaganda by Argentina's military junta; 30 years later, he claimed that he had in fact retired from international duty after he and his family were held at gunpoint in their home in 1977, out of fear of further incidents. Whatever the reason, Cruyff, like Édith Piaf, claimed to regret nothing: "I don't go through life cursing the fact that I did not win a World Cup. I played on a fantastic team that gave millions of people watching a great time. That is what football is all about. . . . There is no medal better than being acclaimed for your style." Although Cruyff's international scoring record was sensational (33 goals in 48 games), he is best remembered not for a goal, but for a move against Sweden, which became known as the *Cruyff Turn*. Trapped on the left-hand side of the penalty area as a Swedish defender tried to marshal him into a harmless position, Cruyff somehow turned his upper and lower torso in two different directions while flicking the ball in a third. Watching the move in slow motion, you can almost see the defender's brain freeze as he struggles to stay upright, while the Dutchman breaks free to deliver a lethal cross.

Jan Olsson, the poor Swede victimized by the move, generously claimed that the moment was "the proudest memory of my career. I thought I'd win the football for sure, but he tricked me. I was not humiliated. I had no chance. Cruyff was a genius."

FULL NAME:	DATE OF BIRTH:	PLACE OF BIRTH:	NATIONAL TEAM:	CAPS / GOALS:
Hendrik Johannes Cruijff	*April 25, 1947*	*Amsterdam, Netherlands*	*Netherlands, 1966–77*	*48 / 33*

KENNY DALGLISH

IN THE SUMMER OF 1977, LIVERPOOL fans were devastated when Kevin Keegan, the team's curly-mopped star forward, announced he was moving to Hamburg. His replacement was a 26-year-old Scottish player named Kenny Dalglish, for whom Liverpool had paid what was then a record British transfer fee of £440,000. The Anfield faithful were reduced to scrounging for mentions in the local football rags and calling up friends with Glaswegian cousins to verify the extent of Dalglish's abilities. Keegan was a known quality, having led Liverpool out of their late-'60s trophy drought with three league titles in five years. Dalglish was an unknown. Everyone was nervous and skeptical, endearingly innocent to the knowledge that within 15 years, Keegan would remain a mid-level character in LFC's pantheon of heroes, and Dalglish would be their patron saint.

Upon first glance, Dalglish had no immediately apparent skills. He was neither remarkably fast nor remarkably deft-footed. On the pitch, his posture was often ambivalent, giving off an almost apathetic air of directionlessness as he hovered on the periphery of the action, lulling marking defenders into relaxing their guard. And then, with the sudden drop of a shoulder, Dalglish would make space where there had been none, collecting the ball in a flash and curling it into the net with an unexpectedly versatile right foot. In December 1977, Dalglish scored the sixth goal against Keegan's own Hamburg in the second leg of the European Super Cup final, clinching the win for Liverpool. "Keegan was quicker off the mark," manager Bob Paisley remarked, "but Kenny runs the first five yards in his head." In May 1978, Dalglish scored the winning goal in the European Cup final against Brugge, driving Liverpool to their second European Cup in two years. By the end of his first season, "Keegan, who?" could be heard echoing around the stadium as the Anfield faithful coronated a new sovereign: King Kenny.

Dalglish stayed at Liverpool for 13 years, ushering in the most successful period in the club's history: six league titles, two FA Cups, four League Cups, seven Charity Shields, three European Cups, and one European Super Cup. Motivator and playmaker in equal measure (a dual role that was made explicit in 1985, when Dalglish was appointed player-manager after Joe Fagan's resignation), he could be prickly and demanding, but his expectations were always followed by an inviting grin and a preternatural pass that seemed to know exactly where you were without Dalglish so much as looking up. By the start of 1989, he was the most decorated man in English football.

Had his story ended there, Dalglish would be remembered as a beloved star and a decent manager, but then Hillsborough happened.

If the heights he reached with Liverpool were the prose of Dalglish's career, the punctuation was Hillsborough, the darkest moment in the club's history. On April 15, 1989, shortly after kickoff in the FA Cup semifinal between Liverpool and Nottingham Forest, catastrophe struck. The pens where the Liverpool fans were gathering became fatally overcrowded, and 97 people were killed with nearly 800 injured. It was the biggest stadium disaster in history, shaking the entire city of Liverpool to its core. Police attempted to cover up their action and blamed the fans, while the fans began a decades-long fight for justice to prove that police actions were truly to blame. The rest of the country watched in horror and dismay at the notion that 97 football fans could go to a match and never return. The entire nation was angry and traumatized and desperately in need of someone to look to. Dalglish was only 38 years old, but he stepped in to fill that void, attending funerals, visiting hospital beds, meeting with families—acting at once as mayor, grief counselor, and guiding light. The effort took its toll. Within 22 months, Dalglish had succumbed to the emotional strain and resigned as manager. But in that year and a half, Dalglish was remade from club hero to national hero. You can't talk about England in the '80s without talking about Hillsborough. And you can't talk about Hillsborough without talking about Kenny Dalglish.

Some legacies are diminished by tragedy, entire careers reduced to the memory of one harrowing event. Dalglish's was amplified tenfold, the immeasurable gratitude of a population beatifying this man from Glasgow, who had come 14 years earlier to prop up a team, and stayed to prop up a city.

FULL NAME:	DATE OF BIRTH:	PLACE OF BIRTH:	NATIONAL TEAM:	CAPS / GOALS:
Sir Kenneth Mathieson Dalglish	March 4, 1951	Glasgow, Scotland	Scotland, 1971–86	102 / 30

ALFREDO DI STÉFANO

N THE SPRING OF 1952, REAL Madrid organized a small celebration for their 50th anniversary, inviting Swedish champions IFK Norrköping and Argentine champions River Plate over to the Spanish capital to participate in a friendly three-day, three-way tournament. When Real discovered in the lead-up to the tournament that the best players in Argentina had left the country en masse in '49 in protest of a 1,500-peso salary cap set by Argentina's Ministry of Labor, they promptly retracted River Plate's invitation and sent one to the Colombian club Millonarios instead. Millonarios appeared at the end of March with Argentina's best prodigal sons in tow—chief among them a blond, surprisingly boyish-looking forward named Alfredo Di Stéfano—and comfortably won the tournament with the help of three goals from the 25-year-old expat.

Up north in Catalonia, Barcelona caught wind of the player who had neatly done away with their rivals, rubbed their hands together, and went straight to River Plate (who still technically owned the rights to Di Stéfano, as the Colombian league was not part of FIFA at the time) to broker a deal. Unfortunately for Barcelona, River Plate couldn't transfer Di Stéfano without the permission of Millonarios. In the meantime, Real Madrid brokered a deal with Millonarios, precipitating a situation the official FIFA term for which is, we believe, "sabotage-laced, corruption-ridden transfer standstill." A mediator was appointed; in a spurt of Solomonic wisdom (and just maybe inspired by a dash of pressure from famed Madridista and local dictator Francisco Franco), he adjudicated that Madrid would take Di Stéfano for the first two seasons of his contract, while Barça would have him for the second two. Twice-frustrated, Barcelona shrugged in defeat, cut their losses, and had Real Madrid buy them out of the contract. Seven months later, Real had won the Spanish title for the first time in 21 years on the back of 27 goals from Di Stéfano, and the steam emitting from Catalonian ears could be seen straight across the country.

There has perhaps never been a more complete footballer than Di Stéfano. He had pace, skill, stamina, superb ball control, and the ability to switch gears at the drop of a hat. Depending on what moment you saw him in action, you might have described him with equal confidence as a striker, a box-to-box midfielder, a classic number 10, or a deep-lying playmaker. Di Stéfano essentially enacted an individual version of total football, zipping around, perpetually popping up at center half or full back to cover a displaced teammate, insistent on influencing the game from all corners at all times. By all accounts a rather pompous, self-interested player, Di Stéfano barely seemed to realize that he had 10 other teammates on the pitch. "If Pelé was the lead violinist," Helenio Herrera once noted, "Di Stéfano was the entire orchestra."

With their new star comfortably settled in, Real went about building the best offense in the world, signing Raymond Kopa in 1956 and Ferenc Puskás in 1958. By the time Di Stéfano left for Espanyol in '64, Real had won eight league titles in 11 seasons and five consecutive European Cups. The club's dynasty was firmly established—and with 34 La Liga titles to Barcelona's 26, they have yet to go more than five years without winning the league since. Of course, there have been other players, other generations who have helped to build the Real legacy, but none more so than Di Stéfano. Success begets success.

Despite his prolificacy, Di Stéfano never accomplished much on the international stage. He was banned from the Argentina team in 1954 after appearing in a handful of unofficial friendlies for Colombia; he finally managed to qualify for a World Cup at age 36 after being naturalized in Spain, but an injury kept him on the bench; by 1966, he was retired. This is likely the reason that Di Stéfano remains somewhat of a niche player as legends go, much less in the public eye than the rest of his GOAT confrères, always half buried under a century of Barcelona–Madrid resentment. But tellingly, when asked who the greatest player of all time was, Diego Maradona overlooked the likes of Pelé, Messi, and even himself in favor of Don Alfredo. It's not simply that Di Stéfano ran the show. He *was* the show. In the words of Arrigo Sacchi, the legendary Italian manager, "Di Stéfano turned still photographs into cinema."

FULL NAME:	DATE OF BIRTH:	PLACE OF BIRTH:	NATIONAL TEAM:	CAPS / GOALS:
Alfredo Stéfano Di Stéfano Laulhé	*July 4, 1926*	*Buenos Aires, Argentina*	*Argentina, 1947; Colombia, 1949; Spain, 1957–62*	*6 / 6; 4 / 0; 31 / 23*

MARIBEL DOMÍNGUEZ

OST OF THE WOMEN IN THIS book have, at one time or other, played on men's teams—often on boys' under-12 teams if they grew up in towns that didn't have organized spaces for young girls to play. Occasionally, you hear about a woman trying to play on a professional men's team—it doesn't happen that frequently, but it's a story that always gets picked up, partly because it has an intriguing gender dynamic, and largely because it reminds everyone of their favorite football film, *She's the Man.*

In December of 2004, Maribel Domínguez made international headlines when she signed a two-year contract with Atlético Celaya, a second-division men's team in Guanajuato, Mexico. Domínguez was the star of the Mexican women's national team; she had 45 goals in 46 games for Mexico, including Mexico's only goal at the 1999 World Cup, two against Canada to qualify them for the 2004 Olympics in Athens, and one at the Games themselves, which was enough to see Mexico into the quarterfinals—the Mexico women's team's greatest international achievement to date. A *Los Angeles Times* profile from the summer of 2004 described her as the Mexican Mia Hamm, but she was essentially an unknown outside of Mexico. Being the Mexican Mia Hamm didn't come with very much clout, since the Mexican team was ragtag and generally underperforming, cobbled together in a country that didn't even have an amateur women's league at the time.

Considering the lack of a women's league, it seemed more than reasonable that Domínguez would want to play for a Mexican men's team. While she lacked the brawn of her would-be teammates, she had the technique, the speed, the desire, and the chutzpah. The idea, unorthodox though it was to the media, could not have struck Domínguez as particularly outrageous—she had spent years playing under the pseudonym *Mario* as a child, her teammates only learning her gender when she was chosen for the subnational women's team. (Her teammates reportedly knocked on her mother's door in disbelief when they heard the news.)

Celaya was more than willing. They were mid-table in the second division, in financial straits, and missing a decent center forward. Candidly, Domínguez, a wiry and intuitive world-class goal-poacher, was by far the most talent they were going to get for that small a price tag, and the signing would provide some free publicity for the club. They had a jersey mocked up specially for her. The international press ate it up, publishing the story far and wide, launching Domínguez straight into the global spotlight. It was by no means the first story of its kind (in 2003, Perugia in Serie A had teased the press for months with a flurry of rumors that they were signing different female players), but this time it was really happening. Maribel Domínguez, affectionately called *Marigol* by fans, was going to be the first woman signed to a men's professional team. You could feel the anticipation in the air, as a thousand Hollywood screenwriters sharpened their quills. Two days later, it was predictably over. The Mexican Football Association couldn't see a problem with it, but they deferred to FIFA, who ruled from Zurich that gender separation had to be maintained, for reasons that they have always deemed prudent to keep to themselves.

Eventually, the early 2000s fad of threatening to put women on men's teams faded. Domínguez was about as close as anyone came to actually doing it. Moving on quickly, she signed with Barcelona's women's team, which was then struggling on the brink of relegation, and helped buoy them back up in the Superliga table. Fittingly, she capped off her career a decade later with a season in the Liga Mexicana de Fútbol Femenil, established a few years after Domínguez's departure for Catalonia. Rarely has a sports league been as obliged to a single athlete as the Mexican women's league is to Domínguez.

It's never been clear whether women playing on men's teams is a good or bad thing for women's football, which is why no one ever particularly advocates for it. But as sports narratives go, it is one of the most enduringly thrilling, if only because it grabs attention like nobody's business. Mexico's women's league was founded largely on the back of the publicity Domínguez garnered during the whole Celaya affair. Ironically enough, it effectively convinced Mexican football, like nothing else had, that people were interested in watching women play football.

FULL NAME:	DATE OF BIRTH:	PLACE OF BIRTH:	NATIONAL TEAM:	CAPS / GOALS:
Maribel Guadalupe Domínguez Castelán	*November 18, 1978*	*Mexico City, Mexico*	*Mexico, 1998–2016*	*116 / 82*

DIDIER DROGBA

IDIER DROGBA IS AN OPTICAL illusion. His legend looms larger than life, casting him as one of the most venerated players of this century, his name woven into song lyrics and national memories and onto the backs of jerseys gifted by uncles who still have his feats swirling around their brains to children born too late to know him. Drogba's mother once claimed on Ivorian TV that he was in the womb for 10 months and was walking seven months later. True or not, the story captures the trajectory of his football career. Slow, then fast. Very fast. After all, the Ivorian spent five years bumbling around Ligue 2 at Le Mans before Ligue 1 side Guingamp picked him up in 2002 at age 23 for a humble £80,000. Just two years later, following a successful season at Guingamp and one brief but heavily lauded season at Marseille, Drogba had made it to Chelsea, walking into a career as the most famous face of a wave of Ivorian players—Kolo Touré and Emmanuel Eboué at Arsenal, Yaya Touré at Man City post–Abu Dhabian purchase—who would come to heavily define that second decade of the Premier League.

For Chelsea fans, Drogba denotes the greatest era of achievement in the club's history. For non-Chelsea fans, the word that comes to mind is *cheaty*. He was prone to dramatics, dives, the occasional Maradona-inspired Hand of God goal. Cynics complained throughout his career that he was overrated, arguing that he was inconsistent and difficult and didn't actually score that many goals—but what did it mean to be overrated when you were Didier Drogba, whose great performances were like sudden thunderstorms? Derbies, table-defining league games, cup finals; if the game was big, so was Drogba. He played 10 finals with Chelsea. He scored in eight of them. Powerful, precise, seismic, awesome: When he was on,

he was completely unplayable. You weren't sure exactly what he wanted, but you were sure he wanted it more than you. In 2012, Drogba propelled Chelsea to their first ever Champions League trophy with an astonishing 88th-minute header in the final against Bayern Munich to take the game to penalties. Drogba—who was nowhere near the ball's trajectory when it was launched from the corner flag—could be heard shouting "mine" as he hurtled towards Frank Lampard teeing up at the far post. Lampard stepped out of the way.

Drogba spent most of his childhood in France, bumping around the country with his uncle, a journeyman striker in Ligue 2. But he was born in Abidjan, a city of 4.4 million on the southern coast of Côte d'Ivoire, and it is there that he exists most clearly in the popular imagination—an entire generation of Ivorian rap songs, dance moves, jumbo beer bottles (referred to as *Drogbas* because of their strength and size), and West African Chelsea fans standing as evidence of his influence.

Drogba rose to fame against the background of Côte d'Ivoire's first civil war. Some credited Drogba for ending it with an impassioned locker room speech after the nation qualified for the World Cup for the first time in the fall of 2005, begging the country to reunite, singing, "We want to have fun, so stop firing your guns." The two factions had in fact already put down their guns—a ceasefire had been in effect for months—and would pick them up again not too long afterwards. The Côte d'Ivoire national team, meanwhile, who were championed as the most talented team in Africa, failed to get out of the group stage, and would fail to exit the group stage in the next two tournaments as well. But one wanted to give Drogba the credit, because ending a war *felt* like just the kind of clutch goal in a big game that Drogba was capable of producing.

FULL NAME:	DATE OF BIRTH:	PLACE OF BIRTH:	NATIONAL TEAM:	CAPS / GOALS:
Didier Yves Drogba Tébily	*March 11, 1978*	*Abidjan, Ivory Coast*	*Ivory Coast, 2002–14*	*105 / 65*

EUSÉBIO

N THE OLD BLACK AND WHITE '60S television footage, Eusébio is often just a blur streaking across the screen. As much 100-meter sprinter as footballer, he moves so fast you can barely make him out. His goals are breathtaking displays of agility and acceleration: breakaway plays with streams of defenders trailing helplessly behind him or poaches where he appears out of thin air in slivers of open space, scoring before the defense has even had a chance to inhale. They called him the *Black Panther*—never has a nickname been more apt.

It is often pointed out that Portugal's most beloved footballer, Eusébio da Silva Ferreira—or simply Eusébio, as he was usually known—was not actually from Portugal at all. He was instead from Mafalala, a slum on the outskirts of Maputo, the capital city of Mozambique (Mozambique being one of the major jewels in the crown of the Portuguese Empire, colonized at the beginning of the 16th century and not decolonized until 1975, by which time Eusébio was 33 and his career was winding down). Among the less talked about advantages of colonial empire is that it vastly extended the possibilities of "local talent," allowing the Portuguese to farm feeder teams halfway around the world. And so, at 18, after playing two years in Mozambique, Eusébio signed with Benfica and was brought over to Portugal to play for them. On his debut against Atlético Clube de Portugal in 1961, he scored a hat trick. If Eusébio had misgivings about the colonial arrangement, he kept them quiet as the Portuguese fans took one look at what he was capable of and embraced him as a native son.

Portugal was not a dominant footballing force in those days: 1966 was their first time qualifying for the World Cup, and they wouldn't qualify again for another 20 years.

But that year, the only World Cup that Eusébio got to play in, they reached the semifinals, Eusébio pushing them up the hill essentially by himself. He scored nine goals in six games, including a Herculean four goals to drag Portugal back from a 3–0 hole against a surprisingly tenacious North Korea in the quarters.

Paradoxically, despite ending his career with a dumbfounding 733 goals in 745 professional matches, Eusébio is perhaps most remembered for a shot that he didn't make. It is 1–1 in the dying minutes of normal time during the 1968 European Cup Final against Manchester United. Eusébio picks up a long ball and storms into the box. With the United defense unable to do more than nip at his heels, he bullets a blistering shot from 10 yards. Unflinching, United keeper Alex Stepney lunges to his left and catches the ball. The force of the impact knocks him to the ground. Without even pausing, Eusébio offers him a hand to help him up. As he turns away, he looks back, applauds Stepney, and smiles. United go on to win in extra time.

If it weren't for Pelé, Eusébio likely would have been considered the best player in the world over the course of his 20-year career. But what makes him such an enduringly likable icon is his modesty. He was a world-class footballer, and he was also a man who would address his teammates as *Senhor* when asking for permission to take a free kick. In 2015, Eusébio was interred in the Portuguese National Pantheon in which the nation's greatest figures lie. A kid from Mozambique who learned to play football with a sock stuffed with old newspaper, buried next to Portugal's most historic figures. One can only assume that he'd be pleased as punch and embarrassed as hell, destined to spend all of eternity graciously applauding the achievements of his neighbors.

FULL NAME:	DATE OF BIRTH:	PLACE OF BIRTH:	NATIONAL TEAM:	CAPS / GOALS:
Eusébio da Silva Ferreira	January 25, 1942	Maputo, Mozambique	Portugal, 1961–73	64 / 41

JULIE FLEETING

THE ODD THING ABOUT THE PROTO-professional era of women's football is that the details of it are often disarmingly banal. For most of Julie Fleeting's career, she was a PE teacher in Kilwinning, Ayrshire, a small town about 20 miles south of Glasgow. On Sunday mornings, she'd take an hour-long flight from Glasgow down to London, where legendary Arsenal Ladies coach Vic Akers would pick her up at the airport and drive her to the grounds. She'd warm up, start for Arsenal, and fly back in the evening. Often, she'd be subbed off midway through the second half so that she could make her return flight. She had no sheen of celebrity, none of the gloss of the professional footballer. You likely wouldn't have clocked her in the airport carpark as anything other than a woman who'd had a long day.

Which is to say that you likely would have kept right on fiddling with the retractable handle of your carry-on, never realizing that Scotland's most prolific goalscorer had just hurried past you, well on her way to becoming the sixth-highest international scorer—man or woman—in the history of football.

Sometimes one forgets, given how loudly their football fans sing, but Scotland is a very small place, with a population about three million short of London's. Their national team also has a longstanding tradition of underperforming on the world stage. How difficult could it be then, you ask yourself, to be the country's top goalscorer? Truthfully, not that difficult. The number to beat when Fleeting first debuted for the national team in 1996 at age 15 was 30 goals, a record jointly shared by Denis Law and Kenny Dalglish. To say that Julie Fleeting beat it, however, would be a bit of an understatement. By her 20th birthday, she had already blown well past 30. When she retired 15 years later, she had 116 goals in 121 appearances, dynamiting a chasm so vast between her and everyone else, man or woman, who has ever played for Scotland it's almost laughable.

Fleeting's feat is staggering not because it indicates any particular bounty of talent that Law or Dalglish were lacking. She was a gifted player with good instincts, good footwork, and a flair for taking balls out of the air (during her one-year stint playing for the San Diego Spirit in the Women's United Soccer Association, the American fans had gamely nicknamed her *Air Scotland*), but she is undoubtedly not the sixth-most talented goalscorer in history. Women's football, particularly in those days, tended to be higher scoring than men's. Careers lasted longer. And many of the early fixtures of the Scotland women's team were not exactly what you'd call competitive (the 27–0 rout of the Isle of Man at the 2000 Celt Cup, in which Fleeting scored 16 goals, comes to mind). No, what is staggering is the simple fact that through 20 years of obscure, insignificant friendlies, minor local competitions, and qualifiers for tournaments they knew they had no chance of attending, she kept turning up, unwatched and uncompensated, playing on backwater fields in front of crowds you could count on a child's abacus. And kept scoring.

Fleeting was not some dilettante player who was just happy to be there. She lifted 17 trophies with Arsenal, where she commanded the league for eight years alongside the likes of Kelly Smith and Kim Little. She played professionally in the US, scoring in front of cheering crowds of 25,000. When the English FA asked her to play for Great Britain at the Olympics, Fleeting declined politely. Her goals were reserved for Scotland. A normal footballer would have stopped after a while, lost motivation. Despite her 16 goals against the Isle of Man, Scotland didn't even win that tournament—they were knocked out in the next round by Ireland. The Scottish women did not win even a minor competition until 2020, five years after Fleeting's retirement. They debuted at the Euros in 2017, the World Cup in 2019. Fleeting has no trophy-winning goals, no iconic moments while playing for her country. If a goal is scored in the forest and no one is around to hear it, does it make a sound? Fleeting spent two decades arguing that it does. A world-class player hanging around goal like a madwoman, with no self-consciousness, no sense of stakes, no interest in holding anything back for more important occasions. The result was kind of astounding.

FULL NAME:	DATE OF BIRTH:	PLACE OF BIRTH:	NATIONAL TEAM:	CAPS / GOALS:
Julie Fleeting	*December 18, 1980*	*Kilwinning, Scotland*	*Scotland, 1996–2015*	*121 / 116*

JUST FONTAINE

HIRTEEN GOALS IN A SINGLE tournament. It is a World Cup record slightly preposterous in magnitude, likely never to be matched, achieved by a certain amusingly named Moroccan-born French striker at the 1958 World Cup in Sweden. Achieved, it should be noted, wearing borrowed boots.

Raised in the formerly imperial city of Marrakesh, born to a French father and a Spanish mother, Just Fontaine was 24 in the summer of 1958. He had wide, powerful thighs, an open face with an amiable grin, and great timing. And he was having a good career. He had moved to the Côte d'Azur from the French protectorate five years earlier to play for Nice, before signing to Stade de Reims, France's marquee team, in 1956, to help fill the hole left by the great Raymond Kopa, who was himself off to Real Madrid. And Fontaine was proving well up to the task, driving Reims to a league and cup double in the spring of '58 with a table-topping 39 goals. He was not a regular member of the French national team, with a mere five caps to his name going into the World Cup that summer, but he was off to Sweden with a last-minute call-up as a reserve forward behind his Reims strike partner, René Bliard. One eve-of-finals training injury later, and Fontaine was suddenly a starting forward in his first (and only) World Cup. In his excitement, he wore straight through his shoes in training. "I found myself with nothing," he explained. "Luckily, Stéphane Bruey, one of the second-choice strikers, wore the same size as me and lent me his boots."

Expectations for the French team were about as tempered as was humanly possible on the eve of the 1958 tournament. Les Bleus had spiraled out of the group stage in 1954. Only eight members of the '54 squad had survived to the 1958 team in the intervening years, the rest replaced with younger, less experienced players like Fontaine. Many of the players had never taken the field together in actual competition before. Even the French press couldn't muster any optimism for the event. One newspaper posited that the team had arrived in Sweden so early because they knew they'd be the first to leave.

Chief among the quirks of the French press: They are often wrong. What followed was three weeks of once-in-a-generation alchemy between Kopa and Fontaine, which rocketed the French team all the way to the semifinals—their best result in 30 years of competition. Kopa's playmaking and Fontaine's finishing fused almost instantly into a largely uncontrollable combination, part meeting of the minds, part kismet, and much greater than the sum of its parts, quickly named *le tandem térrible* by a suddenly-enthusiastic-again French press. Together they crafted a dizzying, all-out attacking style of Champagne football, Kopa feeding perfect passes to Fontaine making perfectly timed runs, leaping over oncoming tackles and shouldering his way around opposing defenders to deposit the ball in the back of the net. This was their particular magic. They performed it as if on loop, Fontaine notching goal after goal after goal in every conceivable fashion: seven with his right foot, five with his left, and one with his head. He claimed he could "jump so high to head the ball, when I come down again, I have snow in my hair." A hat trick in the opening match against Paraguay was followed by a brace against Yugoslavia, who had beaten the now-forgotten French '54 team for knockout-round qualification in the group stage of the previous World Cup. One goal against Scotland. Two against Northern Ireland. With the French public following along intently on living room radios and above the din of smoky brasseries, gripped by a heady mix of patriotic fervor and unshakable astonishment, France sprinted all the way to their semifinal matchup against Brazil, where they were finally halted by a young Pelé and an already-leaky defense made leakier by a defender with a broken leg. Just two years later, Fontaine's own career would be stopped in its tracks by a double fracture in his left leg. But not before he scored four more goals against West Germany in the third-place 1958 playoff, to cap his World Cup total off at a tidy, unsurpassable 13.

As for the boots he borrowed from a teammate? Six matches and 13 goals later, he gave them back. "I like to think some of my goals were inspired by combining two spirits inside the same shoe."

FULL NAME:	DATE OF BIRTH:	PLACE OF BIRTH:	NATIONAL TEAM:	CAPS / GOALS:
Just Louis Fontaine	*August 18, 1933*	*Marrakesh, Morocco*	*France, 1953–60*	*21 / 30*

FORMIGA

LMOST ALL BRAZILIAN FOOT-
ballers are known by a single name. This often
strikes people as a charming eccentricity—an
indication of the familiarity and regard that Brazilian fans have for their players. In truth, it's
mostly a practical measure. Brazilians, whose naming tradition involves maternal surnames, paternal surnames, middle names, and even middler names, come into this world
trailing a great many monikers. They often pick up more
along the way. It would be impractical, if not impossible,
to call everyone by their given names. Live commentary
would be an absolute disaster, with balls flying all the way
down the other end of the field while commentators were
still shouting out the names of players who'd just scored.
Official nicknames are the only obvious solution. They're
mostly straightforward. *Neymar, Sócrates, Marta*: pieces of
names tapped to stand in for the whole thing. Occasionally,
they are more involved: *Kaká*, evolved out of his brother's
childhood mispronunciation of *Ricardo. Zico*, which meta-
morphosed from *Arthur* to *Arthurzinho* to *Arthurzico* to
Zico. Cafu, so called for his resemblance to a player named
Cafuringa (whose name was of course in and of itself a nickname—turtles all the way down, as it were). In the highest
tier of Brazilian nicknames there are the silly sobriquets:
stupid childhood nicknames that stuck. This is the surest
way to know that a Brazilian player is good. It requires a
very advanced level of talent to transcend the meaning of
a silly nickname and turn it into a term synonymous with
great achievement: *Pelé*, which as far as anyone knows, is
just nonsense sounds; *Garrincha*, which means *little bird*.

Formiga, which simply means *ant*.

Formiga (Miraildes Maciel Mota to her friends)
first appeared for Brazil's national team at the age of 17,
when she came on as a substitute at the 1995 World Cup
in Sweden. She had been dubbed *Formiga* by teammates
back in São Paulo, a vaguely unflattering if fairly accurate
joke about the head-down, selfless industriousness of her
game style. An all-action defensive midfielder, Formiga
would power around the entire pitch, sprinting in to execute
much-needed slide tackles and get to goalscoring opportunities that her teammates couldn't reach, frequently shouldering much more than her fair share of responsibility for
the team's success. By the 1996 Olympics, the first time
women's football appeared at the Games, Formiga was a
starter for Brazil. When she retired a quarter of a century
later, she was the only woman footballer in the world to play
in every iteration of the Olympics, and the only player, male
or female, to appear at a record seven World Cups. Formiga
used her athleticism, her commitment, and her expertise to
make Brazil a formidable opponent, no matter the situation.

After Brazil suffered a heartbreaking loss to hosts
France in the round of 16 in 2019, Marta gave an
impassioned post-match speech on the side of the pitch.
"There's not going to be a Formiga forever," she cried,
pleading for her country to support and nurture a new
generation of women footballers for when Formiga, who
attempted to step down from international duty in 2016
before being convinced to return, inevitably retired. And
while it was true that Brazil couldn't have Formiga forever, it does not yet feel true, because we are still learning
what women's football looks like without her. She has
been such a consistent, invigorating presence for as long
as—if not longer than—most people have been aware
of women's football. It's hard to imagine a tournament
without her there, head down, braids flying, a gleam of
intense concentration in her eyes.

FULL NAME:	DATE OF BIRTH:	PLACE OF BIRTH:	NATIONAL TEAM:	CAPS / GOALS:
Miraildes Maciel Mota	*March 3, 1978*	*Salvador, Bahia, Brazil*	*Brazil, 1995–2021*	*234 / 29*

GARRINCHA

O ONE EVER ASKED GARRINCHA how he felt about playing football. Maybe this was because he had a widespread reputation as the Forrest Gump of the Brazilian game—sweet, good at running, incapable of self-reflection. Or maybe it was because he was usually swimming in rum by the time he stepped out on the field. More likely, it was because of how he played. Watching Garrincha on the pitch—even today, in the compressed, grainy, black and white of YouTube clips—you can't imagine him doing anything else. Bliss radiates off of him. Garrincha—likely the best dribbler of all time—doesn't just plow through opponents. Nor does he simply go around them. Instead, he toys with them, weaving and feinting and veering every which way, leaving the other team in tangles behind him. He dribbles past defenders, then waits for them to catch up, just so he can have the pleasure of dribbling past them again. There is no malice, only winking, gleeful mischief.

The miracle of Garrincha was not that he became one of the greatest footballers the world has ever seen. It was that he was able to take the football field at all. Born into destitute poverty in 1933 in rural Brazil, with a spinal defect and a left leg that was six inches shorter than the right, Garrincha wasn't supposed to be a professional football player. He wasn't even supposed to be able to walk. Part of the appeal of Garrincha's football for fans—and perhaps for himself as well—was the perpetual surprise of this lopsided man's unexpected dexterity. Described by his biographer as "the most amateur footballer professional football ever produced," Garrincha would ditch training sessions at Botafogo, one of the top teams in Brazilian football, to play pick-up matches in the streets of his hometown, Pau Grande. To him, there was no particular difference between the two, so long as someone was passing him the ball. He was just there to play.

Alongside a 17-year-old Pelé, Garrincha led Brazil to their first World Cup victory in 1958. During his first match, a win over the USSR, he immediately dribbled past five players. A French journalist watching described it as "the greatest three minutes in the history of football." Later, Garrincha twisted an opponent into knots until the man tripped over his own feet. Garrincha turned around, went back, and helped the man up. Then he ran on with the ball. After the match, he asked his teammates why the Russians looked so distraught, completely unaware that, not being a league competition, there wouldn't be a second leg. He didn't even seem to know that he was at the World Cup.

Pelé, the Simon to Garrincha's Garfunkel, had more charisma and an infinitely better ear for PR, and was hoisted into the spotlight after that tournament. Yet Garrincha, even more than Pelé, represented the joy, spontaneity, and individualism at the essence of Brazilian football. When Pelé was forced to sit out most of the 1962 World Cup with an injury, Garrincha stepped out of his shadow and took up the mantle, delivering—essentially single-handedly—a second consecutive victory for the Brazilians. He was the joint top scorer at the 1962 World Cup and was voted the best player at the tournament.

Garrincha's apex was 1962. Eventually, the years of strain on his right knee, his flagrant alcoholism, and his penchant for philandering (by the mid-'60s, he had accumulated no fewer than 14 kids across two continents) caught up with him. He became a shell of his former self. He retired in 1973 and passed away 10 years later in the shadows of football, almost a forgotten man. After his death, Brazil remembered their hero. So many people wanted to attend his funeral that they had to hold it at the Maracanã, Brazil's most iconic football stadium. The national stadium in the capital Brasilia is named in his honor. A fitting tribute to a man who will forever be known as *Alegria do Povo*: *the People's Joy*.

FULL NAME:	DATE OF BIRTH:	PLACE OF BIRTH:	NATIONAL TEAM:	CAPS / GOALS:
Manuel Francisco dos Santos	*October 28, 1933*	*Pau Grande, Rio de Janeiro, Brazil*	*Brazil, 1955–66*	*50 / 12*

PAUL GASCOIGNE

HE AIR OF TORTURED GENIUS, THE lost-boy posture, the facade of impish, reckless lunacy thinly stretched over a bottomless well of existential discomfort: Gazza was the Hamlet of English football. Of course the English adored him. They love a tragedy.

From his debut for Newcastle in 1985, it didn't take Gazza long to catch the eye of English football fans. Gazza resembled a European fantasista, playing with instinct and flair rather than the more cerebral style of the best English players at the time. With a burst of speed and a drop of the shoulder, he'd dribble around defenders as if they were cones; with a physical nonchalance that belied its own precision, he'd disguise shots and passes until it was far too late. He was a raw, intuitive player, bounding with energy and talent the likes of which England had rarely seen before. Off the field, he was a slightly daft, incorrigible kid with pudgy cheeks and a lopsided smile, who spent his free time drinking, horsing around, and playing practical jokes on teammates. The press, dubious but fond of this boy wonder with the penchant for mischief, dubbed him *the Clown Prince of Football.*

Italia 90 transformed Gazza from lovable rascal into national protagonist. And though Gazza spent the tournament running around gleefully, stealing the ball from the bigger kids and charging through the hotel hallways at 4 a.m. looking for people to play with, it is none of this that made him a star. Not the perfectly executed Cruyff Turn he impertinently dropped against an accomplished Netherlands in the group stage, nor the midnight tennis match he played with some American tourists the night before the semifinal. Rather, it was this: The score is tied up in the 98th minute of the semifinal against West Germany when Gazza lunges at defender Thomas Berthold right in front of the German bench. As soon as he does it, he has his hands together in pleading supplication, but it is too late. The yellow, Gazza's second of the tournament, is already out of the ref's pocket; even if England wins, Gazza will not be allowed to play in the final. As the realization dawns on him, his lower lip starts to wobble and the tears well up in his eyes. Gary Lineker goes over to him, has a look, turns towards England manager Bobby Robson, and warningly shakes his head.

It was those tears that engulfed England in a frenzied fever of Gazzamania. They became the tears of the nation, as England, like Gazza, were also forced to sit out the final, after losing to Germany on penalties. But as he wept for England, so, too, did England weep for him. Their grinning imp had been replaced by a vulnerable, pulsing cavity of pain. Like Lineker, everyone took one look and understood on some level that Gazza wasn't going to be okay.

As is so often the case in tragedies, things that appeared comic in acts 1 and 2 took on an increasingly darker hue as the performance rolled on. The way Gazza would bang on the doors of his teammates' hotel rooms in the middle of the night, because he was afraid of the dark and couldn't bear to be left alone, began to seem disturbing rather than endearing. His funny faces seemed more like tics; his drinking more like addiction. Rather than mischievous, his pranks seemed erratic, his inappropriate outbursts compulsive. As he got older, the boyish recklessness fermented into disconcerting self-destruction. He was still capable of moments of brilliance on the pitch, but they became increasingly sparse as he bounced from club to club, struggling with injuries and self-discipline and the taxing work of keeping the demons at bay. In 1999, his wife revealed years of domestic abuse suffered at Gazza's hands during violent, drunken rages. By 2002, his career was over.

There is a temptation to simplify our relationship with Gazza: to split his career into two halves, with daft, laddishly charming, gifted Gazza on one side and troubled, troubling Gazza on the other, and to demarcate exactly where we fell in love and where we fell out again. But the truth is more complicated. The thing about Italia 90 was that it articulated what we had quietly known about Gazza the whole time. That there were cracks in the facade. That his unthinking impulsivity had consequences. That even if we made it, Gazza would not be able to come with us. We didn't have Gazza and then lose him. We were in a perpetual state of losing him. So maybe it was wrong that we exalted the good for as long as we did, ignoring and enabling the bad until that was all that was left. But it was hard to look away, because those moments when he was happy and dazzling and cheeky and lovely burned even brighter in their ephemerality.

FULL NAME:	DATE OF BIRTH:	PLACE OF BIRTH:	NATIONAL TEAM:	CAPS / GOALS:
Paul John Gascoigne	*May 27, 1967*	*Gateshead, County Durham, England*	*England, 1988–98*	*57 / 10*

GHEORGHE HAGI

HEN IRELAND, APPEARING IN their first World Cup in Italy in 1990, reached the round of 16, the entire country lost its mind. Roads stood still, workplaces ground to a halt. When the team scraped by against an equally unlikely Romania on penalties, advancing into the quarterfinals without having won a single game, people wept openly in the streets, hugging neighbors, strangers, blood-feud enemies, and romantic rivals alike. There are those who believe that the victory was primarily responsible for getting Ireland out of the recession of the late 1980s. If you were from Ireland, if you knew anyone from Ireland, if you knew anyone who had ever been to Ireland, you were likely not giving very much thought to the random Eastern Europeans on the other side of the field.

But there they were anyway, the poor Romanians, and I mean literally poor—the second-poorest country in Europe at the time, ahead of only Albania—six months out from the bloody Christmas Revolution and the firing-squad execution of brutal dictator Nicolae Ceaușescu.

And they were a genuinely talented team, the Romanians, in spite of political and economic turmoil. Well-organized and creative, playing decisively non-communist football as if determined to assert their newfound freedom and to remind the world that, former satellite state or not, they were a Latinate people at heart. After the tournament, all of their top players were picked up by big European teams. The Irish celebrated, but the Romanians were the ones who impressed.

The centerpiece of the team was captain Gheorghe Hagi, a small, lithe, mean-faced midfielder referred to as *Maradona of the Carpathians*. Possessing superb technical touch and a knack for brazen long-range shots, Hagi was so good that in 1987 Ceaușescu's son Valentin, charged with the army team Steaua București, had insisted on borrowing him from his club, Sportul Studențesc, ahead of an important European Cup match. As Valentin's pet project and the unofficial football propaganda arm of the Ceaușescu administration, Steaua pretty much had free rein in those days. The scores of their league matches were often known well before kickoff. Three years later, much to Sportul's chagrin, Valentin still hadn't returned him.

After Italy, Hagi signed with Real Madrid, but away from the familiar idiosyncrasies of Romanian football and stripped of the material perks of being the young Ceaușescu's favorite footballer, he couldn't manage to replicate the success of his career in the Romanian league, and four years later he was being relegated to Serie B with Brescia. A disappointing stint at Barcelona and a successful but largely unseen spell at Galatasaray in Turkey followed to round out his club career. But, reunited with his compatriots in the US in 1994, Hagi's magic was once again on full display. In the 34th minute of their opening match against Colombia, he scores one of the most stylish World Cup goals of all time, sending a 40-yard lob from the left touchline whooshing gracefully over the fingertips of Colombian keeper Óscar Córdoba. Romania topped their previous result, making an even more incredible run into the quarterfinals by taking out Argentina (missing Maradona, who had been ejected from the tournament after failing a drug test, but still formidable) in the round of 16, before falling in penalties yet again, this time to Sweden. As nicknames go, one notes, Hagi's bore a striking resemblance to his former dictator's own self-proclaimed moniker: *Genius of the Carpathians*.

Only one Carpathian genius came out on top.

FULL NAME:	DATE OF BIRTH:	PLACE OF BIRTH:	NATIONAL TEAM:	CAPS / GOALS:
Gheorghe Hagi	*February 5, 1965*	*Săcele, Romania*	*Romania, 1983–2000*	*124 / 35*

MIA HAMM

F COOL SOCCER GIRL WAS THE aspirational aesthetic of the '90s (it was), then Mia Hamm was its founding mother. Ask any kid born between 1980 and 2000 who they wanted to be when they grew up. The answer is always Mia Hamm.

Easily the most recognizable female athlete of the 20th century, Hamm is American soccer's most transcendent icon. This is not simply because she was so dominant on the soccer field, although with 158 international goals (tied with Abby Wambach for the most of any player, male or female), two World Cup championships in 1991 and 1999, and Olympic gold medals in 1996 and 2004, she certainly was. Hamm had staggering pace and a knack for flawless finishes. Yet the real difference-maker was her mind. Hamm was hypercompetitive, to the point of near insanity, putting 110 percent into every game she played, every run she made, every tackle she threw herself into. A forward who was perpetually tracking back to midfield, Hamm only had one mode: hard. After spending two hours running furiously under the 105-degree Pasadena sun in the 1999 World Cup Final, she collapsed in the locker room and had to spend two hours recovering with an IV drip attached to her arm. That's how much she wanted to win.

What elevated Hamm from talent to icon, however, was not how good she was, but, rather, how good she made you want to be.

Hamm's iconicity is best encapsulated by a Gatorade commercial that she and NBA icon Michael Jordan made in 1999. Set to the Irving Berlin song "Anything You Can Do (I Can Do Better)," the spot features Hamm and Jordan competing to see who's better at basketball, soccer, fencing, tennis, track, and judo. Hamm, beautiful, charming, with the sleekest ponytail you've ever seen, manages to make wanting something so badly you'd run yourself into the ground to get it look like it was the most natural thing in the world. She manages to make talent, ambition, and intensity look deliciously, irresistibly cool.

The secret to this is that Hamm's talent and competitiveness were tempered by kindness and humility, a team-first attitude, and a shocking disinterest in personal glory. Underneath the ponytails and the sports bras and the perfectly toned legs, the soccer girl was appealing because, modest and down to earth as she was, she had no need to tell you how good she was. But get her out on that field and she'd show you: 158 times.

Bend It Like Beckham, *She's the Man*, Blake Lively's plotline in *Sisterhood of the Traveling Pants*. All inspired by Mia Hamm. An entire generation of women grew up knowing in their souls that they were better at soccer than their brothers. Not because they were particularly ambitious. Or even particularly confident. Simply because Mia Hamm made it cool to think so.

FULL NAME:	DATE OF BIRTH:	PLACE OF BIRTH:	NATIONAL TEAM:	CAPS / GOALS:
Mariel Margaret Hamm	March 17, 1972	Selma, Alabama, United States	United States, 1987–2004	276 / 158

ADA HEGERBERG

DA HEGERBERG IS A PERFEC-tionist. It is a trait so intense it can only be innate, although two decades of vigorous, highly regimented training instituted by her father—a quiet, gentle Norwegian football coach with an almost monastic belief in fundamentals—running through hours of repetitive, painstaking touch drills, in a method they (very charmingly) call "plucking dirt on the little details," have certainly compounded its fervor. The results of this perfectionism are well documented. As a child, Hegerberg was known to bike home sobbing whenever her team lost a game; as a teen, debuting for her first professional club at age 15, she developed a reputation as a prima donna, swearing at managers who thought to substitute her prematurely and berating teammates twice her age. As a 22-year-old, Hegerberg quit from the Norwegian national team in a one-woman protest over what she perceived to be a lack of respect, investment, and consideration on the part of the Norwegian Football Federation, sitting out all international football for five years, refusing to compromise even to attend the 2019 World Cup (which, everyone was quick to point out, Norway could possibly have won with her, but certainly weren't going to win without her).

All of this only matters as much as it does because of the flip side of Hegerberg's perfectionism: Those same endless hours of training, impossibly demanding self-expectations, and refusal to compromise have shaped her into arguably the best female player in the world, spoken of seriously in conversation with Messi and Ronaldo as one of the most skilled footballers ever seen. And she's only 26.

If the Norwegian board of tourism were to imagine their ideal poster woman, she would probably look an awful lot like Hegerberg. She is blond and robust, with round rosy cheeks, an easy smile, and a classic Scandinavian braid carefully woven into her ponytail before every match. The level of detail in her game is readily apparent, her play founded on intricate footwork: muscle-memory touch, defender-evading step-overs, tiny rests that seem to magically imbue Hegerberg with just enough time to reconfigure the pitch into exactly what she needs it to be. And above all, the obsessive hunter's persistence, following every single ball into net to see what she can make of it. There is something almost automatic about Hegerberg in action. She plays without tension or performance, shrouded in a cloud of nearly palpable myopia, fully consumed by her own internal calculations, as if she were still back in Oslo with her father and her sister, running through a complex passing drill for the hundredth time. Already a powerhouse in European women's football when they signed an 18-year-old Hegerberg in 2014, Olympique Lyonnais has been practically unstoppable since her arrival. Six league titles, five Coupes de France, five Champions Leagues, and counting. They are virtually unmatched in women's football. For her efforts, Hegerberg won the first Women's Ballon d'Or in 2018.

One would assume that a perfectionist of Hegerberg's caliber would be frustrated by the five-year international-sized hole in her resume. But Hegerberg doesn't seem to be bothered by it. You don't become the greatest footballer in the world without being a team player, but to a certain degree, Hegerberg seems to sail above any sense of team or collective achievement. She does not want to be the most trophied, the most accomplished; those are vague, symbolic gestures towards greatness. She just wants to be—materially, incontrovertibly—the best.

FULL NAME:	DATE OF BIRTH:	PLACE OF BIRTH:	NATIONAL TEAM:	CAPS / GOALS:
Ada Martine Stolsmo Hegerberg	*July 10, 1995*	*Molde, Norway*	*Norway, 2011–*	*66 / 38 *as of March 25, 2022*

APRIL HEINRICHS

THE MOTHER OF WOMEN'S SOCCER, April Heinrichs debuted for the US Women's National Team in 1986, just four games into the program's existence. The US women, one may have noticed over the years, love to win. Significantly more than other teams. It's not just an ambition; it's an obsession, an instinctive, all-consuming drive encoded into the DNA of the team. That's not an accident. The gene was placed there by Anson Dorrance, first coach of the USWNT, and April Heinrichs, his first captain. Dorrance spent three years coaching Heinrichs at the University of North Carolina at Chapel Hill before they both joined the national team; he described her as "want[ing] to win worse than any player I've ever coached."

Heinrichs's competitiveness is renowned. Every teammate has a story about it. Brandi Chastain has one about trying to take the ball from her during a drill. Heinrichs yelled at Chastain so loudly her face turned red and Chastain backed away in fear. Kristine Lilly's go-to story is of Heinrichs during a team game of *Pictionary*. "You can't draw better than that?" she bellowed at her artistically floundering partner. Her intensity could occasionally ruffle feathers, but Dorrance encouraged it, allowing it to set the tone for the team. He began to think of it as integral to what he called the *USA mentality*, a kind of cowboy irreverence: fearless arrogance and a constitutional unwillingness to concede defeat.

Going into the inaugural Women's World Cup in 1991, the Americans were not in fact the favorites to win. They had no domestic league and significantly less tournament experience than the European teams. But they did have what the Chinese press took to calling *the Triple-Edged Sword*: Michelle Akers, powerhouse; Carin Jennings, speedy and artful; and Heinrichs, captain, catalyst, and maniacal competitor, attacking every game up front with zealous gusto. Heinrichs scored two goals against favored Germany in the semifinal (Jennings scored an additional three—if the US had a statement of intent, it was this game). When Akers powered them to World Cup victory three days later, it was Heinrichs who lifted the trophy first. She hadn't just skippered them to success. She had established a mindset that, although it has undergone endless transformations and adaptations over the years, still permeates the USWNT.

The final against Norway was Heinrichs's last game. Plagued by injuries and a bad knee, she retired after the tournament, moving almost immediately into coaching. In 2000, she became the first woman to manage the national team—to middling success. Silver in Sydney in 2000, third place at the 2003 World Cup, gold in Athens in 2004. Likely not enough victory for Heinrichs's taste, but if anything that just underscored the depths of the desire. After her coaching stint she moved into administration, her appetite for ascendancy unwaning. She was hired by US Soccer in 2011 to oversee their growing girls' development program, where she spent years developing a next generation of American players, including the likes of Mal Pugh and Rose Lavelle. Very few people have devoted more time and energy to the realization of US women's soccer than Heinrichs. She stepped down in 2018. But even now, there is probably no one in the world who wants the US to win more than she does.

FULL NAME:	DATE OF BIRTH:	PLACE OF BIRTH:	NATIONAL TEAM:	CAPS / GOALS:
April Dawn Heinrichs	*February 27, 1964*	*Denver, Colorado, United States*	*United States, 1986–91*	*46 / 35*

THIERRY HENRY

IT'S OCTOBER OF 2000 IN FRENCH- man Thierry Henry's second year at Arsenal. Arsenal are playing Sir Alex Ferguson's Manchester United in their eighth game of the season. With half an hour gone and the score still 0–0, Henry picks up a gently rolling ball on the left edge of the box. United players converge on him from all sides. In a single, deft motion, he scoops the ball with his right foot, assured as you like, pivots away from his marking man towards goal and, ball still hanging in the air, launches a perfectly cresting right-footed volley straight through two additional defenders, spinning high over the hand of his fellow countryman, goalkeeper Fabien Barthez, but quickly dipping, swooshing soundlessly into the far side of the net. Even the United fans are up out of their seats. It is Premier League football for the new millennium.

When Henry arrived at Arsenal in the summer of 1999, he was walking the thin line between stardom and anticlimax. He was the son of Antillean immigrants, spotted by a Monaco scout while playing in the Parisian banlieue of Les Ulis at age 13. He had quickly risen up the ranks at Monaco under the tutelage of Arsène Wenger, who marked his goal-making creativity but chose to place him on the left wing because of his obliterating pace. Three goals in the group stage of France's 1998 World Cup–winning campaign, although not as memorable as Zidane's or Lilian Thuram's respective braces, were enough to see him harvested by Juventus for a reported £10.7 million. But, although the word *flop* is maybe slightly overdramatic, he failed to produce much of anything in an impatient Turin, and seven months later, his bags were packed once again, and Henry was headed to Arsenal to reunite with Wenger

and replace their newly departed striker, international teammate Nicolas Anelka. Fans were on edge: Henry was young, apparently in a slump, and seemingly not the striker the team needed. Wenger, whose entire career was built on the appearance of understanding a great many things that average people didn't, just smiled sanguinely.

What Arsenal got wasn't a left winger or a striker, but a heady composite. Wenger gave Henry the space and the permission to infuse his own confidence into the air of a game, and that's exactly what he did, wholly reimagining the game and his position in it. He became a goalscorer who spent as much time dropping out to the left wing as he did loitering around the penalty box, who fabricated brilliant assists as often and enthusiastically as he did brilliant goals. He could dribble and carry the ball, floating like the best winger out there, but he had the physical presence and positional awareness of the best number 9s in history, and the tactical understanding of a great playmaker. A lot of the best athletes are expert responders, reacting to their environments inhumanly quickly. Henry didn't respond— he generated; his performances felt like acts of creation. Startling, often breathtaking creations. Arsenal's 2003–04 Invincibles season, in which they didn't lose a single game, is revered as the epitome of the Thierry Henry era, not so much for the achievement itself, but for the breathless awe its mention conjures.

There are other players from those first years of the new millennium who were perhaps more integral to the identity-shaping of the Premier League. There are other teams, other styles of play. But no one is more responsible for launching English football into the future than Thierry Henry, who played as if that's where he'd come from.

FULL NAME:	DATE OF BIRTH:	PLACE OF BIRTH:	NATIONAL TEAM:	CAPS / GOALS:
Thierry Daniel Henry	*August 17, 1977*	*Les Ulis, France*	*France, 1997–2010*	*123 / 51*

ZLATAN IBRAHIMOVIĆ

I F ZLATAN WASN'T OMNIPRESENT, you'd have thought we'd made him up. His biography reads like European football *Mad Libs*: the son of a Catholic Croatian mother and a Muslim Bosniak father from the ghettos of Malmö, Sweden, whose childhood hobbies were trick shots, physical altercations, and bike thievery. Who grew into a giant, cartoonish man with supervillain facial hair, a decades-long love affair with the slick manbun, a fetish for talking about himself in the third person even more than the Queen or Adolf Hitler, and an ego so large it seems to be perpetually threatening to burst the seams of his 6'5" frame.

As the story goes, teenage Zlatan—after successfully skirting the petition circulated by the parents of his teammates at Malmö FF to get him kicked off the team for fighting—was invited over to Arsenal by Arsène Wenger. Rather than a contract, Wenger offered him a trial. A trial that Zlatan promptly turned down with a flourish because, as he loves to repeat on every occasion he gets, "Zlatan doesn't do auditions." (One shudders with a kind of sick delight to imagine the sliding-doors universe where Zlatan is slotted into Arsenal's Invincibles era, like a large blustering Yugoslavian-Swedish peg in a round cerebral French hole.) Instead, he stayed on the continent, hopping from one elite club to the next, showing no particular club loyalty as he racked up sensational goals, records, supporters, and detractors in equal measure everywhere he went. Three seasons at Ajax, two at Juventus, three at Inter Milan, one at Barcelona, three at Milan, and four at PSG before finally making it to England for a two-season stint at Manchester United, followed by a characteristically headline-grabbing vacation/retirement tour in MLS with the LA Galaxy, which he chased with a shockingly triumphant return to Milan at age 39, presumably just to show that he can. He is the world's most successful journeyman or the world's least successful club talisman, depending on how you look at it, exiting stage left instinctively each time

he feels his spotlight drifting towards another part of the set. Even Sweden doesn't quite know what to make of him; he is their all-time top goalscorer, but the goals he scores often feel almost . . . facetious. When Sweden qualified for the 2018 World Cup, Zlatan, despite having not made a national team appearance for almost a year and a half, tweeted out a photo of the team. The caption read: "We are Zweden."

Zlatan scores great goals. There is no doubt about that. His putaway against NAC Breda for Ajax in August 2004 is an all-time classic, with Zlatan feinting not once, not twice, but five times to evade every member of the Breda backline as he mazily delivers the ball directly into goal. Skeptical English fans, detached from the Zlatan hype of mainland Europe, used to point out that he was not particularly adept at scoring against them: He had only ever scored three goals against English sides (and all against Arsenal, oddly enough), despite playing against them on many occasions with six different clubs. In response, Zlatan, encountering England in a friendly in 2012, scored four goals, including an outrageous 90th-minute bicycle kick lob that still has Joe Hart shuddering in his sleep. It feels ridiculous to take him seriously—he's a man who trademarked his own first name and frequently refers to himself as *the Lion*.

Whereas most people are 60 percent water, Zlatan is 60 percent pomp. He's the Tommy Wiseau of football, if Tommy Wiseau had accidentally made *Rashomon* rather than *The Room*. We fought it for as long as we could, suggesting that he was perhaps a scorer of great goals rather than a great goalscorer, pointing out that he had never won the Champions League, arguing that he could not possibly live up to his own hype. But 22 years into his career, it's pretty clear that he has. The fact that he shares joint goalscoring records with the likes of Cristiano Ronaldo and Messi is not a fluke. His achievements do not warrant an asterisk. He is a genius clown. But he is also a clown genius.

FULL NAME:	DATE OF BIRTH:	PLACE OF BIRTH:	NATIONAL TEAM:	CAPS / GOALS:
Zlatan Ibrahimović	*October 3, 1981*	*Malmö, Sweden*	*Sweden, 2001–*	*118 / 62 *as of March 28, 2021*

NWANKWO KANU

1N THE SUMMER OF 1996, A YOUNG Nigerian team marched into the Olympic Games in Atlanta. They were led by 20-year-old captain Nwankwo Kanu, just signed for Inter Milan. An overgrown string bean of a forward, with a wispy mustache, size 15–feet, and marionette-ish limbs, Kanu was a strange paradox of a player: awkward and ungainly, perpetually in danger of getting tangled up in his own legs—yet somehow capable of pulling a velvety touch out of this mess of limbs, scoring freakish, implausible goals with his unique blend of clumsy elegance. There was perhaps no one in the world more suited for the oddness of Olympic football than Kanu.

Football at the Olympics has always had a Bizarro World quality to it. Even before the formation of the World Cup in 1930, when the tournament was the pinnacle of international football, it had what can only be described as weird vibes: At the 1908 tournament, Denmark beat France 17–1 in a semifinal so humiliating that the French refused to play in the bronze medal match. Four years later featured a consolation tournament for teams knocked out in the first rounds of the tournament proper, and Germany routed Russia 16–0, which so angered the Czar that he declined to pay for the players' tickets home. When the Games resumed in 1920 after the First World War, hosts Belgium won gold by default after Czechoslovakia stormed off the pitch midway through the final in protest of the referee whom they suspected of being biased. (He definitely had reason to be biased, having survived an attack by a mob of angry Czechoslovakian fans earlier in the year.)

Nowadays, men's football at the Olympics still feels like an alternate reality. As of 1996, eligible players must be under 23 (with three overage exceptions for every team), so as not to compete with the Euros and the beginnings of the club seasons. Most of the big football nations don't pay any attention to the tournament, building halfhearted rosters of young second-string players, with the occasional aging star sprinkled on top for good measure. Which means that not only is the draw often populated by random low-ranked FIFA nations—they also win. It's the dream universe of global football, where history and expectation are dropped carelessly at the door. (On the women's side, it should be noted, the Olympics is a major piece of the calendar, with no caveats or age restrictions.)

Into all of this entered Nigeria in 1996, led by Kanu, already a rising practitioner of the laughably improbable. The team inched their way through the group stage on goal difference, paying out of their own pockets for minivans to get themselves to training and putting up with the indignity of suspicions that the laundry staff at the hotel in Atlanta were refusing to wash their clothes for fear of contracting AIDS. They had lost a pre-tournament friendly to tiny Togo. They were capable—tapped as a dark horse at World Cup '94 before going out in extra time to Italy in the round of 16—but they hadn't played a meaningful game in 18 months, forced by Nigeria's military dictator Sani Abacha to pull out of the African Cup of Nations after hosts South Africa were critical of his regime's execution of a prominent activist.

The Nigerians' path through the knockout round was far-fetched, to say the least. Down 2–3 in the 90th minute of a semifinal against Brazil—not the same Brazilian team who had just won the World Cup two years earlier, but a team still featuring the likes of Ronaldo, Rivaldo, and Bebeto, who had already neatly beaten them 1–0 in the group stage—Jay-Jay Okocha launches a lofting throw-in by the corner flag. Popping out of a frantic scrum on the edge of the six-yard box, the ball falls to Kanu in front of net, who scrabbles it into the air and gawkily knocks it past goalkeeper Dida on the turn. Four minutes later, Kanu picks up a deflected ball on the 18-yard line and fires it hastily into the far corner, blazing Nigeria, as shocked as anyone, past favored Brazil and into the final with Argentina. Another 90th-minute goal, this time off a (controversially offside) volley by Emmanuel Amuneke, and they'd done it: Nigerian gold. Generators burned out all over Nigeria; bars ran out of beer. The national television broadcast had fans bursting into the studio to celebrate the victory on air. The entire continent was swept up into the celebrations—it was the first time an African football team had ever won an international competition. It glares like a misprint in the annals of football, but there it is, a victory fit for their captain: ungainly and shocking and absolutely glorious.

FULL NAME:	DATE OF BIRTH:	PLACE OF BIRTH:	NATIONAL TEAM:	CAPS / GOALS:
Nwankwo Kanu	August 1, 1976	Owerri, Nigeria	Nigeria, 1994–2011	87 / 13

ROY KEANE

HERE WAS ALWAYS A JOLTING thrill to seeing Roy Keane in close-up, his eyes gazing out at you from the other side of the television. Dead and penetrating, they sucked you in, revealing behind them a raging furnace of white-hot anger that made every strand of hair on your body stand on end. It was like staring into a burning bush of violent, endless frustration, fearsome and awe-inspiring in its stubborn refusal to be consumed by the force of its own flames.

By the late '90s, Keane was firmly cemented as one of the defining players of the Premier League's inaugural decade. Raised in Cork in the economic gloom of 1970s Ireland, he had quite literally fought his way into English football, dabbling in amateur boxing while writing letter after letter to English clubs begging for a trial. Finally Nottingham Forest agreed to take him on the advice of a scout who had spotted Keane playing a local game with the Cobh Ramblers; what they discovered upon his arrival was a relentless box-to-box midfielder who would cover the entire pitch shouting and raving and mowing down opponents to regain possession as if it had never occurred to him that he was playing a game. A genuine hard man in a league of players who fancied themselves hard men, he was nothing short of terrifying—fixated and vicious and impossible to get through. Fans were entranced. Three seasons later, Nottingham Forest were relegated, but Keane was on the rise. Manchester United plucked up the snarling Irishman and added him to their league-dominating collection of characters. When Eric Cantona retired in '97 to pursue his acting career, Keane was handed the reins.

Whereas Cantona had always exuded an eerie, preternatural calm, even at his boiling point, Keane spewed rage even at his most zen. He shared the Frenchman's arrogance and his high expectations, but Cantona had played football as if he didn't really care; Keane left life and limb out on the pitch, with nothing but ferocious contempt for anyone who didn't appear to be doing so as well. The artful nonchalance that Cantona had brought to the team was replaced by a new era of lunatic aggression. Differently flavored but equally effective, Keane drove the club to a treble in 1999 with a man-possessed comeback performance against Juventus in the Champions League semifinal that manager Sir Alex Ferguson described as "the most emphatic display of selflessness I have seen on a football field." In the first two years of the new millennium, Keane led Manchester United to two more league titles while propelling Ireland on an unprecedented World Cup qualification run, beating out the Netherlands for automatic qualification without losing a single match. In 2001, he had also received an eight-match suspension for a brutally acrobatic stud-up revenge tackle on Manchester City defender Alf-Inge Håland. All of which is to say that by the time the 2002 World Cup in Japan rolled around, there was a general feeling in Ireland that this was it: They had been gifted a maniac—perhaps by God, perhaps by Alex Ferguson himself—who was going to slash and burn the country to World Cup glory.

Unfortunately, Keane never made it to Japan. He stormed out of the pre-tournament training camp in Saipan, that formerly offenseless jewel of the Northern Mariana Islands, seething at the lack of professionalism of the facilities. Ireland's best player left the team in the lurch eight days before their first match, a fact half the country has never forgiven him for, and half the country has never forgiven themselves for. (The Irish by nature almost equally prone to self-flagellation as they are to long-term grudge-holding.) He is the only player in this book whose World Cup legend was forged entirely in absentia—the photographs of him coolly walking his Labrador retriever, Triggs, up the street in Cheshire while his team played on without him 6,000 miles away are almost as famous as any image from the tournament itself. An easily disinclined patriot, declaring himself to be from "Cork first, Ireland second" on every occasion he got, Keane had been pushed over the edge by what he perceived to be the amateurishness of the Irish FA, decamping with a colorful tirade directed towards manager Mick McCarthy, raging at, among other things, the dryness of the field on which they were practicing. "We could have watered it if anyone had told us you were coming down" were the FIFA liaison officer's famous last words to Keane. You play with fire long enough, you're bound to get burnt eventually. So it goes.

FULL NAME:	DATE OF BIRTH:	PLACE OF BIRTH:	NATIONAL TEAM:	CAPS / GOALS:
Roy Maurice Keane	August 10, 1971	Cork, Ireland	Republic of Ireland, 1991–2005	67 / 9

SAM KERR

AM KERR DIDN'T START PLAYING football, as we know it, until she was 12 years old. Before that, her sport of choice was Aussie rules football, a brutal game that is essentially a slightly rules-bound bar fight passing as a nationally specific obsession. It looks kind of like rugby played on a cricket field and requires a serious and varied collection of athletic capabilities. By all accounts, Sam Kerr was a promising player, but the game gets rougher and less co-ed as you get older, and by her tweens, she was coming home with black eyes and bruises all over her body. Kerr's parents—to the detriment of Aussie rules, no doubt, but to the almost immediate benefit of world soccer—elected to move her over to a less dangerous genre of football. Starting out, 12-year-old Kerr didn't even know all the rules of the game; three short years later, she debuted for the Australian senior team.

Although Kerr now seems to have the offside rule down pat, she still plays like an innately gifted kid who has just been sent onto the field for the first time. She gives the impression of being a much patchier, less reliable player than she is, drifting off into no-man's-land, nonchalantly strolling between defenders while the game goes on elsewhere. And then a ball will reach her suddenly, and you realize—to either your absolute delight or your deflating dismay, depending on which side you're rooting for—that she has somehow managed to stroll herself into a perfect scoring position. Once in sight of net, it is virtually impossible to stop her. By her own admission, she's at her best when she's not thinking. Her favorite goals are leaping headers and quick, defender-evading, midrange blasts, attacking the ball with instinctive gusto and living for an emphatic finish. With everything clicking, she often averages more than one goal a game. It is intuitive football at its most unadulterated. She doesn't make scoring goals look easy, per se—the physical effort required, her sheer athletic ability, the consistency with which she does it are all readily apparent. But she makes it look simple. She doesn't beat you with footwork or guile or speed (although she possesses all three); she simply beats you.

It's difficult not to continue thinking of Kerr as the cheeky, wild teenager who first descended on the international scene nearly a decade ago. She sports the same baby face, the same ecstatically elaborate this-is-the-first-time-I've-ever-scored backflip celebration after every goal. But Kerr is now firmly in her late 20s, years out from having been hailed in many corners as the Australian wunderkind destined to be the best player in the world, and it remains to be seen now whether her achievements will live up to the requirements of that title. If she can manage it, she will likely go down as the greatest player of her generation. If she can't, she might have to settle for the most gratifying—playing such pure, enthusiastic, unteachable football that even her opponents seem to enjoy watching her score.

FULL NAME:	DATE OF BIRTH:	PLACE OF BIRTH:	NATIONAL TEAM:	CAPS / GOALS:
Samantha May Kerr	*September 10, 1993*	*East Fremantle, Western Australia, Australia*	*Australia, 2009–*	*102 / 49* as of November 6, 2021*

RAYMOND KOPA

MUCH LIKE A YOUNG JAKE Gyllenhaal in a French *October Sky*, Raymond Kopa was not entirely enthralled by the prospect of becoming a coal miner. Growing up in Noeux-les-Mines in the 1930s, where coalpits loomed over the northern French landscape, he had hopes of being an electrician. But as the son of Polish immigrants, Kopa had neither the connections nor the social cachet to gain an apprenticeship, and a life trapped in the darkness of mine shafts began to feel inescapable. This prospect became even less appealing when at 14, having followed in the footsteps of his grandfather, father, and brother and taken up the family trade, he lost half a finger in an accident down in the mines. Urgently looking for another way to keep the rest of his digits intact and avoid a life of silicosis and shoveling, Kopa headed to France's national youth football trials. He was signed to the second-tier side Angers—les Scoïstes—where he stayed for three years before being transferred to top-flight Reims. By the time Kopa arrived in the cathedral city, it was clear to everyone that what they had on their hands was no ordinary nine-and-a-half-fingered coal miner.

Asked about Kopa's legacy, Michel Platini once reflected, "He put French football in the shop window across the entire world."

Standing a mere 5'6", Kopa was compact and balanced, agile and controlled, capable of helming the ball towards any destination he saw fit. No conversation about the greatest dribbler of all time can be had without invoking Kopa. He wasn't a particularly keen goalscorer; instead, he took it upon himself to act as architect, finessing the ball up the wings to design attack after attack after attack. Every so often, the press would critique Kopa for dribbling too much, for spending too much time on the ball. But, as Reims and France manager Albert Batteux was happy to explain to anyone willing to listen, this was the essence of Kopa's value. With Kopa in possession, teammates had time to breathe and get into position, knowing that he would deliver them a perfect pass whenever they were ready. He was, in his own words, "the greatest collective individualist in French football." Kopa's on-field presence was so imperious that the Spanish press, observing him for the first time during a 1955 friendly with France, nicknamed him *el Pequeño Napoleón* or *the Little Napoleon*. (As a nickname, *Little Napoleon* is of course conspicuously redundant. The fact that this got past the editing department only serves to reinforce exactly how shaken the Spanish press was by what they had just witnessed.) Kopa had gone from being too Polish to become an electrician to France's conquering emperor.

The Spanish were in fact so impressed that a year later Kopa was signed by Real Madrid, where he combined with Ferenc Puskás and Alfredo Di Stéfano to produce one of the most potent attacking forces the sport has ever seen. Kopa's second year at the club, 1958, saw Real secure both the league title and the European Cup for the second time in as many years.

Kopa was at the summit of his powers in '58. That summer, Just Fontaine scored 13 goals for France at the World Cup in Sweden, a record so extraordinary that no one since has even managed to approach it. Radios across the country carried the commentators' cries of "Vive la France!" after every goal. Asked to explain his achievement, Fontaine gestured to Kopa. "He would only pass when he had finished his dribble," he told the press. "And I was always there when he did."

FULL NAME:	DATE OF BIRTH:	PLACE OF BIRTH:	NATIONAL TEAM:	CAPS / GOALS:
Raymond Kopaszewski	*October 13, 1931*	*Nœux-les-Mines, France*	*France, 1952–62*	*45 / 18*

STEPHANIE LABBÉ

STEPHANIE LABBÉ HAS MADE A career of getting back up. In 2008, freshly graduated from the University of Connecticut, she traveled to Beijing as an alternate with the Canadian national team. She was 21, coming off a successful college career. The following spring, she signed her first professional contract, with Piteå IF in the Swedish league. Four years later, though, Labbé found herself further from the Olympic pitch, not closer. Canada still had two highly respected more senior goalkeepers in front of her, so Labbé elected to step away from the national team. She watched on from the stands as Canada won bronze that summer in London.

Over the next couple of years, Labbé slowly worked her way back. When starting keeper Erin McLeod was injured in the lead-up to Rio, Labbé was tapped to step in. Captain and Canadian legend Christine Sinclair was the focal point of Canada's journey that tournament, but out back for Canada stood Labbé, quietly confident, sturdy despite having started only a handful of meaningful international games before that summer, seeing the team through to their second bronze medal. She lifted it proudly, triumph spread across her face, the highest point of her professional career.

But the highest point was followed closely by the lowest, as Labbé plunged into a post-Olympics depression in the year that followed. Forget losing her love of the game—there were days when she couldn't get off the couch to walk her dog. In what felt at the time like a white flag of surrender, Labbé disappeared, retreating back home to Alberta, announcing a medical leave of absence in the fall of 2017 and walking away from her starting position on the Washington Spirit. Radio silence for six months. And then suddenly she was back, training with a local men's team in Calgary, speaking publicly about her depression, suing to be allowed to play in the Canadian men's league. She didn't win the suit—instead, she returned to women's football, first to Sweden, then back to the NWSL. But she was stronger, physically and mentally, happier, more poised, more zen. When the 2020 Olympics rolled around (and when they rolled around again after the pandemic postponement), Labbé was, for the first time in her international career, the obvious first-choice goalkeeper. It was a comeback that felt hard-earned. You couldn't help but root for Canada, North American soccer's perennial also-rans.

In the opening game of Canada's Tokyo campaign, Labbé suffered a rib injury sliding into the feet of an onrushing Japanese forward on a dangerous run into the box. She stayed down for over a minute, writhing in pain on the ground, tears streaming down her cheeks. Then Japan was awarded a penalty for the slide. Labbé got up gingerly, went back into goal, and, mascara still smeared under her eyes from the tears, coolly swatted the penalty away, grimacing in pain as her teammates surrounded her in celebration. Five minutes later, she was subbed off. But two games later she was back, and nine days later, she was on her line, squaring off for a penalty shoot-out against Brazil in the quarterfinals. Fired up, Labbé saved two penalties to take Canada into the semifinals. A win there against an unsteady US team took Canada into the final against Sweden. Drawing 1–1 at the end of extra time, they went to penalties for the second time that tournament. If Labbé looked fired up during the shoot-out with Brazil, then against Sweden, with the most important five minutes of her footballing life on the line and her retirement already tentatively announced for after the Games, she mostly just looked happy, smiling good-naturedly at the Swedish players as they set up their shots. The Canadians, it should be said, are not particularly good at penalties. They missed three in a row, giving Sweden an almost painful lead. Grinning, Labbé saved one, to keep Canada within touching distance. Sweden, shooting for gold, sent their next over the crossbar. Diving to her left and punching away Sweden's sixth shot, Labbé wrested back Canada's chance at gold. They took it with relish. No one was smiling harder than Labbé.

FULL NAME:	DATE OF BIRTH:	PLACE OF BIRTH:	NATIONAL TEAM:	CAPS / GOALS:
Stephanie Lynn Marie Labbé	*October 10, 1986*	*Edmonton, Alberta, Canada*	*Canada, 2008–2022*	*86 / –*

MICHAEL LAUDRUP

I N THE CELEBRATIONS OF DEN-mark's Cinderella-story 1992 Euro win, one man was conspicuously absent. The win was their greatest achievement, and they achieved it without him, their greatest-ever player. (They settled for his brother, Brian, instead, who was, all due respect to Brian, only the brother of their greatest-ever player.) That man was, of course, Michael Laudrup, and he had refused to attend the tournament because of beef with manager Richard Møller Nielsen. Had he known that they were going to win the whole thing, he might have agreed to compromise, but hindsight is 20/20, and Michael Laudrup was nowhere to be found in the story of his country's greatest football triumph.

Laudrup is a complicated figure. From a purely technical perspective, he is easily the most elegant player Europe has produced this side of Johan Cruyff. He was the fulcrum of Cruyff's Barcelona "Dream Team," deployed as a deep-lying center forward to furnish shiver-inducing balls to a roundup of the era's defining players: Michel Platini, Ronald Koeman, Hristo Stoichkov, Romário, Iván Zamorano, Raúl, Pep Guardiola. It has often been suggested that Laudrup's interpretation of his position inspired Pep's use of Messi at Barcelona 20 years later. He skated silkily around opponents; his highlights are a visual essay in subtle motion, tilting towards one side and darting the other way at the final moment, dragging the ball onto his other foot, gliding it through the legs of oncoming tackles, lockpicking passing lanes and tiptoeing into them. One of his signatures was a no-look chip with the outside of his foot into the dead center of the 18-yard box, which, if anything, made football look too easy.

There's a school of football thought that believes the overlooking of Laudrup—for the Ballon d'Or, in conversations about the greatest player of his generation, in conversations about the greatest player of any generation, really—is one of the major snubs in football history. He's a favorite player's player; Beckenbauer claimed he was the best player of the '90s. Romário held that he was the fourth-best in the history of the game.

But there was always something intangibly unsatisfactory about Laudrup's career. Perhaps it was the lack of international achievement, or the fact that, clashing with Cruyff, he left Barcelona on the cusp of becoming a club icon and farmed his talent out to rivals Real Madrid.

Effort is an odd thing in sports. There are some sports where it's crucial—like running or swimming, where that's essentially all there is. In tennis, they can actually fine you if they think you're not trying hard enough. And then there are other sports where it doesn't seem to factor in at all: There is, to the untrained eye, almost no difference between trying and not trying in baseball. Football, though, exists on the fence. We want our players to give everything, and we love when they look like they don't have to. During their time together, Cruyff became obsessed by the idea that Laudrup wasn't trying hard enough. "[He's] one of the most difficult players I have worked with," Cruyff admitted on more than one occasion. "When he gives 80 to 90 percent he is still by far the best, but I want 100 percent and he rarely does that."

To Cruyff, it was a personality defect, something lacking in Laudrup's upbringing that robbed him of the extra drive, the extra push he would have needed to be truly great. But it was really something inherent in his playing style we think, which was captivating and enthralling, but always a little bit jarring, a little empty, entirely premised as it was on never letting anyone know exactly what he wanted or where he wanted to go.

FULL NAME:	DATE OF BIRTH:	PLACE OF BIRTH:	NATIONAL TEAM:	CAPS / GOALS:
Michael Laudrup	June 15, 1964	Frederiksberg, Denmark	Denmark, 1982–98	104 / 37

KRISTINE LILLY

I N 1987, AT AGE 16, KRISTINE LILLY became the youngest woman to score for the United States. In 2010, she became the oldest as well. Joining the national team two years after its inception and retiring 354 caps—the most of any player, male or female—and five World Cups later, Kristine Lilly was, in many ways, the load-bearing column around which the USWNT was built. Rosters changed, uniforms were upgraded, contract disputes were waged, the public's attention waxed and waned. And through all of it, there was Kristine Lilly, stalwart and solid, serving both as a memory of where the team had once been and a guide for where they could go.

Lilly—or Lil, as teammates affectionately called her—was not a flashy player. She didn't have the commanding presence of Michelle Akers; she didn't have the glamour or intensity of Mia Hamm. In the '99 final, she scored the third penalty rather than the fifth, so it was Brandi Chastain who got the glory of that moment. But while her teammates grabbed headlines, Lilly stayed in the background, happy to handle the mundane, unglamorous work that keeps a team like the US in control of a game. A hardworking outside midfielder, Lilly had a remarkable gift for arriving in the right place at the right time. She would wear down the grass on the flanks, sprinting all the way back and all the way forward again to track down every ball and deliver it up the field with a composure and consistency that made you forget how remarkable the feat actually was.

When you ask the members of the 1999 team who they think is most responsible for that World Cup win, they do not say Brandi Chastain, who clinched the victory in the eyes of the public. Nor do they credit Briana Scurry, whose penalty save sealed it in the mind of the Chinese team. Instead, they all point to a fleeting moment in the 10th minute of sudden death extra time (a short-lived FIFA invention where the first team to score in extra time wins the game). Liu Ying lofts a beautiful corner kick towards the far post. It finds Fan Yunjie, who sends it sailing over Scurry's outstretched fingertips towards the top left corner of the net. There is a collective sharp intake of breath as the American players and fans alike float in that millisecond, a quarter of an inch standing between them and sudden death. And then, all of a sudden, there is Lil on the goal line, heading the ball away. Brushing away praise after the fact, Lilly remarked simply, "that's my job."

Long after the rest of the '99ers transitioned into soccer mom– and motivational speech–speckled retirements, Kristine Lilly remained. As each new generation rolled into training camp, there was Lilly, part captain, part matriarch, still grinding away on the field, playing with a tenacity and ability that seemed to be immune to the diminishing returns of age. When asked in 2007 whether she had any plans to retire, Lilly promised, Mary Poppins–esque, that she would stay until the team didn't need her anymore.

During her international career, the US placed lower than third in tournament play just three times in over two decades. Twelve years later, most of the team's leaders are still members of the classes who came of age under Lilly's tutelage, empowered to take risks by the knowledge that she was right behind them. If the history of the US Women's National Team is a gouache of style, flair, and personal achievement, then it is Kristine Lilly, more than anyone else, who provided the canvas, turning up just where you needed her to be, day after day after day. For 23 years.

FULL NAME:	DATE OF BIRTH:	PLACE OF BIRTH:	NATIONAL TEAM:	CAPS / GOALS:
Kristine Marie Lilly	July 22, 1971	New York City, New York, United States	United States, 1987–2010	354 / 130

GARY LINEKER

THE ENGLISH, BEING A RELATIVELY predictable people, have two basic types of sporting heroes, whom they love equally and with equal amounts of self-loathing. The first is the working-class boy made good: your Jamie Vardys, your Wayne Rooneys, your Gazzas. Players who seem utterly incapable of being anything other than their truest selves. Truest selves, which are, as the English always delight in discovering, gauche and vaguely distasteful, prone to outbursts and bad habits and fairly troubling interpersonal snafus. All of which is absolute catnip for English people, as it confirms a perverse but deeply ingrained cultural mythos about the grit and irrepressibility of the English spirit.

The second sporting hero type is the mirror opposite: the utterly decent athlete. Clean-cut and middle class (if not by birth, then by affect), they do not smoke or drink to excess, they do not cause scenes, they do not get booked, they likely have a tense but respectful relationship with their father. They do the right thing simply because it is the right thing to do. If you throw them on television, they will be polite, articulate, and dependable. If you threw them into the trenches of the First World War, one imagines they would be much the same. This too confirms a perverse but deeply ingrained cultural mythos about the grit and irrepressibility of the English spirit. In the '60s, it was the Bobbys—Charlton and Moore—who maintained athletic decency for the nation. By the late '80s, it was none other than Gary Lineker, the clean-cut, large-featured Leicestershire man, dutifully shouldering the mantle.

One of the last great true English poachers, Gary Lineker's sole dominion was the penalty area, his classic goal a camera flash one-touch from the six-yard box. He had scorching pace and a clairvoyant-seeming intuition for where any given ball was going to drop. Often asked about his knack for being in the right place at the right time, Lineker would courteously push back, insisting that he was in fact in the right place *all the time*. Which is just about true. He is, to date, England's greatest modern goal-scorer. He was not an artistic player, but he was marvelously, deliriously reliable. (He famously played on in a World Cup game after crapping his shorts on the field.) Despite Maradona's thorough pulping of England in that notorious Hand of God quarterfinal, it was Lineker who sauntered home with the Golden Boot—the first English player ever to win the award (and the only one, until Harry Kane matched him in 2018). This certainly didn't make up for the loss, which every person in England who was alive and sentient at the time, whether they followed football or not, still feels as a deep searing pain in the core of their being. But it did go some ways to conciliating it.

In 1990, England did what only England can do, one-upping their '86 quarterfinal loss with an even more heartbreaking semifinal penalty-kick crumble against the Germans. Most utterly decent athletes have laddish counterparts. In Italy in 1990, Lineker was gifted his in a 23-year-old Gazza. Despite his 1986 Golden Boot and his four goals in 1990—including an 80th-minute strike against West Germany to send that semifinal into penalties—the moment that lingers most enduringly from Lineker's two World Cup appearances came in the seconds after Gazza's semifinal yellow card. Lineker walks over to Gazza, clocks the tears welling up in his eyes, turns around instantly to England manager Sir Bobby Robson, and apprehensively mouths, "Have a word with him." A pivoting touchline camera captures it in agonizing close-up. It's Lineker's eyes, as much as Gazza's, that seize you. There is no anger—neither at the ref, nor at Gazza, nor at the fact that their star player has just been ruled out of the final. No drama. He is so unflinching: sympathetic but not overly so, pragmatic, mannerly. We were Gazza, but we were also Lineker. Never had the two sides of the English personality been so succinctly proffered for our viewing pleasure.

FULL NAME:	DATE OF BIRTH:	PLACE OF BIRTH:	NATIONAL TEAM:	CAPS / GOALS:
Gary Winston Lineker	*November 30, 1960*	*Leicester, England*	*England, 1984–92*	*80 / 48*

HANNA LJUNGBERG

I**N THE SUMMER OF 2017, ONE OF** those fake news stories that were so in vogue at the time—you know, the ones that start as weird clickbait at the bottom of the page ("She was a star, now she works in New York," "The most beautiful twins in the world," "Check out this letter written by blind pirates in 1676!") and then crawl out of the primordial soup into more legitimate parts of the internet—popped up, declaring that former female soccer star Hanna Ljungberg was dead at 39. If you google Ljungberg, this is still a top hit. Do not click. Hanna Ljungberg is not dead, has never been dead, is, in fact, alive and well and living in Sweden.

There was a time, not too long ago, when Sweden was the best place on the planet to play women's football. The landscape of the sport has changed drastically over the past five years, as the big European clubs put ever more value in fielding competitive women's teams to complement their men's sides, beefing up their respective women's leagues with an influx of new investment. But before there was the NWSL in the US, and long before the Spanish and French leagues had gained any kind of foothold, there was the ever-reliable Damallsvenskan.

The Damallsvenskan, founded in 1988, is a serious place. Factoring in preseason and European competition, they play 10 months out of the year, with just a brief break in the dead of winter when it is literally too cold and too dark in Sweden to do anything outside after about 3 p.m. Semi-pro and well organized, in the early 2000s the league was an odd mecca, the best women's soccer in the world tucked quietly into a constellation of small Swedish towns. The presiding team was Umeå IK, who dominated the league with seven championships, four Swedish Cups, and two Champions League titles in eight years, a huge football powerhouse in a modest university town on the Ume River. They played host to some famous names over the years, including Marta, who was with the club from 2004 to 2008. But their biggest draw was always Swedish star Hanna Ljungberg, a local player who grew up just a couple miles down the road.

Ljungberg was a compact, pacey attacker, relentless in the box but dangerous from anywhere, with a particular penchant for capitalizing on the minor misjudgments of defenders in her path. She played football that was not just technically adept, but also perceptive. Her speed and aggression were exhilarating. Her cleverness, though, provided the real fun of watching her take off with the ball. She is still, nearly 15 years after her retirement, one of the most accomplished Swedish players of all time, with seven Swedish titles, two European cups, and the all-time season scoring record in the Damallsvenskan to her name, a veritable legend of Swedish football lore.

Ahead of the 2003 World Cup, the *Chicago Tribune* published a brief profile of Ljungberg that divulged, among other things, that her favorite meal was reindeer and rice, and that she had once pranked the Sweden national team coach by putting a dead fish in her locker. (In 2003, Sweden still felt like a very foreign place.) Ljungberg was the first fully professional player in the Damallsvenskan, which made her, after that year's shuttering of the Women's United Soccer Association in the US, one of the only fully professional female players in the world. The headline of the article read "Tiny Swede Is a Titanic Scorer," which about summed up the situation. Sweden lost in the final at that World Cup, beaten in extra time by a golden goal from Germany, the only country in the world with a domestic league to rival Sweden's. Ljungberg scored Sweden's only goal of the final, a barreling breakaway in the 41st minute.

In the Damallsvenskan, the top scorer is called the *skyttedrottningar*—which translates into the ABBA-esque *shooting queen*. Showing their appreciation for the small shooting queen in their midst, the crowd in Carson, California, gave Ljungberg a three-minute standing ovation before she walked disappointedly off the field.

FULL NAME:	DATE OF BIRTH:	PLACE OF BIRTH:	NATIONAL TEAM:	CAPS / GOALS:
Hanna Carolina Ljungberg	*January 8, 1979*	*Umeå, Sweden*	*Sweden, 1996–2008*	*130 / 72*

CARLI LLOYD

 OR FANS, CARLI LLOYD WAS ALWAYS a bit of a puzzle. She was not the most skilled member of the USWNT, nor the most consistent. She worked hard, going in on weekends and holidays to run drills (and posting them to Instagram to make sure you knew about it), but that did not stop her from frequently logging in poor performances and making game-deciding blunders. She was on the team for close to a decade and a half, but each time a tournament rolled around, no one was sure if Lloyd would make the roster. No one was even sure that she should.

And yet, during the 16 years she was on the team, no one contributed more directly to the success of US soccer than Carli Lloyd.

This was the remarkable thing about Lloyd: She could be playing some of the worst soccer of her life one minute, and then, seemingly out of nowhere, she'd spring to life and produce a jolting, jaw-dropping, game-winning goal. She did it in Beijing in 2008, scoring in extra time against Brazil to win the gold for the US. Then she did it again in London in 2012 with a brace in the final against Japan. They're consistently odd goals—not so much unexpected as implausible. Often, it looked like Lloyd was in the wrong place, either lagging behind or dragged out of position. There was rarely any buildup, none of the gear-turning troubleshooting you often see with midfielders. Just an exhilarating burst of energy, like a neon sign flashing on abruptly. The ball would roll to her feet, and suddenly, somehow, she'd gotten a shot off before you'd even had time to consider whether or not it was a good idea.

During her tenure on the national team, the US won four major tournaments. Lloyd scored the decisive goals in three of them.

This particular quality made Lloyd "a challenge to coach," as then-USWNT coach Pia Sundhage admitted candidly in an interview before the 2015 World Cup. It also made her a frustrating, captivating player to watch. She would turn up in the wrong place at the wrong time; she gave away possession in dangerous areas; many of the shots she attempted did not, in fact, turn out to be good ideas. And then she rocked up to the 2015 World Cup final and scored a hat trick in the first 15 minutes. Few players in the history of the sport have had such an electrifying, totally mystifying knack for big moments.

The third goal of that 2015 final is the most classically Lloydian of the bunch. In the 15th minute, she picks up the ball outside of the box and takes off towards the halfway line. She has Alex Morgan streaking forward on her left and only two defenders between her and the goalkeeper. But rather than play the ball up the field, Lloyd raises her head, sees the Japanese keeper off her line, and lobs it 60 yards. It's a ridiculous lob—the kind of flippant, harebrained, low-percentage play that no one in their right mind would attempt minutes into a World Cup final. If the Japanese keeper, Kaihori, backpedaling furiously with her right hand stretched as far as it can go, had managed to get two more fingers on the ball, we'd be shaking our heads and wondering why Lloyd threw away such a prime counterattacking opportunity. But instead, Kaihori merely manages to caress the ball, and it slides past her into the bottom right corner. It's an astonishing, once-in-a-lifetime, all-time-great goal. And only Lloyd could have pulled it off. It wasn't just skill; it wasn't just luck. It was an almost preternatural ability to sense a moment, and the reckless, preposterous guts to seize it.

FULL NAME:	DATE OF BIRTH:	PLACE OF BIRTH:	NATIONAL TEAM:	CAPS / GOALS:
Carli Anne Lloyd Hollins	*July 16, 1982*	*Delran, New Jersey, United States*	*United States, 2005–21*	*316 / 134*

DIEGO MARADONA

F DIEGO MARADONA'S LIFE STORY was turned into a Hollywood movie, it would be eerily similar to *Scarface*. Both he and Al Pacino's Tony Montana were swaggering, self-made figures who rose from humble origins to dominate the world, only to flame out in a blaze of glory. While Montana's weapon of choice was his M16 ("Say hello to my little friend"), Maradona's preferred weapons were his legs, in a career of extreme and excess, during which the World Cup was the stage for both his greatest glory and his greatest humiliation. In 1986, he provided one of the singular virtuoso performances in World Cup history. Just eight years later, he was sent home in disgrace for either ephedrine doping or enjoying an innocent energy supplement called Ripped Fuel, depending on whether you asked FIFA or Maradona himself.

Squat and impudent, Maradona was part urchin, part prince. At just 5'5", his career was proof that one need not be a titan to be a world-class soccer player. His low center of gravity was his greatest asset, and he became one of the greatest dribblers in the game, nearly impossible to knock off the ball. When another player managed to kick him off the ball, he would quickly dust himself off and demand it again, drawing strength as he drained defenders of their energy.

In the 1986 World Cup, he single-handedly willed his team to victory, collecting the Golden Ball as the tournament's best player along the way. He scored both goals in the 2–1 victory over England in the quarterfinal, a game played in the shadows of the 1982 Falklands conflict. The first goal, when he used his left fist to reach over a 6'0" goalkeeper and punch the ball into the net, became known as the *Hand of God* around the world, as it was scored, as Maradona himself said, "a little with the head of Maradona and a little with the hand of God." (In England, it was referred to as the *Hand of the Devil*.) Four minutes later, while the English were still reeling, he scored a goal that even God would have had difficulty replicating. He made a spectacular 60-yard dash, a brilliant display of the Gambeta, the Argentine art of dribbling, weaving delicately past five England players, the last two of whom desperately tried to take out the man rather than the ball. Both goals reflect different sides of Maradona's persona: The first required the stealth and pluck of the pickpocket; the second, the daring and polish of Thomas Crown.

Maradona's retirement was marred by cocaine addiction and alleged ties to organized crime, held over from his time at Napoli, and idiosyncratic foreign policy pronouncements on behalf of Cuba, Venezuela, and Iran—all of which, perversely, combined to make him more beloved than ever in Latin America. His left leg featured a tattoo of Fidel Castro, while the image of Che Guevara dominated his right bicep. Rumors of a possible Hugo Chávez tattoo made international news. Perhaps not surprisingly, his talk show on Argentine television, *La Noche Del 10* (*The Night of the Number 10*) was one of the most watched in the nation's history. He was in and out of rehab, and cynics suggested he scheduled his occasional television appearances to prove he was still alive. His erratic coaching career made many wish he had remained a talk show host. Despite his troubles, he will always be remembered as the icon from the semifinal against Belgium in 1986. About to launch an attack. Never mind double- or triple-teamed. Six defenders surround him. You can smell their fear. And you know he likes the odds.

Maradona passed away in November 2020, after years of physical decline in the public eye. Paying tribute to the icon, Pelé commented, "One day I hope we can play football together in heaven." Which was fitting, since that's where Maradona had been playing all along.

FULL NAME:	DATE OF BIRTH:	PLACE OF BIRTH:	NATIONAL TEAM:	CAPS / GOALS:
Diego Armando Maradona	*October 30, 1960*	*Lanús, Argentina*	*Argentina, 1977–94*	*91 / 34*

MARTA

IKE MANY OF HER MALE COMPA-
triots, Marta got her start playing barefoot on the
streets of a small impoverished town in northeastern Brazil. Unlike the men who merely lacked
boots, however, Marta also lacked infrastructure.
From 1941 to 1979—just seven years before Marta was
born—it was literally illegal for women to play soccer in
Brazil (it was deemed dangerously unfeminine), and that
attitude still permeated Brazilian society. Marta not only
had to beat her opponents. She had to constantly prove
women belonged on the football field in the first place.

It was a lonely pursuit. Growing up, constantly
defending herself against jeers and judgment, Marta was
the only girl in the street games and the only girl in the
locker room at her local club. It wasn't until 2000, when
she was invited to join the women's side at Vasco da Gama
in Rio—30 hours away from her hometown of Dois Ria-
chos—that Marta had ever even seen an entire team composed of women.

Marta has since thrived, playing for 10 different
clubs on three different continents and in three different
decades, winning the coveted FIFA Women's World Player
of the Year a record six times. She is the only person in the
world to have scored 17 World Cup goals. Faster with the
ball than most players are without it, Marta has demanded
again and again that women's soccer keep up with her—
both figuratively and literally—forcing them to build clubs
and players worthy of her devastating talent.

Much in the way that the history of the world is
bisected by a certain other one-named superstar, in the
history of women's soccer there is Before Marta and there
is After. Before Marta, women's soccer was a relatively
one-dimensional game. The best players tended to fall into
two categories: Either they were powerful, bulldozing their
way through defenders, or they were precise ball strikers.

With one goal, Marta announced to the world that this
dichotomy was no longer relevant. It's the 2007 World Cup
semis. Brazil is playing the US. The American team, ranked
number one and coming off a slew of tournament wins, is
feeling confident to the point of arrogance. This is quickly
revealed to be ill-advised hubris, as they go down 3–0.
Then, in the 79th minute, Marta gets the ball on the edge
of the penalty box. With her back to defender Tina Ellertson, Marta kicks the ball up with her right foot, bounces
it around Ellertson with her left, runs around Ellertson on
the other side, and picks the ball back up before Ellertson can even process what's happened. At the last second,
Ellertson tries to grab Marta's shirt, but she is already
gone. Marta feints left, wrong-foots the next defender, and
shoots. Goalkeeper Briana Scurry doesn't have a chance.

Around the world, millions of cartoon lightbulbs went
on at once. All of a sudden, it was so obvious. Female strikers could be fast and powerful, technically skilled, stylish,
and immensely creative, all at the same time. The USWNT
limped home, tail between their legs, fired their coach, and
completely overhauled their approach to soccer in order
to make sure they were ready for Marta the next time she
came. Everyone else, shaken but still standing, rushed
home and just googled the word "how." And thus, the After
Marta era was born.

FULL NAME:	DATE OF BIRTH:	PLACE OF BIRTH:	NATIONAL TEAM:	CAPS / GOALS:
Marta Vieira da Silva	February 19, 1986	Dois Riachos, Alagoas, Brazil	Brazil, 2002–	167 / 113 *as of October 26, 2021

LOTHAR MATTHÄUS

ERMANS DON'T LIKE LOTHAR Matthäus. He is the hero of their 1990 World Cup title, their most capped player, one of the most complete midfielders in the history of the game, their second-greatest player of all time barring only Franz Beckenbauer. And the most your average German can conjure towards him is a feeling of perverse indifference.

This is because Matthäus is widely known, in addition to everything else, to be a massive asshole. He played until he was 39. The first half of his career was dedicated to being a world-class footballer, the second half to being a knob. He developed an enthusiastic two-way relationship with the German tabloids, happily playing the role of tawdry playboy, shuffling through one failed marriage after another, and cultivating feuds with everyone he came into contact with, his penchant for them getting worse and worse over the course of his career to the point where he and his fellow teammates at Bayern Munich would only speak to each other through the press. Stefan Effenberg, fellow Bayern and Germany midfielder, devoted an entire chapter to Matthäus in his autobiography. It is entitled, "What Lothar Matthäus knows about football." It's a blank page. During his MLS retirement stint in 2000, Matthäus told his team he was rehabbing his back, only to be photographed sunbathing in Saint-Tropez. "I am an idol and should be treated like one," he petulantly declared, keenly aware of the German public's lack of interest in him. After retirement, Matthäus embarked on a disastrous managerial career, barely making it more than a year in any position, and leaving behind a trail of lawsuits, turbulence, and unhappy supporters. He was vain, insecure, mean, inescapable. To live in Germany from roughly 1990 to 2010 was to suffer through two decades of Matthäus-induced secondary embarrassment. The Germans have accordingly adopted an attitude of aggressive inattention.

But Matthäus could also be amusing, ferocious, persuasive, inspiring, and, crucially, absolutely brilliant. If you experienced Matthäus from outside Germany, you are in a much better position to remember that part. He played in five separate World Cups, with the most appearances of any man in history, showing up as a different iteration of himself each time, from defensive midfielder in 1982 to deep-lying defender in 1998. But the version of Matthäus that lives on most firmly in memory is 1990 Matthäus. He arrived in Italy as the epitome of suave German football dominance, bedecked in one of the greatest kits of all time, a geometric lesson in futuristic cool by Adidas. Operating as a box-to-box midfielder, Matthäus was a machine of a man, rampaging around the pitch with combustion engine–level speed and power. His nickname was *Der Panzer: The Tank*. He had a bullet of a long-range shot, which he showed off and then some in West Germany's opening match against Yugoslavia. Having already scored one goal, he picked the ball up in midfield in the 64th minute. Charging straight over the Yugoslavian sweeper, Matthäus lashed the ball from 30 yards out, splitting the Yugoslavian defense and sending it careening into the bottom left corner. When he was at the peak of his powers, as he was in 1990, he made opponents seem not just ineffectual, but silly as he played on a higher plane of mastery, outrunning, outmaneuvering, and outshooting them like they were paper dolls he could tear right through.

In a rematch of the '86 final, West Germany faced off against Maradona's Argentina once again. But this was a Maradona already in decline. It was an ugly, cynical final with a lot of diving and very little goalscoring. West Germany were by far the better team, but, despite outshooting Argentina 23 to 1, they couldn't find the net. Finally, with five minutes left on the clock, Germany were awarded a penalty. In a move entirely contrary to his personality, Matthäus, the team's captain and regular penalty-taker, declined to take it. (He claimed later that he had changed boots in the middle of the game and wasn't comfortable in them.) Andreas Brehme stepped up instead, earning Germany their third World Cup trophy after a decade of attempts. In Germany, this is tagged as another Matthäus diva turn, pulling a Goldilocks-esque "my boots are too tight" at the crucial moment of a World Cup final. But from a different perspective, it looks a lot like modesty.

FULL NAME:	DATE OF BIRTH:	PLACE OF BIRTH:	NATIONAL TEAM:	CAPS / GOALS:
Lothar Herbert Matthäus	*March 21, 1961*	*Erlangen, West Germany*	*West Germany / Germany, 1980–2000*	*150 / 23*

STANLEY MATTHEWS

WHEN STANLEY MATTHEWS signed for Stoke City at 17, it was agreed that he would be paid the maximum wages: £5 a week, £3 a week over the summer. The year was 1932, George V was king, and Matthews was the third son of a local hairdresser/boxer known as *the Fighting Barber of Hanley*. He came up in the English football of the 1930s. He was a dribbling specialist, so much so that he preferred to train alone rather than with the rest of the team, spending hours each morning by himself working on footwork. By the middle of the decade, he had perfected not only the swerve, but the then-almost-unprecedented double swerve, which would become his trademark move. In the spring of '38, he was part of the now-infamous England squad that traveled to Berlin to play a friendly with Germany and, in line with Chamberlain's policy of appeasement, were forced by the FA to give the Nazi salute before the game. Matthews proceeded to swerve his way around the German defense, and England won the game 6–3. In Germany, they named him *Der Zauberer—the Magician*. War broke out four months later.

Matthews was an individualistic maniac, of the type that you don't often see in team sports. By the time World War II was over, he was pushing 30, and it was expected that his athletic prime, like that of most of his peers, had largely passed him by during the intervening years. He apparently had other ideas. A proto–Tom Brady, Matthews played for another 20 years, until the age of 50. A feat managed, in his estimation, through a strict diet and exercise regimen that included, among other things, teetotaling, boatloads of carrot juice, and never eating on Mondays.

It's not clear that Matthews was ever a good footballer in the usual sense. "When Stan gets the ball on the wing, you don't really know when it's coming back," England teammate Raich Carter once grumbled. He refused to track back to defend. He was an ungenerous passer, and his greatest ambition was very evidently to win every game all on his own (a feat that was perhaps more difficult than he anticipated—he only won one major trophy in his 30-year career). But he was certainly a great footballer. His footwork was so iconic that often television programs would simply show close-ups of his feet when talking about him. It was reported that the announcement of his name on the lineup sheet would add crowds of thousands wherever he played. Rather than slowing down, he seemed to speed up with age. In 1953, he lifted Blackpool to an FA Cup win after they went down 3–1 early in the second half, his performance so dominant, the match is now known as the *Matthews Final*. The team photographs from this era are veritably ridiculous. Matthews, face furrowed and hairline receding, looks like one of the players' dads who's accidentally wandered into the frame. But he was somehow playing the best football of his life—the best football, many believed, in the world.

The invention of the athlete superstar would not occur for another decade, but Matthews's name and feet had already spread around the globe. In 1956, at 41, he was awarded the first Ballon d'Or. England recalled him for a friendly against Brazil that spring, where he stole the show by wiping the floor with Nilton Santos—10 years his junior and regarded as the best left back in the world at the time. Matthews would play for yet another nine years after that; they had to knight him before he retired because it was taking so long. When he did finally retire in 1965, the world that Matthews had grown up in was entirely gone. As was the football. In an incredible act of chivalry—or insanity, depending on how you see it—Matthews insisted on accompanying it all the way to the door.

FULL NAME:	DATE OF BIRTH:	PLACE OF BIRTH:	NATIONAL TEAM:	CAPS / GOALS:
Stanley Matthews	*February 1, 1915*	*Hanley, Stoke-on-Trent, England*	*England, 1934–57*	*54 / 11*

GIUSEPPE MEAZZA

IUSEPPE MEAZZA WAS ROUGHLY everything you could have wanted from a 1930s footballer. He had the scampish movie star aura and the greasy side part; he was an enthusiastic late-night drinker and an inveterate gambler, a serial frequenter of the local Milan brothel scene, and a well-known propaganda tool for Mussolini's fascist government. Long before the likes of Garrincha, Best, or Cruyff, the Italian tabloids were publishing weekly stories of Meazza being hustled out of bed, torn from the arms of two or three women at a time, and rushed to the stadium just in time for kickoff. Meazza's Milanese mother, a widowed fruit seller, hadn't wanted him to be a footballer, which she judged to be a disreputable sort of thing for a young man to become in Northern Italy in the early part of the 20th century, so she took away his shoes. He took to playing barefoot.

The 1934 World Cup was an odd, unsettling affair. Reigning champions Uruguay refused to attend because they were still mad about the European no-shows when they hosted the inaugural tournament in 1930. England was in a self-imposed exile from FIFA at the time, and declined to participate as well. The whole tournament was extremely violent. The fascist party's anthem, "Giovinezza," was played at every opportunity. Czechoslovakia came very close to winning the final, going up 1–0 with 20 minutes left, which would have been the last great Czechoslovakian victory until Václav Havel, but they made the classic mistake of not marking Meazza, who was limping his way through with a leg injury sustained earlier in the tournament. Fast, agile, and nimble-footed, limp or no limp, Meazza set up a trophy-clinching goal by Angelo Schiavio in the first minutes of extra time.

Ahead of the next World Cup, Meazza was appointed captain of the Italian team. By way of congratulations, Mussolini sent him a personal telegram. It read: "Win or die!" Meazza, never one to leave a party prematurely, opted for the former, famously scoring a deciding penalty against Brazil in the semifinals while holding his pants up with one hand. Three days later, Italy hoisted their second consecutive World Cup trophy, to enthusiastic boos from the French republican fans.

It's hard to verify, almost a century out, how good Meazza actually was. Italy manager Vittorio Pozzo swore that "having him on the team was like starting the game 1–0 up," but the only vestiges left of his actual game are a few brief choppy film reels and 100 years worth of nostalgia-tinged anecdotes, which mingle chaotically with accusations of fascist game-rigging. The vestiges of his reputation, on the other hand, are hard to miss. He still holds the Serie A record for most goals scored in a debut season. San Siro is officially named Stadio Giuseppe Meazza in his honor. And, tellingly, when someone scores a great goal in Italy, even now, fans will sometimes still call it a *gol alla Meazza*. A goal worthy of Meazza.

FULL NAME:	DATE OF BIRTH:	PLACE OF BIRTH:	NATIONAL TEAM:	CAPS / GOALS:
Giuseppe Meazza	*August 23, 1910*	*Milan, Italy*	*Italy, 1930–39*	*53 / 33*

LIONEL MESSI

THE FIRST THING YOU NOTICE about Messi is that he looks, well, basically like a normal guy. In the post-Beckham era of the Uncannily Handsome Footballer, Messi is conspicuously nonconforming, standing a diminutive 5'6", squat and thick-necked and illogically pale, sporting a scruffy beard that only goes so far towards obscuring the distinct unchisel of his jawline and a hairstyle that can only be described as Supercuts. The second thing you notice about Messi is that his name sounds an awful lot like messiah. The third thing you notice is that he plays like God.

Whether you consider Messi to be the best footballer of all time is a matter of personal preference, but that he is the most famous player of all time is an indisputable fact. If you have never seen even a single minute of football—even if you couldn't pick Messi out of a lineup of three men, all of whom were him—you know his name. You have heard it tossed about gleefully, chanted solemnly as incantation, cried out in religious ecstasy. It means Barcelona, it means Argentina, it means the World Cup, it means football in the modern era, because to witness Messi is to witness a kind of dream, surreal and grand and moving, which is what modern football at its best has proven itself capable of producing.

There are no real words to describe the experience of watching Messi—which is why his name itself has become a kind of shorthand for it. He makes football look like an individual sport. Not to say that he is selfish, which he is not, nor that he is solely responsible for his teams' successes, which—despite what it may look like at times—he is also not. Simply that when Messi is on the ball, everything else fades into the background. With other players, you talk about ball control, but Messi is beyond control. The Uruguayan poet Eduardo Galeano once said, "Diego Maradona played as if the ball was glued to his shoe, but Lionel Messi played as if that ball was stuck inside his sock." He never appears to be moving the ball so much as moving with it, the two of them—Messi and ball—performing an intricate, magnetic pas de deux, slaloming hypnotically around everything in their path. It is a primarily physical experience, watching Messi: You feel it rustling in the pit of your navel, swelling up in your chest, prickling the back of your neck.

We tend to ascribe our greatest athletes with a sense of unnaturalness—we call their abilities freakish, accuse them of being from another planet. That they are often abnormally attractive (see: Ronaldo, Cristiano; Beckham, David) reinforces this sense, and we reminisce about their feats in terms of how impossible they felt. With Messi, the opposite is true. What he does feels startlingly natural—truthful, even. Like he is playing football—real, honest to god, Plato's Cave football—and everything else is just shadows. He is the materializer of our dreams.

FULL NAME:	DATE OF BIRTH:	PLACE OF BIRTH:	NATIONAL TEAM:	CAPS / GOALS:
Lionel Andrés Messi Cuccittini	*June 24, 1987*	*Rosario, Santa Fe, Argentina*	*Argentina, 2005–*	*156 / 80 *as of November 5, 2021*

VIVIANNE MIEDEMA

IVIANNE MIEDEMA IS TOO YOUNG to be in this book. She is only 25, and looks to be about 15. She has never lived in a time when there was no Women's World Cup, no women's football in the Olympics. She is not old enough to remember professional women's leagues being a pipe dream. She is from a generation of new footballers who have just begun to stake their claim on history, not yet accomplished enough to edge out their predecessors in the pantheon of greats. She is also, at age 25, the Netherlands' most prolific goalscorer, by a wide margin, with (as of this writing) 85 goals in 104 appearances, having rolled right past Robin van Persie's record of 50 (in 102 appearances) in 2018 at age 22.

Miedema started playing professionally when she was 14, the youngest player in the Netherlands' four-year-old women's league. She was called up to the senior Dutch national team two years later. The Netherlands have been slower off the mark than many of their neighbors, not investing significantly in women's football until the mid-aughts. Miedema's career effectively tracks their progress—or perhaps vice versa. Two years into her national career, the team qualified for the World Cup for the first time in their history. In 2017, they won the Euros. Just four short years after their first World Cup, they were in the final in 2019.

Miedema has been gradually stealing her way into the public consciousness. She has been at Arsenal since 2017, but it is only in the past couple of years that people have begun to realize what she has already accomplished. Titles won, records broken. She has snuck in under the radar and popped out as one of the defining strikers of the WSL, of the Netherlands, and, unhyperbolically, of the modern game.

Miedema is an unassuming player. She does not seek the spotlight, does not do very many interviews, is chronically averse to any kind of goal celebration. She oozes the cool of the unbothered, looking supremely relaxed, even in front of goal, even in big moments. Her long legs allow her to zip into spaces ahead of defenders, but she always appears to be jogging. She stalks the pitch not like a predator, but like a person at a park-side pickup game who doesn't want to get too sweaty. She scores at will with incredible variety: surging solo runs, long-range cannons, deft tap-ins, nonchalant little lobs. The goals are addictive—they all have this *yeah, why not* quality to them. She assists almost as often as she scores, dropping deep to collect the ball, trigger presses, and drag defenses out of position, the odd striker who is perfectly happy to cede her own goal opportunities. There isn't a player in the world right now who manages to make scoring seem less urgent—and perhaps it isn't urgent to Miedema, given the frequency and ease with which she does it.

Miedema banked 10 goals in four games at the 2020 Olympics, including two absolutely unstoppable missiles against the US in the quarterfinals, stymied only by a missed penalty when the game went to a shoot-out. Back in 2019, Miedema made the preliminary list of Ballon d'Or nominees for the year—the award ultimately went to Megan Rapinoe—but she didn't feature in the year's FIF-PRO World XI, which put Rapinoe, Marta, and Alex Morgan up front. "I don't really care about individual awards to be honest, but I think it's a joke," Miedema said. Well. Joke's over. The Dutch have arrived with Miedema up front, cool as can be.

FULL NAME:	DATE OF BIRTH:	PLACE OF BIRTH:	NATIONAL TEAM:	CAPS / GOALS:
Anna Margaretha Marina Astrid Miedema	*July 15, 1996*	*Hoogeveen, Drenthe, Netherlands*	*Netherlands, 2013–*	*104 / 85 *as of November 27, 2021*

ROGER MILLA

FTER 11 RESPECTABLE, IF RELA-
tively unremarkable, years as a journeyman for
an eclectic procession of French clubs, Roger
Milla was living in semiretirement on the
French volcanic island of Réunion, 400 miles
off the coast of Madagascar. Playing for a small local team
on the island, the 38-year-old Cameroonian had retired
from international play and was settling into the life of an
obscure but relatively successful aging footballer. Then the
president of Cameroon called.

There was no particular indication that Milla, who
had proven a competent but not what you'd call prolific
goalscorer over the course of his career, would be anything
more than a statistical footnote in a paper about the average age of World Cup players when he showed up for the
1990 World Cup in Italy that summer. Most footballers are
elevated to greatness by their consistency—this many goals
over this many games, this many trophies over a career this
length. This is no doubt what makes those rarer moments
of unforeseen greatness, of rising to the occasion, even
more satisfying.

Milla scored four goals during Italia 90. Had he been
a 20-something football star playing for a top-seeded team,
that still would have been an impressive number. That he
did it at 38, playing for Cameroon, is a staggering feat. The
goals—two against Romania in the group stage and two
against Colombia in the round of 16—were well anticipated, calmly executed. They were also deliciously scrappy.
Every goal seemed to come off of a long ball with a weird
bounce, a mistimed pass, or some other moment of unexpected opportunity. In his fourth goal of the tournament,
which saw Cameroon into the quarters, the Cameroon
defense sends an overly enthusiastic clearance to the feet
of the Colombian keeper. There is not a single Cameroon
player on the Colombian side of the pitch as the keeper,
René Higuita, ambles out of the box to stop the ball and
pass it to his right back. As the right back calmly sends it
back to Higuita, Milla comes streaking in from nowhere,
cherry-picks the ball, and runs it into the net. It had none
of the technical splendor of a perfectly executed lead-up
play or a beautiful cross into the box. But it was a masterclass in offensive optimism, bravado, and the dogged,
unabashed willingness to take errors and glimpses and the
tiniest of chances and convert them into lemonade.

Going into the tournament, Cameroon was such a
noncontender that the Argentine coach didn't even bother
mentioning them when listing the potential perils in the
team's group. Cameroon promptly beat the reigning champions 1–0 in one of the biggest upsets in World Cup history. They topped their group and came within minutes
of reaching the semifinals. FIFA were so impressed by the
performance that they decided to add a third African spot
for the next tournament.

If Milla's legacy from that tournament were merely
giving the European press something else to ask the
Cameroonian team about other than whether they ate
monkeys back home, that would have been enough.
Yet, in addition to forcing the world to respect African
football, Milla also gifted us something arguably just as
valuable: the dancing goal celebration. After each goal,
Milla went to the corner flag and did a little hip-swinging
samba for the fans. It is an image dripping in swagger
and joy. It didn't matter that due to a clerical discrep-
ancy, Milla's name keeps coming up on televisions across
the world as "Miller"; it didn't matter that Cameroon
would be knocked out by a Gary Lineker penalty in the
105th minute of the quarterfinal against England. For
30 years, players have been replicating that dance. Not
just because Milla taught us that celebrations are more
fun with choreography. But because it represents the
defiant optimism of doing something that no one in their
right mind expected you to be able to do.

FULL NAME:	DATE OF BIRTH:	PLACE OF BIRTH:	NATIONAL TEAM:	CAPS / GOALS:
Albert Roger Miller	*May 20, 1952*	*Yaoundé, Cameroon*	*Cameroon, 1973–94*	*77 / 43*

AYA MIYAMA

IT'S THE FINAL OF THE 2011 WOMen's World Cup. Japan's veteran captain Homare Sawa has just scored a 117th-minute equalizer against the US to thrust Japan back into the game and take the final to penalties. Sawa, with her astonishing, improbable flick of a goal, is rightfully the obvious focus of the world's rapture. But standing tranquilly on the dispatching end of that corner kick is midfielder Aya Miyama, nine years Sawa's junior and even smaller, and the obvious heir to Sawa's throne as the éminence grise of women's football in Japan.

Miyama was in a lot of ways the opposite of Sawa. This was perhaps why they complemented each other so well. Sawa had the long glossy ponytail of the American footballer; Miyama had the floppy Bieber crop favored by the Asian players. Sawa was quick, acrobatic, and opportunistic. Miyama was technical, graceful, and patient, one of the best in the world from a dead ball.

To the extent that such a thing existed in Japan in the 1990s, Miyama came from a footballing family. Her father, an enthusiastic member of the first real wave of Japanese football fans, started his own youth club in their hometown of Ōamishirasato, where Miyama learned to play, supplementing her education with hours upon hours of solo kickabouts at the beach down the road. As Miyama got older without getting any taller, coaches began to prepare her for what they perceived to be the inevitable. She was 5'2", neither particularly fast nor particularly strong, and they couldn't foresee her having much of a long-term future in the sport. Undeterred, Miyama focused methodically on the things she could control—her movement, her vision, the ball itself—and by 16, she had landed herself a professional contract; by 18, a spot on the national team.

Eight years later, Miyama was, along with Sawa, at the very center of that team, both figuratively and literally. In the 2011 World Cup final against the US, she was responsible for sending the two teams into extra time, capitalizing on a defensive mistake in the 81st minute to knock the ball in and draw Japan level at 1–1. And her corner kick in the 117th minute, floating, unrushed, precise, bailed the team out again and sent the game to penalties.

Miyama is chosen to take the first penalty. It's difficult to imagine the levels of adrenaline coursing through her blood, because her face reveals almost nothing as she steps up to the spot. Shannon Boxx, who has just missed the first penalty for the US, ran up to the ball like someone was chasing her and pounded it towards the outstretched leg of Ayumi Kaihori, the Japanese keeper. In contrast, Miyama barely lifts her feet off the ground as she ambles up to the ball and calmly taps it past Hope Solo. When Japan wins, six penalties later, Miyama doesn't celebrate immediately. First, she goes around to all the US players, comforting them on their loss. Christie Rampone gets a shoulder squeeze. Megan Rapinoe gets a hug. Heather O'Reilly, a smile and some kind words. Miyama will celebrate with the rest of the team, ecstatically, emotionally. But she's in no hurry.

FULL NAME:	DATE OF BIRTH:	PLACE OF BIRTH:	NATIONAL TEAM:	CAPS / GOALS:
Aya Miyama	*January 28, 1985*	*Ōamishirasato, Chiba, Japan*	*Japan, 2003–16*	*162 / 38*

PORTIA MODISE

HEN PORTIA MODISE WAS about 10, or so the story goes, the local boys' team in Soweto—the township in southwest Johannesburg, once home to Nelson Mandela himself—required that players provide their birth certificates in order to sign up. This was a problem for Modise, for the obvious reason that her birth certificate would indicate pretty explicitly that, as much of a short-haired football-mad tomboy as she was, she was not in fact eligible to play for the boys' team. To her mother, this seemed like a fairly insurmountable hurdle. To the young Modise, not so much. She marched next door, borrowed the birth certificate of the neighboring boy, and handed it in to the coach. An administrative problem with a straightforward solution. Until she moved over to the Soweto Ladies at 13, that was that.

Modise joined the national team—nicknamed *Banyana Banyana*, or simply *the Girls*—aged 16, in 2000. By the mid-2000s, she was a star on the rise in African soccer, easily one of the most recognizable female players on the continent. Modise is small, with hair tightly cropped, cherubic cheeks, and an ear-to-ear grin. It is not difficult to imagine her blending in with the other mischievous Soweto youths. It was perhaps more challenging to picture her as an elite athlete. Until you'd seen her on the field, that is. A nimble-footed, hungry striker, Modise attacked often, poaching possession from unsuspecting defenders, dribbling around opponents, using her technical precision to find simple, obvious ways of getting the ball into the back of the net. And always exuding the same unmistakable air of brazen competence.

Modise drew eyes reflexively, swaggering in with the internal glint of a born scene-stealer. She was brash, roguish, and forthright, an unshrinkingly out lesbian at a time when even players in much more gay-friendly countries, on much more gay-friendly continents, were not yet. Arsenal Ladies offered her a contract in 2003, but the stipend wasn't enough to make the move worthwhile, and Modise elected to stay home, drawing global eyes to South Africa, a country that, up until that point, had been little more than an asterisk in the atlas of world football. It was universally noted that she had the potential to break Africa's international goalscoring record.

Before she could manage it though, Modise suddenly bowed her way off the national team in 2008. She was unhappy with the abuse she and her teammates were facing in a country where homophobia and sexism were still commonplace, even within the small world of South African women's football. Never one to overcomplicate a problem, Modise refused to return until 2012, after their coach of five years, Augustine Makalakalene, a major contributor to the culture of abuse, was finally fired for sexual harassment.

Freshly reinstalled, Modise turned back up just in time to accompany Banyana Banyana to the London Olympics. The team was vastly outmatched that summer, grouped with Sweden, Japan, and Canada, and they only managed to find the back of the net once during the tournament. That goal, however, is widely agreed to be the most magnificent ever scored at the Olympics. In the 60th minute of their first match, against a formidable Swedish side, Modise plucks the ball from Sweden captain Nilla Fischer on the halfway line. She springs forward a few strides and sanguinely launches it over the keeper from 45 yards out. It is uncomplicated, unapologetic, and just a little bit cheeky. Quintessential Modise. Despite the four-year hiatus, she proceeded to end her career with 101 goals, which was in fact enough to send her into the African record books as the continent's top goalscorer, where she has remained ever since. Asked recently about her own legacy, Modise, never one for false modesty, proclaimed succinctly: "Back then, I didn't even think that women's football would be powerful in South Africa, but I made it powerful. I made people recognize that there is women's football."

FULL NAME:	DATE OF BIRTH:	PLACE OF BIRTH:	NATIONAL TEAM:	CAPS / GOALS:
Portia Modise	*June 20, 1983*	*Soweto, South Africa*	*South Africa, 2000–15*	*124 / 101*

BOBBY MOORE

T IS A FACT BITTERLY REMARKED upon whenever English people get together that despite having invented the damn game, England's national football team has only managed to win one major tournament in its entire century and a half of existence. Aside from the glory of invention, it is that single World Cup trophy—won in a nation-rousing extra-time 4–2 victory against West Germany at home at Wembley in the summer of 1966 that has come to represent in the mind of the country the pinnacle, the apex, the platonic realization of English football. The iconic image of that summer is of the England players in the moments after receiving the trophy, gathered in a semicircle sporting their stylish blood-red long-sleeve jerseys and terrible English teeth. Hoisted onto their shoulders in the center of the shot, with a grin on his face and the cup in his hand, is team captain and star defender Bobby Moore. If '66 is the platonic realization of English football, Bobby Moore is the platonic realization of the English themselves.

Born in London's East End in the dying days of the Blitz, Moore advanced quickly through the ranks of the West Ham academy. By 17, he was a starter for the senior team. At 22, he became the youngest player to captain England, inheriting the position from Jimmy Armfield, who was sitting out the summer with a groin injury. If James Bond and Mr. Knightley had a child, he would not have been closer to the ideal Englishman than Moore. He was polite, reserved, conscientious (he famously wiped his muddy hands on the tablecloth before shaking hands with and receiving the trophy from the Queen at Wembley, because he was worried about messing up her clean white gloves),

strong enough to muscle you off the ball, but intellectual enough not to have to. On top of that, Moore was virtually unflappable; patrolling the English side, he read every ball, waiting patiently for the exact right moment and picking each off with a perfectly timed tackle or interception. There are no hasty, panicked clearances—no matter how quickly the offense is closing back in, Moore, uncannily calm, always finds time to look up and weigh his options before releasing the ball again. As he does in the final minute of extra time of the '66 final, sending a perfect long pass out to Geoff Hurst, who in turn sprints for the 18-yard line and blasts the ball into the back of the net, sealing the English victory with a kiss.

Pelé called Moore the best defender he ever played against. Sir Alex Ferguson called him the best defender he ever saw. George Best once proclaimed, "If I could wish for my son to turn out like someone, it would be Bobby Moore." The Empire was crumbling, but the country still had Moore to defend it. With one foot in the restrained composure of the old world and one foot in the loose camaraderie of the new one, Moore redefined English dignity for the postcolonial era.

To that end, perhaps the most iconic image of Moore is actually from four years after the 1966 victory: Moore congratulates Pelé just after Brazil beat England in the group stage at the 1970 Mexico World Cup. Swapped shirts in hand, both men grinning from ear to ear, Moore is the model sportsman. As gracious in defeat as in victory.

In life, and even more so in death, Moore became a kind of talisman, an illustration of the England the country wanted to believe in. Part fantasy, part metonym, he remains the best version of England we have on offer.

FULL NAME:	DATE OF BIRTH:	PLACE OF BIRTH:	NATIONAL TEAM:	CAPS / GOALS:
Robert Frederick Chelsea Moore	*April 12, 1941*	*Barking, Essex, England*	*England, 1962–73*	*108 / 2*

CAROLINA MORACE

ROUND MIDAFTERNOON ON August 18, 1990, Manchester United and Liverpool faced off at Wembley for the Charity Shield, the annual charity match between England's top-tier champions and the winners of the FA Cup. With a handful of Manchester United's starters out injured and the preseason's traditional low stakes, it was a relatively uneventful match. The teams drew 1–1 and shared the trophy. More technically minded historians will remember the day as the penultimate Charity Shield to end in a draw, as penalties were introduced two years later in an attempt to up the stakes and simplify the award ceremony. Emotionalists will remember it as the final trophy Kenny Dalglish would lift with Liverpool before his abrupt midseason departure in February of '91 in the tragic aftermath of Hillsborough. Only a very small subset of the population—the roughly 30,000 fans who came early to witness the first half of that day's Wembley doubleheader, a friendly between the English and Italian women's national teams—will know it as the day that Carolina Morace absolutely trounced the Lionesses, scoring four goals in one of the most dominant individual performances the storied ground has ever seen.

Reporting on the match back home, the *Gazzetta dello Sport* noted Morace's "cascade of blond curls," her "class and grit," and her "masculine power goals." Needless to say, Italian women's football was a niche genre at the time. The fact that the women had been playing at Wembley at all was about as surprising to people as Morace's one-woman blowout. Owing to the particular coupling of the privileged role of men's football in Italian society and the national brand of sexism, women's football in Italy in those early days, more than being perceived as either a good or a bad idea, was just kind of a funny one. Football fell just far enough outside the realm of recognizable female behavior as to make it comedic. When at 14, Carolina Morace's father came home and informed her she'd been called up to the national team, she had replied, skeptically, "Which national team?" But there was only the one, so for better or for worse, the Italians got Morace—and on the flip side, Morace got the Italians.

The country never really knew what to do with her. She was too talented to ignore, a bit too beautiful, definitely too outspoken. The national team itself, entirely amateur and little more than a side project for the Italian Football Federation, didn't make much of a splash either in competition or with the Italian football-watching public. But Morace demanded attention. She scored the first hat trick in Women's World Cup history in 1991, walking away with four goals for the inaugural tournament. The press took to calling her *Baresi in gonnella* (*Baresi in a skirt*), after Franco Baresi, the Italian men's captain. She led Italy to UEFA championship finals in '93 and '97. They put her on the covers of fashion magazines wearing fur coats and heels, with a football at her feet. She was the top scorer in women's Serie A for 11 years, from 1988 all the way up until her retirement.

In 1999, Luciano Gaucci, the famous Italian club owner, appointed her manager of his Serie C team, Viterbese, making her the first woman ever to manage a professional men's side. The tabloids mocked her, the club executives micromanaged, and so, unimpressed, Morace packed up and moved on, leaving Viterbese after only two games. People loved that too. To the Italian public, she was an object of curiosity, mild fear, ironic pride, and genuine admiration. Her favorite writers were Sartre, Simone de Beauvoir, and André Gide. She had 12 Italian league titles and a law degree. "I have discovered in the past few days that the Italian male is scared of women," Morace pontificated in her final days at Viterbese. "It makes me angry to be judged before I have even started. I might fail but that has nothing to do with my sex." Always in conversation with the public, Morace bore her role with patience, obstinance, the aforementioned great hair, and an almost pathological compulsion to score goals. Which was, in short, exactly what you'd have hoped for: a perfect first female footballing star for a country that didn't even know it wanted one.

FULL NAME:	DATE OF BIRTH:	PLACE OF BIRTH:	NATIONAL TEAM:	CAPS / GOALS:
Carolina Morace	*February 5, 1964*	*Venice, Italy*	*Italy, 1978–97*	*150 / 105*

ALEX MORGAN

IN THE BEGINNING THEY CALLED her *Baby Horse*, which wasn't the most flattering nickname one could have imagined, but it was remarkably apt: the way she sprinted clear of opponents with a sort of prancing, powerful, head-first gallop on the balls of her feet and that long mane of glossy brown hair trailing behind her. She was a 21-year-old California native, brought in as a pacey super-sub to complement the power of Abby Wambach and the creativity of Megan Rapinoe up front for the US. She took the assignment seriously, galloping on in the 86th minute to score a stoppage-time goal against Italy that assured the US's admission to the 2011 World Cup after the team missed out on automatic qualification at the Gold Cup earlier in the year. She replicated the feat twice that summer, scoring almost identical goals, first in the semis, then in the final, hurtling past defenders with that signature stride to send the ball cresting in with her left foot. The team she had joined was certainly not short on stars, but it was still sporting a Mia Hamm–sized gap in its roster six years after her retirement, operating without the kind of marquee player who could command the interest of women's soccer enthusiasts and the general American public alike. No one was more perfectly positioned to fill this gap than Alex Morgan.

Mia Hamm may have invented soccer girl cool, but Alex Morgan has, for the past decade, been its finest virtuoso. In interviews, she is chatty but circumspect, speaking a language of modest, eager self-assurance with that elusive SoCal accent that always sounds the slightest bit hoarse, like she's just come back from a fun night out you weren't invited to. She has the glossy ponytail and the confidence and even makes headbands look blithely chic—the iconic thin strip of pink pre-wrap, like she's just pulled it out of the first-aid kit at the last minute to deal with some unanticipated flyaways. Hope Solo passed as cool for years just by virtue of looking kind of like her. On the field, Morgan seems capable of endless bursts of speed and agility, exuding hyper-competence and a sense of relaxed excellence, as if you have not even seen her at her highest gear. She runs like she knows exactly where she's going and how she's going to get there. And usually she does.

Owing to a combination of prodigious talent, precocious business savvy, and massive pop-cultural appeal, there are very few things that Morgan has yet to accomplish. Two World Cups, Olympic gold, three league titles in three different leagues, one Champions League, individual awards out the wazoo. Since her first year as a starter, she has been the face of the USWNT, appearing in centerfold magazine spreads, doing TV appearances, her smile plastered onto the sides of buses. She has authored a series of soccer-themed children's books, which rocketed immediately to the top of the bestsellers list. She was the first woman to feature on the cover of a *FIFA* game. She has attained rare, John Malkovich–type celebrity, starring in a vastly underdiscussed children's film about an Alex Morgan superfan who begins to hallucinate her after an unfortunate head injury. She has also dedicated herself to the fight for equal pay—a vital but historically unglamorous thing. An endorsement whose legacy will likely reverberate long after Morgan herself has receded from the spotlight.

On her 30th birthday, Morgan scored the game-winning goal against England in the semis of the 2019 World Cup, speeding into the box and lofting herself into the air to put away a header in the 31st minute. She ran to the corner, arms out on either side of her—her signature celebration—stopped, and mime-sipped a cup of tea, pinky finger raised ironically to the sky. Devastating, if you were an inhabitant of the British Isles. In 400 years of trying, no Briton had ever managed to make tea drinking look that ecstatic. Such is the power of Alex Morgan.

FULL NAME:	DATE OF BIRTH:	PLACE OF BIRTH:	NATIONAL TEAM:	CAPS / GOALS:
Alexandra Patricia Morgan Carrasco	*July 2, 1989*	*San Dimas, California, United States*	*United States, 2010–*	*190 / 115 *as of October 26, 2021*

GERD MÜLLER

 ERD MÜLLER'S NICKNAME WAS *Kleines dickes Müller—short, fat Müller—* bestowed on him upon his arrival at Bayern Munich by Croatian manager Zlatko Čajkovski, who was making no attempt to hide the fact that Müller did not look the way he thought a footballer should. Müller, 5'9" with thighs like oak trees, was in fact neither short nor fat, but the nickname got at the distinct just-some-guy-ness of Müller's aura. Both on and off the pitch, he didn't seem like the kind of player who was going to produce anything spectacular.

And in a sense, this is true. Müller, the man who single-handedly dragged the art of striking onto the celestial plane, is perhaps the most illustrious virtuoso of the unspectacular the sport has ever seen. Fans called him *Der Bomber*, but it was almost an ironic nickname, because Müller's goals rarely exploded into the net. They trundled, bumbled, teetered, ricocheted, and pea-rolled over the line. If you witnessed any specific goal, you would have thought that Müller was an average hack of a striker blessed with a moment of fortune. But witnessing the goals in aggregate, goal after goal, week after week, season after season, you quickly saw just how spectacular Müller's unspectacular-ness was—the magnificence of these goals in totality, which defied traditional technical ability and common wisdom to add up to one of the greatest goalscoring careers of all time.

"I was never into performing magic tricks for the crowd," Müller proclaimed unapologetically. "I just wanted to score." It wasn't an exaggeration—he really wasn't picky. He'd put the ball in with any part of his body that was available: right foot, left foot, shins, knees, thighs, chest, you name it. You'd often find him seated on the ground while the ball inched past the goalkeeper; he'd score from all sorts of strange, awkward positions, twisting and contorting off balance, tumbling to the ground while sticking out an instinctive leg to send the bouncing ball into net. His motto: "If you think, it's too late."

Müller is one of a very small number of players to average more than a goal per game on the international stage, with 68 goals in 62 appearances for West Germany. He ripped through World Cup 1970 with 10 goals, demolishing the optimism of an entire generation of English fans with a gawky leaping 108th-minute karate tap-in in the quarterfinals to put an end to England's back-to-back dreams. (Müller would score two goals against Italy in the semifinal, but it wasn't enough to see West Germany past the eventual runners-up.)

Four years later, Müller took West Germany all the way on home turf. The Netherlands was famously the better team in that tournament, the team that should have won, if you subscribe to a merit-based theory of artistic athletic justice. But after trading penalties in the first 25 minutes, Müller snagged the only goal from open play to give West Germany a lead that, with Beckenbauer patrolling the West German half, the Dutch were unable to reverse. It was an exquisitely Müller goal. Rainer Bonhof, with the ball on the edge of the box, flipped it to Müller, who had made the run with him and was rushing towards goal with a defender on his heels. The pass bounced off Müller's shin and rolled behind him. Staggering backwards with his body contorted in a double helix, Müller hoofed the ball through the legs of the defender on top of him, the ball not traveling particularly fast, but just a foot too far for Dutch keeper Jan Jongbloed to reach from the near post, and bowling into the back of the net. In Müller's words, "The ball jumped off my left foot, I turned a little and suddenly it was in."

FULL NAME:	DATE OF BIRTH:	PLACE OF BIRTH:	NATIONAL TEAM:	CAPS / GOALS:
Gerhard Müller	*November 3, 1945*	*Nördlingen, Germany*	*West Germany, 1966–74*	*62 / 68*

NADIA NADIM

ADIA NADIM HAS ONE OF THOSE stories that is literally unbelievable. Like if you saw it in a movie you would think (or more realistically, when you see it in a movie, you will think), *Huh, that's a great story, which they have clearly embellished at will*, when in reality, the writers have intentionally left out the most incredible details for fear of seeming like they were just making things up.

Nadim was born in Herāt, an ancient oasis in the northwest part of Afghanistan, at the tail end of the Soviet-Afghan war. Her father was a general in the Afghan army; when Nadim was nine years old, he was captured by the Taliban and secretly executed. After three years of moving house to house, trying to stay under the radar of the Taliban, hoping against hope that her husband was somehow still alive, Nadim's mother sold all their possessions, gathered Nadim and her four sisters, and fled: minivan to Karachi, two months to acquire false passports, flight to Italy, days in a dark Milanese basement, 50 hours in the back of a truck on their way to what they believed to be London and turned out to be a refugee camp in rural Denmark.

It is not in this refugee camp, but in a second one, that Nadim discovered football, coming across a group of girls playing on the other side of a fence. She still spoke no Danish, no English, but she kept coming back, and with some enthusiastic gesturing the coach figured out that Nadim wanted to participate. He started including her in drills. After three months, he threw her a kit and invited her to play her first match. Nadim's family was eventually offered asylum. She went to school, got a newspaper route, and progressed up the ladder of the Danish football system. In 2009, Nadim was naturalized and debuted for the Danish senior national team, becoming the first non-Danish-born player in the team's history.

Nadim is a fleet-footed forward, with long, rapid strides and the ability to lose almost any defender on a quick turn. She has won the NWSL championship with the Portland Thorns and Division 1 Féminine with PSG. In normal circumstances, becoming a professional female footballer feels like scaling a mountain full of misleading trail signs and thorny shrubbery. Nadim makes it seem like the easiest path she's ever climbed. She spends so much time doing ludicrously challenging things outside of football that she makes Troy Bolton look like an extracurricular-juggling dilettante. Her mother must have a field day when she runs into rival mothers at the supermarket. "How's *your* daughter? Mine speaks seven languages fluently, is a qualified reconstructive surgeon, was voted Dane of the Year in 2017 by Denmark's leading newspaper, ranked number 20 on the *Forbes* list of Most Powerful Women in International Sports in 2018, and is the face of UNESCO's campaign for girls' and women's education." To mention just a few of Nadim's other accomplishments. It is as if she took the old adage *stick to sports* and dangled it by its feet out the window. Professional football is almost a side gig for her. But it is an important side gig, both to her and to those of us watching at home. It is a wordless lesson in resilience, unlikely achievement, and the wide, inclusive reach of football. Her enthusiasm diffuses out onto the field like pollen.

FULL NAME:	DATE OF BIRTH:	PLACE OF BIRTH:	NATIONAL TEAM:	CAPS / GOALS:
Nadia Nadim	*January 2, 1988*	*Herāt, Afghanistan*	*Denmark, 2009–*	*99 / 38 *as of September 12, 2021*

HIDETOSHI NAKATA

NO ONE EXPECTED JAPAN TO MAKE much of an impact at the 1998 World Cup. They were a nation of sumo- and baseball-lovers competing in their first World Cup; their domestic league was only six years old. It was not clear that Japan itself was interested in football, so it didn't seem particularly worthwhile for anyone else to be. And on paper at least, this was right. Japan lost all three of their group stage matches and were on the plane home before any of the fun had even started. They were politely golf-clapped at the time by neutral onlookers who praised their effort, their classy play, their willingness to take their own game to intimidating opponents like Argentina, but 1998 was the year of Zidane, Ronaldo, Beckham's red card. In the retelling of that tournament, Japan does not feature—should not, by all logic, feature. Except that in their midfield was 21-year-old Hidetoshi Nakata, making mazy runs through the Argentine defense with his striking copper-colored dye job. Cynics scoffed that no one would have even clocked him if not for the hair, but Nakata, already a rising star in Japan, had officially caught the eye of the global public.

Stylish, exceptionally handsome, charming, and possessing an artistry that vastly outstripped the rest of the Japan team, Nakata was singled out in France and dubbed the Asian David Beckham by admiring observers. Within weeks of the tournament, he was off to Italy with a fresh $4 million contract from Perugia in his pocket—only the second Japanese player ever to make the leap to Serie A. Perugia was notorious at the time for their headline-prioritizing transfer strategy (this is the same Perugia who would seriously contemplate adding female players to their men's side and then handed a contract to Muammar Gaddafi's son in 2003), and Nakata's signing was originally dismissed as a silly publicity stunt. As if in direct response, Nakata came out and scored two goals against Juventus on his debut, with 5,000 Japanese fans sitting in the stands. The signing had garnered Perugia their fair share of publicity to be sure, but silly it clearly was not.

New deals were quickly inked to broadcast Perugia games live in Japan as Nakatamania exploded across the island nation. Replica jerseys flew off shelves as Nakata's face suddenly appeared on every poster, every front page, every magazine insert. Average Japanese attendance at Perugia matches rounded out around 3,000 fans a game as Japanese tour operators began including day trips to Perugia in their Italian vacation packages. Nakata was, wrote the *New York Times* just months into the 1998–99 season, a "one-man tourist attraction and a small merchandising gold mine." He was trailed at all times by a corps of Japanese journalists who, often stymied by Nakata's fierce privacy measures, would simply publish stories about his refusal to give interviews. Nakatamania was primarily a Japanese phenomenon, but by virtue of being really famous somewhere, Nakata became famous everywhere, launched into the spotlight as the most recognizable Asian footballer of all time by the sheer force of the Japanese adoration.

Nakata's on-field achievements do not necessarily match the scale of his off-field presence. As a player, he was tenacious, with quick feet and good balance, capable of dribbling out of tight spots with an eye for incisive passes and a fondness for dramatic goals (like the 30-yard strike he fired against Juventus in May 2001 to help keep Roma's title usurpers at bay), but his career was patchy, hampered by Serie A regulations limiting the number of foreign players teams could have on the pitch at once and a revolving door of record-breaking transfers that saw Nakata passed around from one Italian club to another, each hungrier than the last for a piece of this new Japanese football market. Nakata won the Scudetto with Roma in 2001 and the Coppa Italia with Parma in 2002, playing meaningful roles in both campaigns, but they were supporting roles, his position always that of journeyman super-sub. He played Japan into the round of 16 at the 2002 World Cup, but the accomplishment was overshadowed by their cohost South Korea's fairy-tale run to the semifinals. And yet none of this matters, because from the get-go, Nakata's significance was never particularly resume-dependent: his indelible legacy in making Japan care about football, and in turn, making world football care about Japan.

FULL NAME:	DATE OF BIRTH:	PLACE OF BIRTH:	NATIONAL TEAM:	CAPS / GOALS:
Hidetoshi Nakata	*January 22, 1977*	*Kōfu, Yamanashi, Japan*	*Japan, 1997–2006*	*77 / 11*

LOUISA NÉCIB

WEEK BEFORE THE 2011 WORLD Cup, three members of the French team posed nude in the German daily *Bild*. "Is this how we have to show up before you'll come to our games?" the caption underneath sneered in the direction of an apathetic French public. Cutting, attention-grabbing, and, in retrospect, totally off the mark. Because the French did finally start showing an interest that tournament. But it turned out that what they needed wasn't nudity at all. It was Louisa Nécib.

Debuting in her first World Cup that summer, the 24-year-old from Marseille stepped onto the pitch in Germany with mesmerizing, dynamic touch, a commanding presence, and an Arabic surname—similarities striking enough that it was near-impossible to talk about her without reflexively shouting the name of the player she evoked. Both were from the Marseillaise housing estates, both were children of Algerian immigrants; both were raised on foot de rue, street football; both were midfielders who seemed to have the ball on a string. The press nicknamed her *Ziza* to Zinédine Zidane's *Zizou*. Nécib's game was technically quite different than Zidane's; whereas Zidane was also an expert finisher, Nécib was almost exclusively a playmaker, bringing the ball down, dancing it into space, and then threading the needle with carelessly perfect passes to teammates streaming towards goal. Zidane tended to play centrally, while Nécib favored the left wing. Zidane's great strength was his elegant efficiency, his ability to find the cleanest way of getting the ball from point A to point B. Nécib played looser, more complex, street performer–type football. But the raw talent was the same. The thrill was the same. The French men's team had fallen into something of a rut since Zidane's retirement in 2006, spinning their wheels in the depressing murk of poor results, infighting, and political scandals; the women were both a novelty and a throwback. With

each game, more and more French viewers tuned in to bask in the glow of this team: fresh, unknown, playing entertaining, mouthwatering football as if it were Paris in 1998. It was nostalgic, it was surprising, but mostly it was just exciting, as they dominated all the way to the semi-finals with Nécib in the spotlight. "There's so much sunshine when she touches the ball," France manager Bruno Bini proclaimed.

There were those who took issue with the constant Zidane comparisons. Some argued that it overrated her abilities, others that it underrated them. Over the next five years (until her abrupt retirement at the early age of 29), Nécib went on to become a household name in her own right, but she could never shake the title of *Zidanette*. In some ways, this was a dark cloud over her time as a player, perpetually forcing her to play second banana in her own career. But if Nécib lost personally in the association, the French women's team won collectively. The public had been waiting patiently for a successor to Zidane, only to realize that they had been watching at the wrong door. When they discovered that the renaissance of cunning and craftsmanship had happened on the women's side of Clairefontaine rather than the men's, they headed right over. What they were looking for wasn't Zidane, but rather his legacy. And here it was. A woman born 15 years after Zizou, eight kilometers down the road, who, like the rest of the country, had grown up emulating him, and who—thanks to France's significant investments in women's football as well as men's in the wake of his World Cup success—was being given a chance to do it on a global stage. Zidane was the great song, but Nécib was the remix: less serious, less distinguished perhaps, but also more unexpected, more interesting—frankly, more fun. Left and right, people happily pulled up their seats to bear witness. France now counts itself among the biggest women's football–watching nations in the world.

FULL NAME:	DATE OF BIRTH:	PLACE OF BIRTH:	NATIONAL TEAM:	CAPS / GOALS:
Louisa Nécib Cadamuro	*January 23, 1987*	*Marseille, France*	*France, 2005–16*	*145 / 36*

PERPETUA NKWOCHA

ONLY SIX AFRICAN NATIONS HAVE participated in the Women's World Cup. Of them, South Africa, Ivory Coast, and Equatorial Guinea have each participated once. The ratio of World Cup berths to member nations makes Africa statistically the most difficult qualifying region in the world. Cameroon has appeared twice, Ghana three times. The variable nature of African soccer and the lack of funding and infrastructure mean that most teams, even good ones, have a hard time making it to the World Cup at all, let alone repeating the feat.

And then there are the Nigerians.

The Nigeria Women's National Team, or the Super Falcons, as they are known, are the grand monarchs of African women's soccer. They have dominated the continent with a clenched fist since their inception in the early '90s. Of 13 Africa Women Cup of Nations (AWC), the Super Falcons have won all but two, sweeping the floor with their continental competition. They are, along with the six powerhouses of women's football (the US, Germany, Norway, Japan, Sweden, and Brazil), the only country to have appeared in every iteration of the World Cup.

It's a curious feat: Their dominance on the continent is almost unparalleled, but the Nigerians rarely make a significant impact at the World Cup itself. They have finished in the group stage on all but two occasions (their '99 run to the quarterfinals being their crowning achievement to date)—which, for comparison, is not much better than Cameroon, who have made it to the round of 16 on both times of asking. They rarely win games; they rarely even score goals. And yet no one ever begrudges them their spot, because they also play some of the most consistently enjoyable football at the tournament. And this is largely thanks to Perpetua Nkwocha.

The Super Falcons of the '90s were a team based on raw power and pace. Nigerian football as a whole is famous for its flair and speed, but the women leaned heavily towards speed in those early days, tearing aggressively past opponents as they famously did in their '99 quarterfinal run. Nkwocha joined the national team shortly after that World Cup. She brought flair. Often compared to her countryman, Bolton Wanderers cult hero Jay-Jay Okocha, Nkwocha played with a distinctive combination of pace and panache. She was not flamboyant like Okocha, who was famous for playing completely untrainable, almost impractically stylish football, but she had the same inventive eye and mesmerizing ability to accelerate on the ball and dribble out of tight spaces.

The Nigerian women are not a national team with extensive camps or training sessions. Their squads are usually cobbled together out of disparate pieces right before tournaments. For the 15 years that Nkwocha played on the team, she was their defining player, setting the tone, the style. She never managed to make anything of Nigeria on the world stage, but she kept them competitive; you never wanted to blithely rule Nigeria out when they turned up at a tournament, given their unshakable dominance in Africa. Highlight reel–wise, Nkwocha's crowning achievement is undoubtedly the four goals she scored against Cameroon in the 2004 AWC final, emphatically quashing the ambitions of Nigeria's dark horse rivals and sealing the country's sixth consecutive win. Until 2019, Nkwocha was the only woman to have won the African Women's Player of the Year award four times. She now shares the record with the Super Falcons' current superstar, Barcelona forward Asisat Oshoala. This, too, is Nkwocha's achievement: a young generation of creative, skilled Nigerian women playing Nkwocha-style football for some of the best teams in the world.

FULL NAME:	DATE OF BIRTH:	PLACE OF BIRTH:	NATIONAL TEAM:	CAPS / GOALS:
Perpetua Ijeoma Nkwocha	*January 3, 1976*	*Ngor Okpalla, Nigeria*	*Nigeria, 1999–2015*	*99 / 80*

LILY PARR

URING THE FIRST WORLD WAR, thousands of English women flooded into munitions factories to fill the assembly-line spaces left by drafted men. Most factories in those days had football pitches on-site, fielding factory teams to provide the workers with exercise and entertainment. On their lunch breaks, the newly hired women did as the men had done before them, heading out for kickabouts on the factory pitches, and quickly a women's-works league was born. With the men off at the front and official association football suspended for the course of the war, women's football emerged as a surprisingly well-attended alternative.

Lily Parr came along right at the crescendo of this first golden age of women's football, debuting for St. Helens Ladies in 1919, at the age of 14. She was a tall, chain-smoking teenager with sharp features, jet black hair, and a monster left foot. (Once, challenged to get a penalty past a local man, Parr struck the ball so hard that, although he did manage to save the shot, all the man could say in the aftermath was, "Get me to the hospital as quick as you can, she's gone and broken me flamin' arm.") After playing a handful of games with St. Helens, her local team, Parr was offered a spot on Dick, Kerr Ladies, the factory team in Preston. In addition to a job at the Dick, Kerr & Co. factory, Parr signed for 10 shillings and a packet of cigarettes per game. Shortly after arriving in Preston, a local newspaper declared feverishly that there was "probably no greater football prodigy in the whole country." Others grumbled about the women's insistence on wearing shorts, avowing that the huge crowds they were attracting were a passing fad (which, in retrospect, would turn out to be more of a threat than a premonition). Lily Parr and the Dick, Kerr Ladies were veritable celebrities. They became the first touring women's team that year, conquering French teams sporting stylish berets as British cinemagoers watched on delightedly via Pathé newsreels screened across the nation.

On Boxing Day of 1920, the Dick, Kerr Ladies played a match against St. Helens Ladies, Parr's old team, at Goodison Park. Fifty-three thousand spectators poured into the stands, with around 12,000 more left outside the grounds unable to get in. It was a record attendance for a women's match—one that wouldn't be broken until the 2012 Olympic final. This was the highest peak of the interwar women's football surge. It was effectively stopped in its tracks by the FA, who banned women's teams from using FA-affiliated pitches in 1921. The men's league had been restarted in the fall of 1919, and the FA—concerned about competition for spectators, and signing on to a wave of war casualty–induced population anxiety that called for women to stay home and focus on their reproductive duties—felt it their responsibility to quash the burgeoning sport.

They didn't succeed in fully quashing it. Not quite. Parr and the Dick, Kerr Ladies kept playing for another three decades. They toured the US, competing against men's teams in front of tens of thousands of fans, and they maintained the English women's league, albeit playing on smaller and smaller pitches, in front of fewer and fewer fans.

When Parr stopped playing in 1950 at the age of 45, she had scored over 900 goals, but she and her teammates were no longer household names, all but erased by mainstream English football. She settled down near Preston with her partner, Mary, and lived just long enough to see the FA ban repealed in 1971, dying seven years after its reversal. It is only in the past decade, as we've entered the second golden age of women's football, that Parr has been reclaimed posthumously as its foremother. A statue of her now stands in the National Football Museum in Manchester, England. A fitting tribute to a player who was a pioneering lesbian sporting icon before the concept had even been invented.

FULL NAME:	DATE OF BIRTH:	PLACE OF BIRTH:	NATIONAL TEAM:	CAPS / GOALS:
Lilian Parr	*April 26, 1905*	*St. Helens, Lancashire, England*	—	—

CHRISTIE PEARCE RAMPONE

THE CONNOISSEUR'S PICK FOR greatest American player of all time, Christie Pearce Rampone, sometimes known as *Captain America*, is, as of this writing, the most decorated American international footballer in history, with two World Cups and three Olympic golds to her name.

The best athlete Ocean County, New Jersey, has ever produced, Rampone, like many of her teammates in the mid-'90s, was a multi-sportswoman, going to college on a basketball scholarship, playing starting point guard for Monmouth University (the Harvard of the Jersey Shore), and moonlighting as a goalscoring forward on the soccer and lacrosse teams in the off-season. In the winter of 1997, Tony DiCicco, then-coach of the USWNT, called Rampone up to the national team to try her out as a defender. Electing to miss part of the basketball season for the opportunity, Rampone headed to camp to join a team of seasoned veterans like Carla Overbeck, Joy Fawcett, Michelle Akers, and Julie Foudy, who had started off the decade with World Cup–, Olympic gold–winning oomph. Rampone was shy and quiet; DiCicco asserted once that she was basically silent for her first two years on the team. She preferred to hover unobtrusively on the edge, watching and observing her illustrious teammates from the periphery of the action. But she was also, as it quickly turned out, an immensely capable central defender, even better than she was as a forward, utilizing tenacity, acuity, and athleticism to make up for the fact that she was only 5'6". So despite her silence, she evolved quietly into a steadfast fixture of the USWNT's starting 11.

Rampone ultimately played for the US for 19 years, her international longevity second only to that of Kristine Lilly. She stayed the course through two pregnancies, three presidencies, coaching changes, roster changes, one global recession, one reversion back to her maiden name, chronic Lyme disease, and bone spurs to become the last member of the '99 team left standing. Her grit was subtle but always palpable, the bedrock behind the wall of comforting dependability that she provided. When Pia Sundhage took over as head coach in the fall of 2007, she announced that she was appointing Rampone captain. Rampone balked more than anyone: she was not a talker, not an assertive presence, not a natural leader. Why not appoint Abby Wambach, who sweated natural authority out of every pore? Sundhage, who has made her managerial career out of unexpected ideas, suggested that Rampone try leading by example.

That she did. Rampone was a steadying force, clearing balls out the back without fuss, transmitting quiet confidence and unruffled sense of purpose out to her teammates. You felt the difference when she was on the field—the US women had a mature assurance to their play. Rampone had the '99 World Cup win and the 2004 gold in Athens already tucked under her belt when she inherited the captaincy, but most of her teammates from those victories—particularly the '99 win—were either gone by that point or quickly sidling into retirement. By the time Rampone retired from international duty at the end of 2015, she had ensured that every one of her younger teammates was equally as decorated. There is no one moment of brilliance to point to in Rampone's career; only collective achievement. Her personal portfolio as a player is a cumulation of moments that slipped by unremarkably, because Rampone was there with her hand firmly on the tiller. She's a footballer's footballer. When you ask other US women who they'd put on their footballing Mount Rushmore, Rampone, along with Michelle Akers, is one of the first names that comes to them. Hence the nickname, Captain America.

FULL NAME:	DATE OF BIRTH:	PLACE OF BIRTH:	NATIONAL TEAM:	CAPS / GOALS:
Christie Patricia Pearce	*June 24, 1975*	*Fort Lauderdale, Florida, United States*	*United States, 1997–2015*	*311 / 4*

PELÉ

ESUS. GANDHI. BONO. THE TRULY great are universally known by only one name. Pelé, formerly known as Edson Arantes do Nascimento, is no exception. If your knowledge of soccer is one player deep, odds are it is him you know, mostly thanks, we assume, to his brief but thrilling role as the face of American soccer with the New York Cosmos from 1975–77. But long before his American cameo, he was the finest soccer player the world had ever seen. The gold standard against whom all are measured. A prolific goalscorer who combined power, speed, and a masterful control of the ball to embody the joyous soccer fantasy that was the Seleção Brasileira in their prime.

Pelé's career with the Brazilian national team saw them world champions three times in 12 years. His legend began the instant he made his debut at the age of 17 in the 1958 World Cup. Scrawny enough to be mistaken for the team mascot, he showed few nerves in the final, nonchalantly lobbing the ball over a defender's head, running around him, and volleying it into the corner of the net for his first of two goals. But perhaps Pelé's ingenuity and audacity were equally well captured by his misses. Against Uruguay in 1970, he galloped in one-on-one to the top of the box, allowing the ball to run one way while he swept the other, using his body as a decoy to fake out the goalie. While the open goal beckoned, Pelé reconnected with the ball only to slide his shot inches wide of the post. A move that, like the *Venus de Milo*, was perhaps all the more beautiful for its imperfection.

In his autobiography, Pelé attributed his success to his dazzling control, and his dazzling control to the poverty of his youth. Legend has it he learned to play the game barefoot, using a ball made of worn-out socks. Benefiting from his great skill, his success was also the product of great timing.

His debut coincided with the first live broadcasting of the World Cup; that good timing, combined with telegenic good looks and otherworldly skills, made him the world's first soccer superstar. The only Brazilian of his generation to have an agent and a manager, he became a global brand. He trademarked his name, lending it to Mastercard and Coke; invented the celebrity computer game genre with the Atari 2600 classic *Pelé's Soccer*, which was *FIFA* before *FIFA*; and even appeared alongside movie legends Sly Stallone and Michael Caine in the Hollywood action blockbuster *Victory*, in which he pretty much played himself, scoring a magnificent goal in the climax.

Pelé had enough talent to stop a war. His appearance in Lagos, Nigeria, for an exhibition game led to a ceasefire in the country's civil war so that both sides could say they had seen him take the field. His record of 12 World Cup goals in 14 matches was bettered perhaps only by his longevity in an era when loose refereeing meant the game was at its most punishing. Despite the beatings he received, which led him to threaten to retire on more than one occasion, he dominated the game for over two decades. In the words of Henry Kissinger, upon inducting Pelé into *Time* magazine's 100 Most Important People of the Century, "Performance at a high level in any sport is to exceed the ordinary human scale. But Pelé's performance transcended that of the ordinary star by as much as the star exceeds ordinary performance."

FULL NAME:	DATE OF BIRTH:	PLACE OF BIRTH:	NATIONAL TEAM:	CAPS / GOALS:
Edson Arantes do Nascimento	*October 23, 1940*	*Três Corações, Minas Gerais, Brazil*	*Brazil, 1957–71*	*92 / 77*

MICHEL PLATINI

IF YOU'VE HAD ANY ENCOUNTERS with global football in the past five years, even casually, it's difficult to see Michel Platini as anything other than a Falstaffian *Where's Waldo?*, grinning recklessly in the background of every shot in the FBI's dossier against Sepp Blatter. Despite a UEFA presidency dedicated to curbing the power of the European super clubs, Platini's bureaucratic career will forever be defined by the answer he gave when asked why he had accepted a £16,000 watch from the Brazilian football federation literally while being investigated for corruption: "I'm a well-educated person. I don't return gifts."

Yet, as hard as it is to imagine in the era of Qatar 2022, before he was a sniveling sidekick in the decade's biggest sports corruption scandal, Michel Platini—*Platoche*, as he was affectionately known, his name lovingly affixed with the French diminutive—was the toast of Europe.

Ahead of his time, Platini fused the creative ingenuity of a midfielder with the goalscoring instinct of a striker, controlling the pace of the game and making free kicks appear as deadly as penalty shots. The French teams he captained are characterized by his confidence, flair, and ruthlessness. Playing alongside Alain Giresse and Jean Tigana as the Three Musketeers, Platini formed them into one of the most elegant and potent attacking forces of the 1980s. Their system gave him the freedom to initiate every move his team made. Platini seemed as if he could make the ball come to him, and that superpower, combined with his vision and ability, enabled him to place a pass where few others could, dismantling backlines with the practiced ease of Magnus Carlsen deconstructing an opponent's Sicilian Defense.

Platini became a legend in 1982. After signing for Juventus in Italy shortly before the tournament, he led an inexperienced French team into the semifinals against West Germany in what became one of the great matches of World Cup history. Billed as a battle between the artistes and the automatons, the game ended 3–3 after extra time, and the match went to a penalty shoot-out, which Germany won 5–4. But what stayed with people from that game was not West Germany's win. It was the image of Platini walking off the field, grasping the hand of his unconscious teammate, Patrick Battiston, as he was stretchered off after having been callously crushed by the German goalkeeper Toni Schumacher. In defeat, France became the world's darlings. And at the center of this team was Platini: scrawny, mop-topped, heavily stubbled, notorious for sneaking a cigarette just before kickoff and at halftime, more 1980s Madison Avenue advertising executive than world-class athlete. Also widely agreed to be the best player of the decade.

Although hampered by late-career knee injuries, in 1986 Platini inspired his team, now known as the *Brazilians of Europe*, to victory against the genuine article in a majestic quarterfinal game in the heat of Guadalajara. During the post-game locker room celebrations, Platini somehow managed to reach the apex of French bobo cool, sporting only a pair of flowery boxer shorts and an oversized baseball cap. Exhausted by the win over Brazil, France was eliminated from the second tournament in a row by West Germany in the semifinals. When Platini retired the following year, he did so without a World Cup, but with the love, adoration, and reverence of an entire generation.

It is difficult to overstate how important Platini was in the French footballing imagination. The World Cup proved to be beyond Platini, though he led France to Euro triumph in 1984 (scoring an amazing nine goals in just five matches). France would have to wait until 1998 to win on the global stage—by which time Platini was well retired and already wading into the murky waters of football politics. Yet, it was Platoche who had shown the 1998 French team what was possible. The star of that team, Zinédine Zidane, put it best: "When I was a kid and played with my friends, I always chose to be Platini. I let my friends share the names of my other idols between themselves."

FULL NAME:	DATE OF BIRTH:	PLACE OF BIRTH:	NATIONAL TEAM:	CAPS / GOALS:
Michel François Platini	*June 21, 1955*	*Jœuf, France*	*France, 1976–87*	*72 / 41*

BIRGIT PRINZ

HEAD OF THE 2011 WORLD CUP, German movie theaters ran a commercial in which a group of men sit around a bar debating the best footballer of all time. They bandy around the usual candidates: Pelé, Beckenbauer . . . eventually, the bartender turns to a leather-clad loner sitting by himself at the end of the bar, who settles the debate authoritatively. "Birgit Prinz."

With an intense aversion to interviews of all kinds and a personal style that was two parts tuba-playing tomboy and one part harried camp counselor, you would likely not have glanced twice at Birgit Prinz if you saw her walking down the street. On the field, however, it was impossible to take your eyes off of her. *Killer instinct* was the phrase tossed around most often, but the cliché belies the extent to which Prinz's ability was unusual. She had pace and timing and vision, but what was most remarkable about Prinz was her physical presence. Every move, every run, every pass had an intensity and an exactitude to it, as if the image became ever so slightly sharper when she got on the ball.

In 2003, Prinz scored seven goals, winning the Golden Boot as well as the Golden Ball, and leading the German women to their first-ever World Cup victory. By the time Germany destroyed Russia 7–1 in the quarterfinals with the help of a brace from Prinz, her status as superstar was already secure. It had been cemented by a goal against Argentina on the final match day of group stage play. In the 32nd minute, Prinz gets a looping cross into the box. Launching herself backwards into the air, she does a half bicycle kick, reversing the direction of the ball and sending it curving expertly around a hapless Argentine keeper. When Prinz strikes that ball, you forget entirely about gender and age and language and nationality. All you see is the searing focus of one body, slicing its way through space and time, like a sushi knife wielded by a skilled Benihana professional, propelled forward by the dovetailing forces of palpable determination and immense physical precision.

Following that tournament, Prinz was approached by Luciano Gaucci, the eccentric owner of Perugia in Serie A, about signing with the club. The jury is still out on whether it was a publicity stunt or a genuine offer. On the one hand, Gaucci had become the first owner to hire a female coach for a men's side when he put Carolina Morace in charge of Viterbese. But then again, after Prinz turned him down, Gaucci opted to sign the son of Muammar Gaddafi instead (about whom, after finally coming off the bench following a three-month drug ban, *la Republicca* noted, "Even at twice his current speed he would still be twice as slow as slow itself."). It is a testament to Prinz's wisdom and good judgment that she declined the offer. But it's a testament to her ability that a lot of people at the time—including many Perugia fans—felt that the transfer was actually a rather good idea.

In China in 2007, Marta stole the spotlight and the Golden Ball from the German as she thrilled fans with unprecedented shows of flair and technique. But it was Prinz, coasting into the box in the final against Brazil and sending the ball careening decisively past the keeper, who ultimately led Germany to their second consecutive World Cup victory. Never particularly interested in aesthetics, Prinz didn't have Marta's artistry. But she had a force—fluid and powerful and exact—that proved, over the course of her glittering career, almost impossible to stop.

FULL NAME:	DATE OF BIRTH:	PLACE OF BIRTH:	NATIONAL TEAM:	CAPS / GOALS:
Birgit Prinz	*October 25, 1977*	*Frankfurt am Main, West Germany*	*Germany, 1994–2011*	*214 / 128*

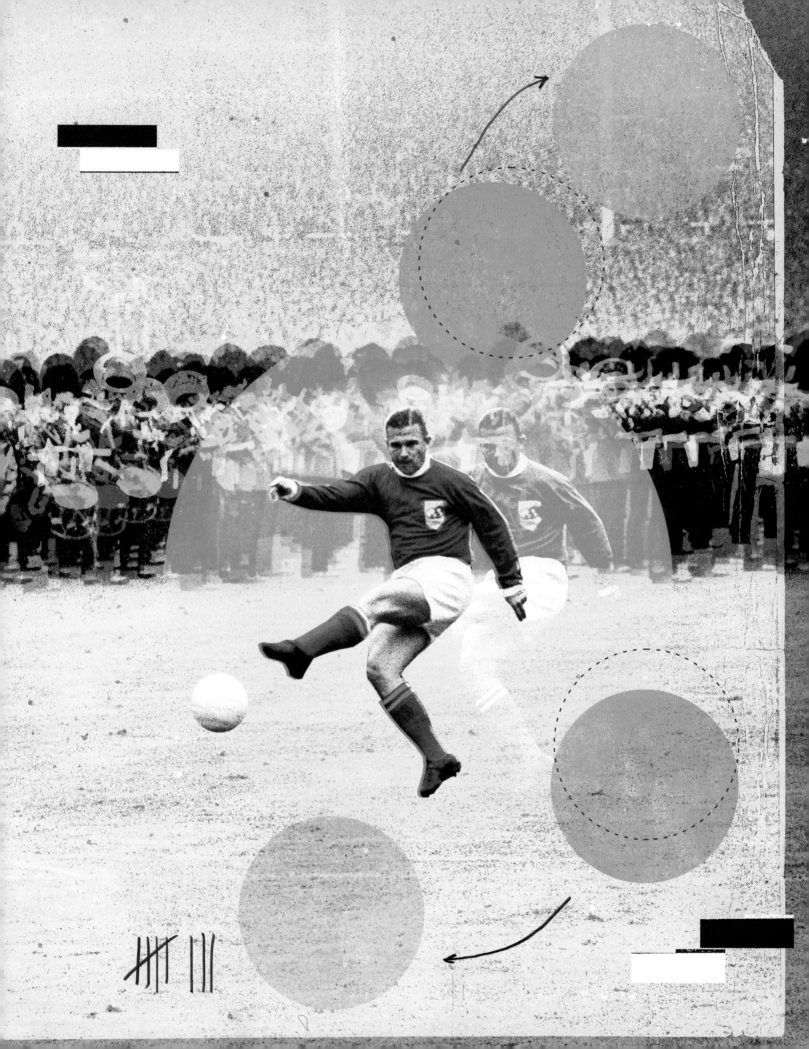

FERENC PUSKÁS

HEN WE TELL YOU THAT MODERN football was born not in England, where they invented the game, nor in Brazil, where they perfected it, but rather, in the Hungarian People's Republic, everyone's favorite former Soviet satellite state, you'll give us a look. "Hungary," you'll say skeptically. "That place with the goulash and the thermal baths and the largest per capita concentration of bachelor parties on the continent? Come on. They haven't even qualified for the World Cup since 1986." When we tell you that the driving force behind this birth of modern football was a man about whom the BBC wrote, "He was short, stocky, barrel-chested and overweight, could not head the ball and could use only his left foot," you'll snort in smug disgust and walk away.

And yet, would we lie to you, dear reader? So begins the 2006 BBC obituary of Ferenc Puskás, the best finisher European football has ever seen.

In your defense, Hungary—paradoxically best known for an intense nightlife scene and having been one of the most oppressive police states in the Eastern Bloc—is not a particularly intuitive footballing nation. But when the Communists took over in 1949, among their first political moves was to hand over the country's major football clubs to the armed forces. Puskás's club, Honvéd, went to the army. Honvéd's rivals, MTK Budapest, were taken over by the secret police. The result was a highly regimented, tactically advanced national team filled with military-rank players (Puskás was appointed a major—hence his nickname, *the Galloping Major*). They played versatile, dynamic football, moving about the pitch in complex collaborative patterns and using decoy forwards to move defenders out of position—essentially inventing Total Football 20 years before the Dutch and Johan Cruyff came to the same conclusion. In November 1953, a famous friendly with England, dubbed *the Match of the Century* by the English press, declared the official time of death on old-style rigid football. The hubristic English team—unbeaten at Wembley against countries from outside the British Isles since 1863—was decisively humiliated, running themselves ragged chasing down Hungarian forwards who uncooperatively refused to remain in the positions where the English expected them to be, allowing the Hungarian team to sneak in behind them. "It was like playing people from outer space," England center half Syd Owen noted afterwards.

From 1950 to 1956, the Mighty Magyars recorded 42 wins, seven draws, and just one defeat (that defeat being a miraculous, capitalist-face-saving comeback by West Germany in the 1954 World Cup Final). That their star striker was, as noted by an apparently still-salty English press corps in 2006, short, unathletic, and 40 pounds overweight is a testament both to Hungary's confidence in their system and to Puskás's copious natural talent. With 84 goals in 85 international matches for Hungary—a ratio that puts him well beyond the likes of Pelé, Cristiano Ronaldo, and Lionel Messi—Puskás was a class unto himself. What he lacked in fitness and versatility, he made up in touch. If you could get him the ball anywhere in the box, he could score.

In October 1956, Puskás was in Spain playing a European Cup game with Honvéd when revolution broke out in Budapest. Puskás refused to return home, for which he was disowned by the Hungarians and banned for two years by FIFA. By the time the ban was up in '58, he was pushing 31 and appeared to be sliding quickly into semi-forced, country-less retirement. The communists wouldn't touch him, the Italians thought he was too old and too fat, the English were still smarting from '53. When Puskás finally turned up at Real Madrid in the fall of 1958, critics and supporters alike took one look at the plump, middle-aged man playing keepie uppie with the local street kids and laughed. This was the captain of the invincible team who had once inspired awe, fear, and whispered reverence in the hearts of Europe?

Five La Liga titles and three European Cups later, no one was laughing.

FULL NAME:	DATE OF BIRTH:	PLACE OF BIRTH:	NATIONAL TEAM:	CAPS / GOALS:
Ferenc Purczeld Biró	*April 2, 1927*	*Budapest, Hungary*	*Hungary, 1945–56;* *Spain, 1961–62*	*85 / 84; 4 / 0*

MEGAN RAPINOE

IT WAS NOT OBVIOUS THAT MEGAN Rapinoe was going to become the most prominent female footballer in the world, although in retrospect it probably should have been. Talent is a precious commodity in professional football, but it is not, all things considered, all that rare. Charisma, on the other hand—not simply charm, or sex appeal, or wit, but that intense, intangible personal magnetism of the genuine icon—comes along maybe once in a generation. Megan Rapinoe has it in spades.

At first glance, Rapinoe looks small. She has always had an impish quality to her, scrawny with a young face and cropped hair. Back-to-back ACL tears at the start of her career kept her out of the 2007 World Cup and the Beijing Olympics the following year. When she rolled up to the global stage in 2011, her hair was dyed bleach blond, she was 26 years old, a veteran of the soon-to-be-no-more Women's Professional Soccer. And she was an absolute revelation. Even when you expect a Rapinoe goal (which, if you've ever seen her in action, it would be foolish not to), it comes at you totally unexpectedly. She is an idiosyncratic, imaginative player. A lot of great football has a sense of post-facto inevitability to it—the ball was played this way because that was the way the ball needed to be played. But Rapinoe plays like she's seen the way the game is supposed to go and is going back to embellish. She plays like she's already won.

She shoots from ridiculous angles, whipping balls around walls of defenders, stepping away from goal and using her weirdly loose hip joints to torque balls on astonishing trajectories into the net. She is one of the best in the world from a dead ball, with such a clean strike her free kicks can feel like gasps. Each goal is a piece of theater in miniature—curtain rising when Rapinoe gets the ball, hush falling instinctively over the crowd, the climax, the plot twist, the denouement, and of course, the curtain call: arms outstretched, chest puffed, chin raised, the fabulist out to collect her applause. Rapinoe was subbed into the US' second group stage match against Colombia in the 45th minute in 2011. Four minutes later she scored, an electric, twisting strike straight over the head of the goalkeeper. She ran to the touchline, grabbed the sideline mic, and sang "Born in the USA." In the quarterfinals, she launched the astonishing 45-yard diagonal cross that Abby Wambach headed in to keep the Americans in the tournament. At the Olympics the following summer, she scored a goal directly off a corner kick—the first ever in Olympic competition—not even intentionally, her ball just curling ever goalward on a path of its own creation. The entertainer had arrived.

Drama is innate in Rapinoe's personality: She's naturally attention-grabbing. This makes for great football; it also makes for great headlines, and Rapinoe has, better than almost any athlete in history, figured out how to wield her magnetism to make people pay attention to the things she cares about. She was the first soccer player to kneel in solidarity with Colin Kaepernick and the Black Lives Matter movement. She is outspoken about gay rights and gender discrimination. During the 2019 World Cup, she found herself thrust forward as the figurehead of the USWNT's equal pay lawsuit and embroiled in a Twitter war with President Trump (if anything, this only served to buoy her as she twirled the Americans to her second World Cup victory). She is one of, if not the most, visible lesbians on the planet, and it is this ability to command attention, more than her football itself, which has ballooned her legacy, expanding her outwards into the cultural conversation. We talk about using football as a force for good. Rapinoe doesn't use football for good; she just is good. Football is an outlet, the same as the activism. They emanate out of the same instinct for invention and revision—Rapinoe out there unattended, creating the world she wants to inhabit. The power of her conviction is palpable. It draws you to it like a tide.

FULL NAME:	DATE OF BIRTH:	PLACE OF BIRTH:	NATIONAL TEAM:	CAPS / GOALS:
Megan Anna Rapinoe	*July 5, 1985*	*Redding, California, United States*	*United States, 2006–*	*187 / 62 *as of October 26, 2021*

WENDIE RENARD

ENDIE RENARD TOWERS. THERE is no other verb for it. At a conspicuous 6'2" with hair that juts out from her head at a perfect 30-degree angle, she is the focal point of any frame she enters.

Born and raised in Le Prêcheur, a sandy village of about 2,000 people on the northern tip of Martinique, Renard is a leading member of France's post-Zidane generation. She was one week from her eighth birthday when the men's team won the World Cup in 1998, watching on from the lush Antillean overseas department as her countrymen lifted the trophy in Paris, 4,000 miles away. Eight years later, Renard was on a plane to France for a trial at Clairefontaine, the country's national youth development center. She didn't make the roster at that trial, but a little finagling from her coach back in Martinique won her a trial at Lyon a few days later. Within the week, Renard was a French footballer—not yet a member of the national team, but well on her way to becoming a regular fixture in Lyon's starting 11. Sixteen years later, there is a strong argument to be made that Renard is *the* French footballer.

One of the best center backs that women's football has ever produced, Renard is poised, collected, and cool under pressure, her aggression almost casual—the way she appears to civilly nudge opponents off the ball with a genial glint of serious concentration in her eyes. She has played her entire career at the center of dynastic Lyon's backline; the *New York Times* once described her astutely as "an institution." In addition to being a stalwart presence at the back of the pitch for both OL and France, Renard also happens to be the French women's 7th-highest goalscorer (and rising), a stat fairly mind-boggling for a defender, thanks to an implausibly consistent capacity for putting away headers. A lot of talented headers launch themselves into the air like heat-seeking missiles. Renard does not. She floats, a bit like Mary Poppins, elegantly nodding the ball home on every occasion she is given.

Since the early part of the last decade, France has been steadily gaining momentum as an ascendant power in women's football. Renard, who began her international career in the months leading up to the country's breakout performance at the 2011 World Cup, has been the cornerstone of that ascendancy. Chic, composed, immediately recognizable, French in the way that much of the country is French—simultaneously an immigrant and a proud native daughter—Renard is not necessarily the most talented or most instrumental member of the generation that has raised France, but she is, undoubtedly, their lifting force.

FULL NAME:	DATE OF BIRTH:	PLACE OF BIRTH:	NATIONAL TEAM:	CAPS / GOALS:
Wéndèleine Thérèse Renard	*July 20, 1990*	*Schœlcher, Martinique*	*France, 2011–*	*126 / 29 *as of September 17, 2021*

HEGE RIISE

HE NORWEGIAN WOMEN'S NATIONAL Team, for abstruse, inside joke–type reasons, are officially nicknamed *the Grasshoppers*. Their men's team bears the very staid and very common nickname *the Lions*. (There are a lot of Lions in international football, Lions being a traditional symbol of power, cropping up on a great many national crests.) But the women are, oddly enough, the Grasshoppers. This gives the misleading impression that the men's side is a very serious team, whereas the women are quite silly, leaping directionlessly around the pitch. In reality, the Norwegian men are somewhat of an also-ran; much like in the US, it is the women who have been, for close to half a century, the main jewel in Norway's football crown.

The 1991 inaugural Women's World Cup was, more than anything, a proof of concept for FIFA, and it established two main things. First, that there was an audience willing and ready to dive into a self-contained world of women's football; second, who the dominant forces in that world were going to be. There were the global superpowers. Hosts China, with pace and a large, tangible fanbase. The US, with their Title IX–fueled talent pool and their athletic might. Germany, with their eminence as a football nation on the men's side. And, somehow, Norway, with a population of just over five million, which had emerged in the late '80s as the chief powerhouse of European women's football, despite a later start than some of their fellow Scandinavian countries. The US walked away with that first trophy in the end, assuming their place in the center of the women's football orbit. But it could very well have been Norway, a penultimate-minute strike by Michelle Akers in the final the only thing wedged between them and a deciding penalty shoot-out.

That early Norwegian team was a famously physical side, able to return the power of the US women blow for blow. But their driving force was the vision of Hege Riise, an attacking midfielder called *the woman with six pairs of eyes* because of her ability to dictate the game from midfield, threading passes through tiny needles, materializing space in front of her that moments earlier seemed not to exist, dismantling the oppositions' defenses by laser-focusing straight through them. With gap teeth and a mum-did-it-in-front-of-the-bathroom-mirror haircut, Riise certainly did not look like the kind of player who could slice expertly through a game. She always claimed that her great strength was not in seeing, but rather in feeling. "I also felt the game more than others—I had a feeling of where my teammates would move to," she once explained.

Riise was 21 at that first tournament, only one year into her international career. Four years later, she was a primary fixture on the Norwegian roster. The US were hampered in 1995, losing Akers to an injury in the first match. But the tournament was Norway's regardless. They thrashed through the group stage with a machete, scoring 17 goals and conceding none, and taking down Denmark and the US in the knockout stages with very little resistance. Norway lost their captain to two yellow cards ahead of the final against Germany, but it didn't matter. Riise drew first blood 37 minutes in, dribbling through three German players before launching a clean strike from 20 yards out. Because the US bookended the decade with wins in '91 and '99, we think of them as being at the top of the 1990s football pyramid. But for much of the decade it was, in fact, Norway: They won the Euros in '93, the World Cup in '95, and the Olympics in 2000, with Riise becoming one of only three women to have completed that treble. A quarter of the Norwegian population watched the 1995 final. The entire country watched on as they flew back from Sweden, escorted home to Oslo by F-16 fighter jets for a hero's welcome.

FULL NAME:	DATE OF BIRTH:	PLACE OF BIRTH:	NATIONAL TEAM:	CAPS / GOALS:
Hege Riise	*July 18, 1969*	*Lørenskog, Norway*	*Norway, 1990–2004*	*188 / 58*

RONALDO

HE 1998 WORLD CUP WAS SUP-posed to be Ronaldo's. No, not that Ronaldo. Get your head out of the gutter. The original one. The Brazilian, with the gap tooth. O Fenômeno. He was 21 years old and widely agreed to be the best player in the world. In 1996, he became the youngest player ever to win the Ballon d'Or. In 1997, he became the youngest player ever to win it twice. With breathtaking pace, cartoonish acceleration, and clinical finishing, he was more video game than human, blowing past defenders in a blur of motion and deft touch. "He's not a man," mused Real Madrid striker Jorge Valdano once, "he's a herd." Going into the 1998 final in Paris, Ronaldo had notched up four goals and three assists. Brazil's fifth World Cup was close enough to touch, and Ronaldo's name was written all over it.

The evening of the final, July 12, 1998, the world turned on their TVs, salivating at the prospect of a matchup with France, to find Ronaldo's name mysteriously left off of the lineup. It seemed like a glitch. By kickoff, he was back on. But when he stepped onto the pitch that evening, it was clear that something was wrong. Ronaldo was the last one out of the tunnel. As the camera followed him onto the field, he was subdued and glassy-eyed. The rumor mill went into overdrive: He was suffering from an ankle injury maybe, or some kind of stomach complaint. He barely touched the ball. When he did, he was lethargic, slow to react, almost dazed, missing all the pop and power of the usual Ronaldo. With their star player sleepwalking around the field, Brazil went down 2–0 by halftime. They conceded again in the final moments of the second half, slinking off the field as France erupted around them in jubilation. As the Brazilian team trudged up the steps through the euphoric crowd to accept their runner-up medals, the camera trained itself on the face of Ronaldo. He was not angry, not in tears like some of his teammates. He looked bewildered and slightly bemused. The look of an extraordinarily gifted athlete who woke up in someone else's body.

In the ensuing months, it came out that Ronaldo had suffered a seizure on the afternoon of the final. Speculation abounded. Had it been the nerves? Had he been poisoned? And why had he been put back into the lineup when he was clearly not fit to play? It was the grassy knoll of sports mysteries, filled with dark, convoluted conspiracies and unanswerable questions. The Brazilian congress held an inquest to investigate. Meanwhile, Ronaldo's physical woes were just beginning. In November of 1999, playing for Inter Milan, he tore a ligament in his knee and was forced to sit out most of the next three seasons. He underwent two surgeries and months upon months of rehab. When he turned up in Japan for the 2002 World Cup with his now-iconic monk-like Tonsure haircut (one of the few elite footballer hairstyles to never catch on), ready to play for the first time in many moons, the world had moved on without him. Fans regarded him with the suspicion of Hamlet staring at the specter of his dead father. He had been idolized, he had been poisoned, he had been eulogized, he had been mourned. And now here he was, dressed like a medieval spirit and risen from the dead.

Ronaldo doubled his previous record, scoring eight goals that tournament. The most quintessentially Ronaldo of the eight is his first goal of the final against Germany. After losing a tackle on the edge of the box, Ronaldo is up on his feet again and has stolen the ball back before you've even blinked. He quickly spins to evade the German midfield and taps it to Rivaldo, who shoots from 15 yards. The shot goes straight to the keeper, Oliver Kahn, but it bounces off of him and rolls about a meter out in front of him. Ronaldo is barely even in the frame when Rivaldo shoots. Yet when Kahn looks up as he scrambles to retrieve it, Ronaldo is already there, blasting the ball past him into the open net. Watching it back in replay, it looks like there are four Brazilians involved in that play. And there are. But three of them are Ronaldo.

Scoring both goals of the final, Ronaldo led Brazil to World Cup glory for that elusive fifth time. When asked in the press conference what felt better, winning the World Cup or sex, he thought for a moment. *This*, he replied. You can see it in the smile as Ronaldo scores his second goal in the final. The emotion he is experiencing is not just the joy of winning or the orgasmic satisfaction of scoring on the biggest stage in the world. It is also the sheer relief of the world's best striker in finding himself, finally, back in his body.

FULL NAME:	DATE OF BIRTH:	PLACE OF BIRTH:	NATIONAL TEAM:	CAPS / GOALS:
Ronaldo Luís Nazário de Lima	*September 18, 1976*	*Rio de Janeiro, Rio de Janeiro, Brazil*	*Brazil, 1994–2011*	*98 / 62*

CRISTIANO RONALDO

RISTIANO RONALDO MAY BE THE only person in the world whose wax figure looks more lifelike than the real thing. It stands in the Museu CR7, a museum/shrine Ronaldo built for himself in 2013 in his hometown of Funchal, Portugal. There is an eeriness about Ronaldo—it has gotten progressively worse with age—not robotic, but uncanny, like Alicia Vikander in *Ex Machina*, an actor playing a robot playing a human programmed to score goals just so he can take his shirt off and reveal his abs once again to an admiring world. The leading men's international goalscorer of all time, he is arguably the most widely disliked footballer in history, partly because he makes it very easy to dislike him, doing things like building museum/shrines to himself, and partly because he is also the most widely adored, with the largest personal fan base of anyone on the planet, excepting Ariana Grande and Rihanna and also God.

Which is not to say that the pervasive disdain for Ronaldo is based in jealousy. He is a sneering, preening, showboating show pony of a footballer, who seems, on and off the pitch, to have no particular interest in anyone other than himself—and even his interest in himself seems deficient somehow, as if it emanates from an impulse both more mechanical and more maniacal than good old-fashioned egotism. To object to Ronaldo is to object to the gaudy flash of the modern game. He plays ostentatious, high-octane, unnatural football, filled with elaborate step-overs and flamboyant goals, crafted by sports science and self-consciousness and endless hours of repetition, designed to live in perpetuity in GIFs and slow-motion replays and YouTube highlight reels. He plays to a crowd, but it is not the crowd in front of him (he has been known on occasion to be booed by his own teams' fans), but rather a larger, faceless global crowd.

If Messi represents the wonder of the modern spectacle, then Ronaldo is its glare. He is mercenary, self-merchandising, the dark prince of conspicuous consumption, a Ferrari-crashing billionaire with diamonds in his ears and the scent of Drakkar Noir–infused yacht trailing behind him. His preferred goal celebration is to lift his shirt or the leg of his shorts and show off his perfectly sculpted muscles to the crowd. He has attempted to steal many millions of dollars of taxes from the Spanish government. He has been credibly accused of sexual assault by multiple women. Whether he is, deep down, a good person—charitable, authentic, playing for the love of the game—is beside the point. He is a collection of all the most distasteful aspects of billionaire football, and, crucially, he is its wealthiest, most successful, most visible brand ambassador.

There are, no doubt, a small number of fans who like Ronaldo because of this. But for the most part, if you're a fan, and, as previously stated, he has many, you tend to look past the glare. Because Cristiano Ronaldo is, for better or worse, the closest football has ever gotten to a mythic hero. The moments he creates, the things he is able to do on the field, are inhuman—discomfiting and intoxicating in equal measure. His movement and his Adonis musculature seem unreal; he is a mutant superman in a game of mortals. Your breath catches in your throat; even his biggest detractors can't stop their pulse from quickening.

Like all the best Greek heroes, he came into this world unwanted—his mother reportedly attempting a home abortion while she was pregnant with him—devoting his entire being to football while his father drank himself to death. One thing that you can't help but notice about Ronaldo is that when he scores a goal, any goal really, but particularly important ones, the first emotion that flashes on his face is not joy. It is relief. Brian Phillips once wrote for ESPN that Ronaldo's "drive to be perfect is so desperately acute that surviving it looks like a test of sanity."

The obsession with his physical appearance, which has transformed him over the years from handsome teen into spooky Ken Doll, the narcissism, the unabashed exhibitions of his exorbitant wealth are compelling—we love the gods because they behave like humans. He is trapped in a quest for perfection that is both alien and entirely familiar; it is glorious and gripping to watch him climb, constantly anticipating the hubristic fall that may or may not be around the bend.

Or maybe we're reading too much into it and they just like him for the very reasons to which Ronaldo once ascribed his unpopularity: "It is because I am handsome, rich, and a great player, because I am envied. I have no other explanation."

FULL NAME:	DATE OF BIRTH:	PLACE OF BIRTH:	NATIONAL TEAM:	CAPS / GOALS:
Cristiano Ronaldo dos Santos Aveiro	*February 5, 1985*	*Funchal, Madeira, Portugal*	*Portugal, 2003–*	*182 / 115 *as of October 12, 2021*

PAOLO ROSSI

N LATE 1979, TWO ROMAN SHOP-
keepers set up a clumsy but ambitious match-
fixing network involving seven clubs and dozens
of players from across Serie A and B. The shop-
keepers being neither discrete nor competent, by
March of 1980 the operation had come crumbling down
and the police, accompanied by the Italian Football Federation, stepped in to pick up the pieces. AC Milan and
Lazio were both relegated to Serie B, Milan's president
was disbarred, and 20 players received bans ranging from
three months to six years. Among them was a 23-year-old
rising star named Paolo Rossi. A cunning striker with great
hair, Rossi had briefly become the most expensive player in
the world in 1976 after Vicenza bought him from Juventus
for 2.612 billion lire (about $3 million, give or take); two
years later, he had risen to international prominence after
scoring three goals in the 1978 World Cup. Despite vehe-
ment protestations of innocence (or if not innocence, then
at least naive ignorance), Rossi received a ban of two years
and was forced to spectate the Italy-hosted 1980 Euros
and nearly two seasons of top-tier football.

Rossi's ban finally came to an end in May of 1982, pre-
cisely one month before the World Cup in Spain. Looking
to jump-start a drooping national team, the Italian head
coach, Enzo Bearzot, immediately called Rossi back up—
disregarding the almost unanimous conviction that he was
not match fit. Even Rossi himself seemed to think this was
a bad idea, warning the press, "In this condition, you can't
expect me to solve all the problems of the Italian team." As
if intent to make good on this promise, Rossi spent most of
the first three matches wandering ineffectually around the
pitch, unable to make any kind of meaningful impact. The
Italian team swayed listlessly through the first group stage,
drawing all three of their matches and slipping through to
the next round on goal difference alone.

The tournament had two rounds of group stage play
back then, with the top of each second-round group progressing to the semifinals. For the second group stage,
Italy was paired with Maradona's Argentina and that stylish, grotesquely talented Brazilian team led by the likes of
Sócrates, Zico, and Falcão. Girding their defensive loins,
Italy bucked up and managed to beat Argentina, who were
also not playing their best that tournament. Argentina lost
to Brazil the following day (a frustrated Maradona, four
years short of World Cup glory himself, kicked Brazilian
midfielder João Batista in the groin and was sent off in the
85th minute, marking his main contribution that tournament). With goal difference, all Brazil needed to advance
was a draw. And this was a team that could draw with their
eyes closed.

Newton's third law of motion: For every team that
should have won but didn't, there is an equal and opposite
team that shouldn't have won but did. Rossi, reanimated
perhaps by the win against Argentina, a particularly effective pep talk from Bearzot, and a whiff of possibility, suddenly sprung to life during that game, personally outscoring
Brazil with a hat trick that propelled Italy directly into the
semifinals. To Italy's shock as much as anyone else's, they
blew past Poland in the semifinal and West Germany in the
final, tying Brazil with a then-record third World Cup. Zico
pronounced the Brazil game afterwards to be "the day that
football died," as the Italians' conservative, defense-focused
style won out over the Brazilians' aesthetic attacking football. To the Italians, it was salvation, as they were finally
able to wallpaper over the scandal of 1980 with something
more exciting to talk about. For Rossi, of course, it was
redemption. Scoring both goals against Poland in the semi
and one against West Germany in the final, he transformed
from miscreant back into hero in the eyes of the Italian public as he delivered the World Cup trophy for his country.
The irony of a match-fixer responsible for one of the most
unexpected wins of all time was not lost on the fans, but if
anything, it just showed Rossi's versatility. This was Italy in
the '80s. Players who could lose for money were a dime a
dozen. But a man who could both lose for money and win
for glory? That was a player to be revered.

FULL NAME:	DATE OF BIRTH:	PLACE OF BIRTH:	NATIONAL TEAM:	CAPS / GOALS:
Paolo Rossi	September 23, 1956	Prato, Italy	Italy, 1977–86	48 / 20

HUGO SÁNCHEZ

I N 1981, ATLÉTICO MADRID PICKED up Hugo Sánchez, a bushy-haired Mexican center forward with a recently acquired degree in dentistry. Five successful seasons in the Mexican league had attracted the attention of European scouts, and Sánchez was headed to Spain.

In North America, Mexico has always had football bona fides—with their endemic football culture, their fútbol to the US' dilettante soccer. Outside of North America, however, Mexico was perceived for many years as a country whose enthusiasm for the sport vastly outweighed their stature. They were an ocean removed from European football, cloistered off from their South American cousins' stake on the game by the Panama Canal. Mexico '70, easily the most famous iteration of the tournament to date, had gone a ways to associating the game with Mexico in people's minds, but the country had yet to produce a player to match the prestige of the Estadio Azteca, the monumental, instantly iconic stadium the Mexican government had inaugurated in '66.

It took Sánchez a few years to warm up to life in the Spanish top flight. He won his first Pichichi—La Liga's top scorer trophy—in the spring of 1985, followed by a crosstown move to rival Real Madrid that summer. By the end of the decade, he had won five Pichichis, four on the run, and was widely agreed to be the best player Mexico had ever produced (a title he has yet to concede). It wasn't even how many goals Sánchez scored that made him notable. It was how he scored them. Sánchez was a spectacular goalscorer in the most basic sense of the word. His specialty was the chilena (the bicycle kick), but he had just about everything in his wheelhouse: spinning free kicks, diving headers, aerial volleys, polished acute-angle tap-ins. There

was even a rumor going around that he had invented the famous scorpion kick, traditionally credited to Colombian goalkeeper René Higuita, though unlike Higuita, he had never actually attempted it in a game. If Sánchez's goals themselves weren't spectacle enough, each one was celebrated with a signature triumphant front flip, an acrobatic tribute to Sánchez's sister, a former Olympic gymnast, which quickly became one of the most dominant visuals of 1980s football.

When Mexico became the first country to host the World Cup twice, winning tournament rights again in 1986 after first-choice hosts Colombia, mired in an economic crisis, reluctantly pulled out, people expected Sánchez to make an impact. He was, after all, one of the best strikers in Europe at the time, and he was playing on home turf. But it was not to be. World Cup 1986 belongs entirely to Maradona; secondarily, it belongs to the likes of Gary Lineker, Michel Platini, and Lothar Matthäus. Sánchez barely featured, eking out only one goal that tournament (his only goal in the three World Cups he participated in, actually), in Mexico's opening win against Belgium. He sat confined to the bench with a cramp as Mexico lost out in a quarterfinal penalty shoot-out with West Germany.

But reinstalled in Spain the following fall, Sánchez continued his rise. He would reach his La Liga apogee in 1989–90, scoring 38 goals on the season. Incredibly, he scored every single goal with one touch—a feat, to the best of anyone's knowledge, yet to be replicated by any player, anywhere in the world—each an expert display of finesse, coolheadedness, and indomitable positional awareness. And each followed by a flawlessly executed midair somersault, Sánchez's penchant for acrobatics providing the world with a belated but emphatic testament to Mexican football.

FULL NAME:	DATE OF BIRTH:	PLACE OF BIRTH:	NATIONAL TEAM:	CAPS / GOALS:
Hugo Sánchez Márquez	July 11, 1958	Mexico City, Mexico	Mexico, 1977–98	58 / 29

HOMARE SAWA

THERE ARE FOUR MINUTES LEFT IN extra time at the 2011 Women's World Cup Final. By all logic, Japan shouldn't be here. In five previous World Cups, they've only made it out of the group stage once. Back home, Japan is in the midst of a national disaster, struggling to deal with the aftermath of the magnitude nine earthquake, tsunami, and subsequent nuclear meltdown that devastated the country's eastern coastline just three months earlier. They weren't even sure they were going to send a team.

Yet, send a team they did, and that team shimmied past Mexico and New Zealand in the group stage, Germany and Sweden in the knockouts. Now here they are, somehow, face to face with the US at the end of the line. To say that the odds are not in their favor is an understatement: In 25 previous encounters with the US, Japan has never won. The US team is taller, better funded. They've led the entire game and have taken twice as many shots on goal. Japan, through a combination of belief, resilience, and pure luck, has managed to hang on, evening things up at 1–1, taking the game into extra time. But they've gone down again, and with just four minutes left in the tournament, they're running out of time and second chances.

After the fact, people will speculate that a higher power was involved. That the Japanese team was spurred on by something larger than themselves. And maybe it was God or two monks high up in the Kii Mountains or a burning sense of responsibility to a nation who desperately needed something to hope for that made the final difference. But in that 117th minute, out there on that pitch in Frankfurt, there is no God. No Nation. There is only a Hail Mary corner kick and the sheer audacity of Homare Sawa.

Sawa, a mainstay of the Japanese national team since her 15-year-old debut in 1993, is only 5'5", but you wouldn't know it from the way she commands the field. She is an aggressive, cunning midfielder; she has scored four goals already this tournament, including a hat trick against Mexico. She has been playing professionally since the age of 12; 20 years later, no one more fully personifies the history of women's football in Japan than Sawa. At 32, she's in the back half of her career. But she's not quite done yet.

Aya Miyama drives the ball into the edge of the six-yard box. With 20 years of experience coursing through her veins, Sawa runs to it and leaps into the air. One foot off the ground and rotating quickly, she gives the ball the tiniest of flicks with the outside of her right foot and sends it flying into goal.

Japan will go on to win on penalties, becoming the first Asian country to win the World Cup. But the second the ball goes in, everyone in that stadium already knows what's going to happen. It's one of those moments where you can see the future being rerouted right in front of your eyes. Sawa will win the Golden Ball, Golden Boot, and FIFA Player of the Year, becoming the most decorated footballer in Asia. She's already won though, in that moment. You can see it on the faces of everyone around her. With one gorgeous, improbable flick, she has rewritten history.

FULL NAME:	DATE OF BIRTH:	PLACE OF BIRTH:	NATIONAL TEAM:	CAPS / GOALS:
Homare Sawa	*September 6, 1978*	*Fuchū, Tokyo, Japan*	*Japan, 1993–2015*	*205 / 83*

PETER SCHMEICHEL

THE MYTH IS THAT THE DANISH national team was on the beach when they found out that they were due at the 1992 Euro 10 days hence. The truth is slightly less interesting— they were at Brøndby, preparing for a send-off friendly against the former Soviet Union before going on their summer holidays when they got the call. Yugoslavia, who had edged them out by one point in qualifying, had been banned from the competition because of their ongoing civil war, and Denmark were the lucky losers. Since they weren't attending the tournament, Hummel hadn't prepared them any kits, so they had to wear hand-me-ups from the under-21 team to their first match against England, which, as you can imagine, were quite tight. Peter Schmeichel, a massive hulk of a goalkeeper at 6'3" and 224 pounds, looked particularly snug.

The summer of the Euros, Peter Schmeichel was 28, one season into his career at Manchester United. He had a shock of white-blond hair and a conspicuous presence— describing the experience of trying to score against him, Sir Alex Ferguson once amusedly warned that you'd have to contend with the "big blond Viking flying out at you" to do it. The son of a Polish jazz musician, Schmeichel had risen in stature in Denmark, first with Hvidovre, then with Brøndby in the Danish first division, before Ferguson picked him up for £500,000 in 1991, one of only 13 non-British or Irish players in the top tier at the establishment of the Premier League. Schmeichel's trademark was the starfish save, sprawling his arms and legs out in all four directions to block off every available angle. Today, every keeper worth their salt has the starfish in their arsenal to deploy against onrushing strikers. When Schmeichel, who had borrowed the technique from handball, debuted it, it looked like he had abruptly decided to audition for dance captain in a Fosse musical.

If you are a person born in the back half of the last century, Schmeichel is likely the greatest goalkeeper you have ever witnessed live. (If you were born in this century, you have likely only witnessed his son Kasper, who preserves the family mantle dutifully, but without the resplendence of Schmeichel in his prime.) Aggressive, elastic, and razor sharp, he brickwalled Manchester United to '90s glory. His save against Rapid Vienna in the group stage of the 1996–97 Champions League, a preconscious, hurtling dive to swipe the ball out of his right corner, rivals Gordon Banks's save against Pelé for the 20th century's most miraculous. His presence in the Bayern Munich penalty area for a 90th-minute corner kick in the 1999 final was enough to fluster the German team into conceding two goals in the span of two minutes, allowing United to charge back in and nab the third piece of their season treble. Schmeichel left for Sporting Lisbon a few weeks later; his cartwheeling trophy celebration was his final act in a United shirt. (A few seasons later, Schmeichel was back in the Premier League with Man City and showcased the same celebratory cartwheel against his former club, a gesture of such intense treachery that many fans have yet to forgive him.)

Back in that Euro summer of 1992, reoutfitted in hastily fabricated, appropriately baggy kits, Schmeichel navigated the Danish team all the way to the championship, in a run so improbable that *fairy tale* is an undersell. Schmeichel's save against Marco van Basten in the semifinal shoot-out against reigning champions the Netherlands sent the Danes into the final. But it was the Danish love of the back pass, mind-numbingly rolling the ball back to Schmeichel over and over and over to run down the clock and prevent the opposition from gaining possession that sealed the deal. It was so egregious that back passes were outlawed directly after the tournament.

FULL NAME:	DATE OF BIRTH:	PLACE OF BIRTH:	NATIONAL TEAM:	CAPS / GOALS:
Peter Bolesław Schmeichel	*November 18, 1963*	*Gladsaxe, Denmark*	*Denmark, 1987–2001*	*129 / 1*

BRIANA SCURRY

HAT BRIANA SCURRY ENDED UP in goal for the US is, in a certain way, the product of happenstance. Scurry was born in Minneapolis in 1971. An athletic kid, her first love was basketball, but she also played tackle football, softball, and floor hockey, ran track, and did karate. Had her family stayed in Minneapolis, Scurry would likely have focused on basketball. Mid-'70s American city kids didn't play soccer. African American girls definitely didn't.

But the Scurrys didn't stay in Minneapolis. In a scene straight out of the Old Testament, shortly after Scurry was born the family home in Minneapolis was swallowed into an underground lake. Searching for a place where they'd be safe from vengeful subterranean bodies of water, the family relocated 30 miles north of Minneapolis, to the small town of Dayton, Minnesota.

Dayton, Minnesota, in the 1970s was not a place you'd go looking for racial diversity. It is in fact still not a place you'd go looking for racial diversity—at 93.7 percent white, according to the 2010 census, it is one of the whitest cities in America. The Scurrys were the only African American family in a four-town radius. Practically speaking, this meant two things. First: that Scurry was the only person of color on each and every one of her sports teams growing up. Second: that if you were an athletic kid, you played soccer, the official sport of the white suburban class. So in addition to basketball, softball, and track, Scurry played soccer too.

When she was nine, Scurry joined the local soccer club. As was common in the '80s, there was only a boys' team, so that's the one Scurry played for. Worrying about the boys being too rough on her, the coach put her in goal. A successful turn in peewee gave way to a stellar high school soccer career, a soccer scholarship at the University of Massachusetts at Amherst, and finally a contract for the national team.

That national team contract blossomed into an illustrious 15-year career playing for the US, replete with two Olympic gold medals and a World Cup. Scurry's most famous moment is no doubt the penalty save she made in 1999, swatting away Chinese midfielder Liu Ying's kick and two-handedly clearing the way for the US' victory. No matter what goalies tell you, successfully saving a penalty is principally good luck. Mind games help, as does cheating a bit (a tactic that Scurry has admitted to taking full advantage of, moving off her line well before Ying struck the ball). But, ultimately, you still have to guess a side. If Scurry's save against Liu Ying was one part mind games and one part cheating, it was still three parts just a very lucky guess. Yet when you ask Scurry about it, she'll tell you that she knew before Liu Ying even stepped up to the ball, with utmost certainty, from Ying's body language, but also from the weight of the moment itself, that she was going to make that save. Rather than chance, it was, in Scurry's telling, something more akin to Calvinist predestination.

There is no doubt that we have Briana Scurry to thank for the fact that women's soccer in this country is less white than it was 15 years ago. Over her first decade on the USWNT, Scurry was the only African American starter on the roster. But every time a young kid turned on the TV, whether it was Atlanta in 1996, Athens in 2004, or Pasadena on that fabled afternoon in 1999, what they saw was Briana Scurry standing stalwartly in goal with the conviction that it was not luck or a weird fluke of circumstance that there was a Black woman on the pitch. It was simply how things were supposed to be.

FULL NAME:	DATE OF BIRTH:	PLACE OF BIRTH:	NATIONAL TEAM:	CAPS / GOALS:
Briana Collette Scurry	*September 7, 1971*	*Minneapolis, Minnesota, United States*	*United States, 1994–2008*	*173 / –*

CHRISTINE SINCLAIR

HEN CHRISTINE SINCLAIR WAS 18, in her second year on Canada's senior squad, head coach Even Pellerud gathered the team in the lobby of their Portuguese hotel for a pep talk ahead of that year's Algarve Cup. When he informed them, midway through, that they had the best player in the world on their roster, Sinclair swiveled her head quickly around the lobby. The rest of the team looked at her. "Who?" she asked incredulously.

Who, indeed. At 18, it was already clear. At 38 and still going strong, it is all the more so. In Canada, they gleefully call her the Wayne Gretzky of female sport. Her achievements—international records, Olympic medals, league titles, commemorative postage stamps, national honors— speak for themselves, even when Sinclair modestly declines to. In her game as in her personal life, she is a humble, unflashy player, her greatest strength a quiet, meticulous attention to detail. She is lanky but fast, every move she makes calculated and efficient, lying patiently in wait for an opening, arms barely swinging as she soundlessly accelerates to full speed in tight spaces, bolting into defenders' blind spots to put the ball away with clean, expert finishes, time and time again.

At the 2011 World Cup, Sinclair had her nose broken 48 minutes into the tournament. Waving off the trainers, she played on, nose smeared all over the side of her face as she lifted a millimeter-perfect free kick over the German wall and into the top corner. Unfortunately, this was not enough to win Canada the game, and, despite the Batman mask Sinclair donned to play the next two matches with her still-broken nose, her free kick would be the team's only goal for the tournament as they crashed out of the group stage. After their third and final defeat, 1–0 to Nigeria, Sinclair was photographed slumped on the grass with her head in her hands, nose jagged, the rest of her face a block of dejected gloom. Then-coach Carolina Morace was promptly replaced by John Herdman. The first thing he did was hang that photo of Sinclair in his office. No one wanted to disappoint her a second time.

One year later, Sinclair, backed by a much more buoyant team, found herself facing the US in the semifinals at the London Olympics, where she put in quite possibly the best individual performance in the history of women's soccer, scoring three goals, which, were it not for an Alex Morgan header in the 123rd minute, would have been enough to lift Canada past a commanding US team into the finals. Sinclair, usually polite and self-possessed to the point of reticence, received a fine and a four-game ban for berating the referee over what she perceived to be a slew of unfair calls. She then stormed into the locker room and gave a rallying speech so impassioned that Herdman could think of nothing to add afterwards other than a solemn nod. When Canada won the bronze against France three days later, Sinclair did not feature in most of the celebratory team photos. This was because she was lying on the ground bawling. Within the decade, Sinclair became the most accomplished international goalscorer of all time, besting Abby Wambach's 184 career goals. A record unlikely to be surpassed by anyone, man or woman—and one that Sinclair insists on brushing aside, shuddering with embarrassment each time it is brought up. Practically allergic to individual accolades, she cries only for Canada.

At the 2020 Olympics, after a decade of trying, Canada finally did it, flying past the US in the semifinals and Sweden in the final to win Gold in Tokyo. The Canadian women buckled to the ground, diving on top of one another in tearful celebration. At the top of the pile was Christine Sinclair.

FULL NAME:	DATE OF BIRTH:	PLACE OF BIRTH:	NATIONAL TEAM:	CAPS / GOALS:
Christine Margaret Sinclair	*June 12, 1983*	*Burnaby, British Columbia, Canada*	*Canada, 2000–*	*308 / 188 *as of August 6, 2021*

MATTHIAS SINDELAR

HE TOAST OF COFFEEHOUSES across the city of Vienna, Matthias Sindelar was the first iteration of what you might call the thinking man's footballer. As beloved by the intellectual bourgeoisie as he was by working-class fans, Sindelar was a far cry from the big, stocky men of prewar European football. He was slight, almost dainty, with small, sharp features and a prematurely receding hairline. They called him *Der Papierene, the Paper Man,* because there was something fragile—insubstantial, even—about him, tripping and fluttering his way around menacing challenges. Viennese theater critic Alfred Polgar once wrote dreamily, "He had brains in his legs . . . and many remarkable and unexpected things occurred to them while they were running." His subtlety on the field lent itself to this kind of lyricism. Walking down the street, you would hear snippets of serious theoretical discussions of Sindelar and Austrian football wafting out of open windows alongside talk of Freud, Klimt, Mahler, Zweig, and politics, the smells of coffee, and flaky Viennese pastry.

With Sindelar front and center, the Austrian national team emerged in the early 1930s as the golden team of Europe's interwar era, playing a sophisticated, fluid, quick-passing style dubbed the *Danubian Whirl,* which elevated football beyond the pragmatic into the realm of the romantic. They were called the *Wunderteam,* and they embarked on a tour of awe around the continent. They demolished Scotland 5–0. Germany was vanquished 6–0. Switzerland went down 8–1. Hungary, 8–2. They were favored to win the 1934 World Cup, but the Italians managed to get the better of them in the semifinals, aided by a combination of mud and malice and Mussolini. And by the next tournament, of course, Austria was no more.

After the Germans annexed Austria in March of 1938, the Austrian team was absorbed into the German side. Sindelar was a committed Social Democrat with close ties to the Vienna Jewish community—his club, FK Austria Wien, labeled a *Judenklub* by the Nazis, was also annexed that spring; the Nazis renamed the team and forced out its mostly Jewish board, replacing them with Party members—and declined to join the newly merged national team. He played one final match for Austria in early April, three weeks after the Anschluss, a ceremonial farewell friendly against the Germans. As the story goes, Sindelar flubbed a handful of easy chances in the first half. Some say that he was deliberately missing to appease the Nazis, for whom a draw would have been the most politically useful result. Others say he was toying with the Germans, taunting them with shots that edged just wide of goal. Or maybe he was intimidated, or flustered, or simply having an off day. All we know for sure is that 62 minutes in, Sindelar perked up. He landed a rebound at net and casually flicked it into the corner past a flailing German keeper. Then he did a celebration dance in front of the Nazi officials' box. Teammate Karl Sesta added a second goal eight minutes later, a free kick from near the halfway line that went sailing into net. When the final whistle was blown, chants of "Österreich! Österreich!" echoed around the stadium in the last demonstration of unabashed Austrian nationalism until well after the war.

Sindelar retired shortly after that game. Within the year, he was dead, found asphyxiated in his apartment along with his girlfriend. Rumors swirled immediately: He had been murdered by the Nazis because of his friendships with local Jews, because his girlfriend was secretly Jewish (she was not), because he was secretly Jewish (also not true). The romantics went even further than the conspiracists: He had committed suicide in protest of the annexation, of the dissolution of the Austrian league, of the death of the lovely bourgeois, intellectual, Jewish Vienna that had raised him up in the first place. Rumors swirled into myths, as anti-Nazi obituaries grandly declared Sindelar's death to be a symbol of the noble death of Austria. In reality, Sindelar likely died of carbon monoxide poisoning, seeping out of a faulty chimney while he slept in the next room. In reality, Austria's was not a particularly noble death, the majority of the populace embracing Nazi annexation without much objection. But Vienna's love of Sindelar had never been about reality. Twenty thousand mourners attended his funeral.

FULL NAME:	DATE OF BIRTH:	PLACE OF BIRTH:	NATIONAL TEAM:	CAPS / GOALS:
Matthias Sindelar	*February 10, 1903*	*Kozlov, Moravia, Austria-Hungary*	*Austria, 1926–37*	*43 / 26*

SISSI

HEN SISSI GOT OFF THE PLANE with the rest of the Brazil squad at Newark in June 1999, onlookers glanced over, their eyes automatically drawn to her. Waif-like, head shaven, some of the bones in her face still out of place from a futsal injury she hadn't had time to treat before flying to the US. In a World Cup dominated by solid-looking women with flowing manes of hair, Sissi made an immediate impression.

Like many of the veterans of the Brazilian national team that tournament, Sissi had come of age in a country where women's football was perceived to be an illicit endeavor. Members of the medical community had raised public concerns about the effect of football on the female reproductive system, and the administration of Getúlio Vargas, Brazil's populist dictator, passed a 1941 law that proclaimed women "not be allowed to practice sports incompatible with the conditions of their nature." It stayed in place for 38 years. Small women's clubs would pop up every so often, operating until they were shut down by the local authorities, but officially, women were barred from playing in clubs, at schools—even playing on the streets, although never actually policed, was technically illegal and heavily discouraged.

Born in 1967 in Esplanada, a small municipality about an hour inland from the northeastern coastline, Sissi grew up wading through jeers and disapproving looks to play with the boys from the neighborhood. When she couldn't get her hands on a ball, she'd tear the head off of one of her dolls and use that instead. She was 12 when the ban on women's sport was finally lifted. By 14, she had moved three hours away to join the newly formed women's club in Feira de Santana.

To see Sissi play was to understand the impact of Brazil's ban. Cautious and watchful, she would spend much of the game lurking in no-man's-land between the forwards and the midfield. For long stretches she would almost disappear, skulking on the outskirts, shrinking into the background of the action. And then, all of a sudden, she would spot an opportunity and reemerge, equally capable of putting a perfect pass into the box or scoring herself with a lethal left foot. When she was on the ball, she had the same trademark artistry that the Brazilian men had introduced to the world. But unlike the men, who always played with a kind of stylish, carefree abandon, Sissi's game was measured, restrained, founded on years of participating in games where she wasn't supposed to be, with people who didn't think she should be there. Like a comedian playing to a fractious crowd, she learned to pick her moments.

And pick her moments she did. Sissi quickly made a name for herself that summer of 1999, scoring a hat trick against Mexico in Brazil's first match out of the gate, and a brace against Italy in their second. Another goal against Germany saw Sissi streaking into the quarterfinal with six goals in three games.

The quarterfinal against Nigeria proved more challenging. After charging to 3–0 in the first half, Brazil watched their lead slip through their fingers as Nigeria tore through the shaky Brazilian defense, evening things up at 3–3. And then, 14 minutes into extra time, Sissi reappears. Stepping up to a free kick from 25 yards out, she channels her predecessor to the number 10 shirt to expertly whip a free kick, Zico-esque, into the top-left corner. It's a beautiful, virtuosic piece of skill. Sissi runs to the far corner, shouting ecstatically, flapping her shirt up and down, beaming from ear to ear. Extra time is sudden death at this tournament. For the first time in their history, the Brazilian women are into the semifinals of the World Cup.

The US '99 team are in many ways the antithesis of Brazil that tournament, their athletic, reach-every-ball style of play standing in stark contrast to Brazil's more artful, thoughtful game. The US beat Brazil decisively in the semis and went on to win the final, so it was Brandi Chastain's penalty kick celebration that transcended the tournament to become the enduring symbol of female athletic empowerment. But you can only truly appreciate Brandi's moment for having seen Sissi's. Because to witness Brandi is to witness the power of giving women the chance to win. To witness Sissi is to witness the power of giving them the chance to play the game at all.

FULL NAME:	DATE OF BIRTH:	PLACE OF BIRTH:	NATIONAL TEAM:	CAPS / GOALS:
Sisleide do Amor Lima	*June 2, 1967*	*Esplanada, Bahia, Brazil*	*Brazil, 1988–99*	*19 / 8*

KELLY SMITH

"**OMEN'S FOOTBALL IN ENGLAND** is a joke." So declared striker Kelly Smith in 1999. After a brief stint at Arsenal Ladies during her final year of school, the Watford native had decamped to the States in '97 on a scholarship from Seton Hall University. When asked by a tabloid journalist whether she would return to play in England after graduation, the answer was a decisive, dismissive, absolute no.

Women's football in England spent a long time lagging behind its FIFA brethren. A result of an overzealous commitment to traditionalism, coupled with a famously sluggish bureaucracy, and a serious case of chauvinism, their Football Association was a stuffy, conservative body, and had banned women's teams from playing on their fields until 1971, when the pioneering girls who began to play were met with scorn by their male counterparts. By the 1990s, most Premier League teams ran women's teams, but they remained unpaid, unfunded, and usually unseen. It was an odd whiplash, to turn from the testosterone-soaked Premier League of the '90s, dripping in fresh hundred-million-dollar broadcast deals and newfound global celebrity, to the women's teams, jogging onto the practice pitch after the men were finished with it, outfitted on their own dime and already tired from day jobs in kennels and laundries required to pay the rent. In their first four attempts, the England Women's National Team qualified for the World Cup just once, in 1995. If you were a woman trying to play football in England, this was essentially your lot, and there tended to be a kind of *you get what you get and you don't get upset* attitude. Stiff upper lip and all.

That is, until Kelly Smith decided she wanted more. In 2000, when the Women's United Soccer Association (WUSA), the world's first fully professional women's soccer league, was set up in the States, Smith was at the front of the line, signing with the Philadelphia Charge, and becoming the first—and, at the time, only—English woman to play professional football. Other than occasional highlights smuggled into the country on pirated VHS, there was no way to watch the WUSA in England, so the idea of Smith in America, paid to play football, took on an almost mythical quality, her name relayed with hushed reverence by one aspiring English football girl to another.

In reality, Smith only played one full season in the WUSA. She tore her ACL in 2002 and spent much of the next two years battling injury and alcoholism. The WUSA collapsed in 2003, and in 2004, Smith's father came to shepherd her back to England, where she went into rehab. When she returned, she was welcomed not as a hypocrite or a failure, but as a conquering hero back from the wars. She had played professionally. She had seen Jerusalem. An incredibly technical player, Smith's football was clean, precise, and purposeful, utilizing a level of ball control and awareness that had no real comparisons in the women's game at the time. She had been the outstanding talent when she left seven years before, and she was the outstanding talent when she came back. Smith rejoined Arsenal Ladies at the end of the 2004–05 season, clinching the title for the team with a goal against Charlton Athletic from 30 yards out.

The comparison people most favored when discussing Smith was with Zidane—both for the masterful ball control that the two possessed, and for the rage control the duo lacked. During the UEFA Women's Cup semifinals in 2007, Smith scored two goals for Arsenal. Then she found herself suspended the rest of the tournament for flipping off the Danish fans after she was sent off in the final minutes of the game. Off the field, Smith tended to be rather shy, demure even, but her time in the US, her ability, and her hair-trigger temper mingled together to create a larger-than-life aura about her.

In 2007, England appeared at the World Cup for the first time in 12 years. In their opening game against Japan, Smith scored a stylish equalizer with nine minutes remaining. She took off her boot, held it up for the crowd, then put it to her lips for a kiss. She scored again two minutes later; this time, both boots came off. If you remember one image from the 2007 World Cup, it is, without a doubt, Kelly Smith, mouth to shoe, standing in front of goal in her stockinged feet. There was always this feeling that Smith was too big for the league, too big for the national team. England reached the quarterfinals that tournament. They did it again in 2011. They were on the rise. English women's football had their star. They stretched themselves accordingly to fit her.

FULL NAME:	DATE OF BIRTH:	PLACE OF BIRTH:	NATIONAL TEAM:	CAPS / GOALS:
Kelly Jayne Smith	*October 29, 1978*	*Watford, England*	*England, 1995–2014*	*117 / 46*

SÓCRATES

 ITH HIS THICK BEARD, LUSCIOUS locks, and impeccable taste in headbands, Sócrates appeared at times to have been transported straight from Woodstock onto the football pitch. He was 6'4" and smoked two packs of cigarettes a day. His idols were Fidel Castro, John Lennon, and Che Guevara. He had a medical degree and a taste for revolutionary politics. He was, in short, the least likely footballer you could possibly imagine. "I am an anti-athlete," Sócrates once said. "You have to take me as I am."

The epitome of '60s-kid cool, Sócrates often seemed, even while playing, to have no particular interest in being a professional footballer. His club president at Corinthians in the Brazilian top tier had to beg him to celebrate after scoring goals, as his apparent disinterest was putting off the fans (and thus, his iconic celebration—two arms reaching to the sky in praise of the unseen football gods—was born). Never rushed, never harried, Sócrates oozed nonchalance. Where other players ran, Sócrates sauntered to the beat of a Jefferson Airplane song the rest of us couldn't hear. Perhaps the last great football philosopher, he was all elegance and imagination, guiding the ball along as if that were the point of football and scoring was just an interesting byproduct. He played better going backward than most footballers going forward, Pelé once remarked.

Sócrates played in two World Cups, won 60 caps for his country between 1979 and 1986, and scored 22 goals, but he is probably best known for his performance in the 1982 World Cup, where he captained a Brazil team widely recognized as the most aesthetically beautiful team to fail to win the tournament. His Brazilians soared through the first group stage before flying too close to the sun and losing abruptly to Italy in the final game of the second-round group stage. Dr. Sócrates, as he was known, became the first qualified medical professional (as far as we can tell) to score in the World Cup, snagging two goals that tournament, including a spectacular, highlight-reel shot against Italy. Down 0–1, Sócrates receives a beautifully angled pass from Zico. Watching it, you're absolutely sure he won't reach the ball in time. Yet, as was so often the case for Sócrates, time seems to slow down for a moment as he somehow ambles past the defender, finds a tiny gap between keeper Dino Zoff and the post, and bullets the ball in, as if it were the easiest thing in the world. Brazil ultimately lost that game 3–2, devastating a nation whose hopes were pinned on their team of swaggering football poets. Sócrates, for whom football was more art than sport, didn't take the loss as hard as others. He wrote in his book, *Football Philosophy*, "Beauty comes first. Victory is secondary. What matters is joy."

FULL NAME:	DATE OF BIRTH:	PLACE OF BIRTH:	NATIONAL TEAM:	CAPS / GOALS:
Sócrates Brasileiro Sampaio de Souza Vieira de Oliveira	*February 19, 1954*	*Belém, Pará, Brazil*	*Brazil, 1979–86*	*60 / 22*

HOPE SOLO

IT IS A TRUTH UNIVERSALLY ACK-nowledged that all goalies are crazy. It is also true, however, that some goalies are crazier than others. Hope Solo would tend to fall into this second category—not the kind of player you'd want to be stuck in an elevator with. This principle was clearly demonstrated in 2007, when, after losing to Brazil in the World Cup semifinals, Solo stepped onto a hotel elevator and the rest of the US team promptly filed off. Solo, who had been benched in the semi in favor of veteran Briana Scurry, had gone immediately to the press, claiming that they would have won had she been in goal. The rest of the team called her statement a betrayal; Solo called it the truth.

As a rule, footballers tend to be two-faced by professional necessity. On the field, they are balls of competitive fire, petty outrage, exhibitionism, myopic, single-minded focus; when the game is over, we ask them to leave all of that behind, transforming with a handshake and a quick drink of water into banally charming celebrities: chill, mildly introspective, affable in press conferences, and infinitely I'd-have-a-beer-with-her-able.

Solo was a coin with only one side. Conceived on a conjugal visit while her father was in prison for embezzlement, raised in a hardscrabble neighborhood on the southern border of Washington State in a home where the common love language was kicking and screaming, Solo's childhood mythology, peppered with stories of minor kidnapping, domestic disputes, and violent sibling clashes, is a far cry from the manicured fields, soccer-mom minivans, and orange slices that constitute the foundational myths of American soccer culture. She could be charming and funny both on and off the field, but she lugged that filterless, rage-driven intensity, born out of circumstance and honed on the soccer field, wherever she went. Determined to be the best, she trained longer and focused harder and yelled louder, flattening you under the weight of her ferocity. She wanted to win so badly it was almost offensive, but of course, you can't win games in goal, you can only save them, so she would glare and gnash her teeth and run to the edge of the box shouting instructions maniacally, trying to force the other team into submission. Which, to her credit, did seem to be an effective technique, as she racked up a staggering world record 102 shutouts in international competition. In 195 starts in goal for the US, Solo lost only 11 games. Her presence had a palpable force to it, emanating from the goal all the way up the pitch, hitting you in the face as if someone just opened the oven door while you were admiring the 400-degree bread rising inside.

Parallel to her growing list of accomplishments, though, sprouted a list of misdemeanors: drunken belligerence, domestic assault charges, beef with just about everyone in the soccer community. If she wasn't happy about something, you would know, her team would know, the media would know. She was weapon and liability in equal measure, attacking both roles with the fierce, self-destructive dedication of someone who's paid to punch balls away from their face for a living.

In 2016, the US lost to Sweden in the quarterfinals of the Rio Olympics—a loss that would turn out to be the last of Solo's career. Speaking to the press after the game, Solo called the Swedes "a bunch of cowards" for doubling down on defense rather than trying to win offensively. In the Solo post-game insult oeuvre, it was a fairly mild statement, but it proved to be the straw that broke the camel's back. Her USWNT contract was terminated and, though arguably still at the peak of her powers, Solo's career was over. Thus, much like Denmark in World War II, so folded the best goalie women's soccer has ever seen: not with a bang, but with a whine about Swedish cowardice.

Solo will likely be redeemed as a working-class feminist icon via a charmingly revisionist biopic, à la Tonya Harding, with the more distasteful parts of her character reshaped into a palatable Hollywood version of female unlikeability. Until then, she will remain our most fascinating thorn in US Soccer's side: outspoken, intimidating, alluring, unsavory, perpetually lionized and permanently disgraced. A vocal reminder that athletes are rarely the people we want them to be.

FULL NAME:	DATE OF BIRTH:	PLACE OF BIRTH:	NATIONAL TEAM:	CAPS / GOALS:
Hope Amelia Solo	*July 30, 1981*	*Richland, Washington, United States*	*United States, 2000–16*	*202 / –*

HRISTO STOICHKOV

HE LEGEND OF HRISTO STOICHKOV was born in Sofia in the summer of 1985, at the little-remembered Bulgarian Cup final between CSKA Sofia and Levski Sofia. A fierce intra-city rivalry played out in the crumbling, corrupt infrastructure of communist football. The match had already featured a handled goal, two heavily suspect penalties, innumerable scuffles, three red cards, and the referee being struck twice by the Levski goalkeeper before it climaxed in a full-on post-game tunnel brawl that saw both teams stripped of their state connections, renamed, booted from the league, and stripped of their silverware. The two teams' managers were permanently barred from coaching and five players handed lifetime bans for "violations of socialist morale and football hooliganism." Determined to be the chief instigator among the five was CSKA's newly acquired striker, a scowling 19-year-old with a gleam of madness in the corner of his eye. The ban was reduced to a yearlong suspension, but the reputation was there to stay. Hristo Stoichkov had arrived.

On lists of the angriest men in football, Stoichkov rarely fails to make the top five. Snarling, surly, thickset, and violent, Stoichkov confirmed everything seven seasons of *Mission: Impossible* had taught us about Bulgarians. When, in 1990, Johan Cruyff, then managing Barcelona, was looking for a player to help pry La Liga out of the clenched fists of archrivals Real Madrid, there was only one man for the job.

Cruyff's mad Bulgarian lived up to expectations—and then some. Spanish observers described Stoichkov as having mala leche—bad milk. Just three months into his Barcelona career, a contentious El Clásico against Real Madrid in the first leg of the Supercopa in December 1990 had him stomping on the referee's foot after being sent off on a red card. Egotistical, seething, and perpetually unsatisfied, Stoichkov picked fights left and right, barreling through opponents (not to mention officials) like a bowling ball who's just heard that some of the pins were speaking ill of his mother. In Bulgaria, Stoichkov was known as *the Dagger*. The Barcelona faithful rechristened him: *el Pistolero—the Gunslinger*.

Whereas most players slow down as they close in on goal, Stoichkov's trick was to appear to speed up, charging forward, fury mounting, with red flashing in his eyes and the ball lashed to a lethal left foot. A maniac on a mission (his allegiance to Barcelona so intensely felt that years later, when managing the Bulgarian national team, he was reported to have kicked a seven-year-old boy out of training for wearing a Madrid shirt), Stoichkov combined with Romário to form an opposition-devastating strike partnership. He changed the entire complexion of the Barcelona team, imbuing each game with a rage-filled hunger you had to see to believe. "Stoichkov is a predator—a beast who is only satiated by the flesh of his victims," Real Madrid manager Jorge Valdano once wailed. Stoichkov's arrival had completely toppled their reign.

At the 1994 World Cup, Bulgaria lost to an ebullient Nigeria in their opening match. No surprise perhaps, as Bulgaria had failed to muster a single World Cup win in 30 years of trying. Yet Stoichkov rallied the Lions, inspiring them to embark on a *Revenge of the Nerds* rampage straight through champions Argentina and heavily favored Germany all the way to the semifinals. When asked about the team's success, Stoichkov demonstrated a surprising modesty. "God is Bulgarian," he philosophized sagely to the press, echoing the divinely grateful commentator who had coined the phrase earlier in the year after the team bashed into the tournament with a shock win against France on the final day of qualifying. Six months later, when presented with that year's Ballon d'Or, Stoichkov clarified the sentiment: "There are only two Christs; one plays for Barcelona, the other is in heaven." It wasn't the one in heaven, he of turn-the-other-cheek fame, who had made the difference on the field.

FULL NAME:	DATE OF BIRTH:	PLACE OF BIRTH:	NATIONAL TEAM:	CAPS / GOALS:
Hristo Stoichkov Stoichkov	*February 8, 1966*	*Plovdiv, Bulgaria*	*Bulgaria, 1986–99*	*83 / 37*

LUIS SUÁREZ

O UTTER THE NAME LUIS SUÁREZ in the modern era is to conjure Jungian nightmares of giant, disembodied Uruguayan teeth closing in on you as the sound of urgent whistling pierces through the air. This is Luis Suárez, the ruthless striker, friend of Messi, opponent-biter extraordinaire, who has set up camp at the forefront of popular Luis Suárez–regarding imagination. Which is misleading. Because not only is he merely the second-most important Luis Suárez in footballing history, he is in fact only the second-most important to don the blue and garnet of Barcelona. A rabid but less historically significant sequel to the original Luis Suárez, Luis Suárez Miramontes, the only Spanish player ever to win the Ballon d'Or.

When Suárez (the first), Luisito to friends, turned up at Barcelona in early 1955, the club was still reeling from the Di Stéfano transfer debacle of 1953; Real Madrid had just beaten Barcelona out for two consecutive league titles, and they seemed to be in danger of sprinting away with the rest of the decade. Suárez, a stealth contender for handsomest man in this book, arrived at the Catalan giants with slicked-back hair and thick, impressive eyebrows, but with little else to show for himself. A 20-year-old from the working-class port city of A Coruña in northern Galicia, he had just been promoted up from Barcelona's reserve side following a very brief stint at Deportivo. He was unknown, unproven. He was also, as it turned out, northern Spain's answer to Di Stéfano.

Like his southern counterpart, Suárez was his team's primary playmaker. A deep-lying attacking midfielder, his touch had a flamenco-like quality about it, his feet barely lifting off the ground as he smoothly shuffled the ball around opponents, releasing it finally into the penalty area with abrupt, clever passes. Fans called him *el Arquitecto*. Combining with Barcelona's Hungarian refugee front three, László Kubala, Sándor Kocsis, and Zoltán Czibor, Suárez transformed Barcelona once again into a powerful attacking threat, capable of matching Real Madrid blow for blow. By '59, they were back on top of the league, winning a domestic league-cup double in the 1958–59 season and a league-European Fairs Cup double in 1960. Suárez was rewarded with the 1960 Ballon d'Or for his trouble, beating out Madrid rivals Di Stéfano and Ferenc Puskás for the honor.

One imagines that if Suárez had played out the rest of his career at Barcelona, he would never have been pipped for that top Luis Suárez spot. But Suárez was becoming unhappy in the Catalonian capital. The Spanish press had invented a rivalry between him and Kubala, which led to a contentious stand-off between the two players' official fan clubs: Los Kubalistas versus Los Suáristas. All fairly tame, but unpleasant nonetheless, and so in 1961, Suárez left Barcelona and followed manager Helenio Herrera to Inter Milan, where together they won three Scudetti and two European Cups. Suárez's position on the pitch, which had already gotten progressively deeper during his time at Barcelona, appeared to retreat with his hairline, his command of the game becoming more and more dominant the further back he sat.

By the time Suárez returned to Spain for the 1964 Euros, his hair had receded quite a bit indeed, and he led La Roja to their first and only international trophy until well into the new millennium. They played compact, organized football, orchestrated by Suárez, who was, at 29, the oldest player on the team and the only real Spanish star. It was, for many years, a perplexing quirk of Spanish football, that their clubs dominated Europe while their national team floundered, propped up—but only just—by nationalized foreign players. Suárez is now pub trivia fodder, relegated to the odd factoid and sentences that begin, "No, not that one." But for the half century that preceded, he was the country's main homegrown talisman—wielded as proof that the Spanish were more than just discerning importers of foreign talent. That they were part of the conversation.

FULL NAME:	DATE OF BIRTH:	PLACE OF BIRTH:	NATIONAL TEAM:	CAPS / GOALS:
Luis Suárez Miramontes	*May 2, 1935*	*A Coruña, Galicia, Spain*	*Spain, 1957–72*	*32 / 14*

DAVOR ŠUKER

NE OF THE ALL-TIME GREAT CULT World Cup teams, Croatia showed up to their debut tournament in 1998 brandishing the red, white, and blue flag of a nation that was only seven years old and just three years removed from the horrifying, casualty-heavy Yugoslav Wars that had been the cost of that independence. They strode into France with a patriotism that felt urgent and uncynical, with instantly iconic red-checked shirts paired, in a truly inspired move of football fashion, with matching red-checked wristbands, and an infectiously audacious sense of eager-eyed self-belief.

The team also sported a wide, colorful array of characters. There was Robert Prosinečki, the permanently scowling, crafty midfielder who was rumored to smoke upwards of 40 cigarettes a day. Slaven Bilic, handsome and earringed, who played in a prog rock band on the side and, despite being, by all accounts, a pretty nice guy, would become the tournament's villain after taking an egregiously theatrical dive to get French center back Laurent Blanc booted out of the semifinal in the 76th minute. There was Petar Krpan, a substitute striker who had spent six months, rifle in hand, fighting off Serbian forces in his hometown of Osijek at age 17. And then, of course, there was captain Zvonimir Boban, nicknamed Zorro, who was folklorically credited with having started the Croatian War of Independence by attacking a police officer during a riot at a match between Dinamo Zagreb and Red Star Belgrade in the spring of 1990.

But the team's brightest star was indisputably Davor Šuker, who had announced Croatia to the world two years earlier at the 1996 Euros by chipping a gorgeously impertinent ball over the head of Peter Schmeichel, the Danish keeper—arguably the best goalkeeper in the world at the time—as Croatia marched right past them into the knockout rounds. Languid, with a smug smile and a face that made him look 18 rather than his actual age of 30, Šuker

was coming into the World Cup in France at the end of a successful decade in La Liga. He had already proven himself a talented striker in Spain. That summer in France, he was on another level, scoring six goals and clinching the Golden Boot as Croatia ripped its way to the semifinals.

All six of Šuker's goals are delectable works of artistry: cool, controlled, and canny, pulling chances out of thin air with the nonchalance of a veteran illusionist. His chef d'oeuvre is the fourth of the collection, an 85th-minute strike in the quarterfinal against Germany, which put Croatia up 3–0, avenging their Euro quarterfinal defeat from two years earlier. Šuker retrieves the ball on the edge of the German box. Charging to the front of the net, head down, falling to his right while aiming to his left, Šuker, neither foot on the ground, sends the ball careening through the legs of defender Jörg Heinrich and whizzing inches to the left of keeper Andreas Köpke's right foot. Each time Šuker scored, the smug coolness of his play would melt instantly away into the purest, most triumphant smile you had ever seen. His ecstatic pride a stand-in for that of his nation.

Croatia's downfall four days later was almost as unlikely as their rise—after going up 1–0 in the semifinal against France, they were defeated by two goals from defender Lilian Thuram. Thuram, a consistent presence in the French backline, made 142 appearances for his country. Those are the only two goals he ever scored.

If anything, the unlikeliness of the Thuram goals adds to the Croatian legend. Brazil, whom they would have met in the final, were conquerable that summer. If not for that small French twist of fate, they could have won the tournament. Having experienced so many larger twists of fate that decade, the Croatians didn't particularly seem to mind this one. They headed enthusiastically to their third-place playoff against the Netherlands. Šuker scored the winning goal in the 36th minute, once again sending the ball straight through the legs of the opposition. He celebrated as if he'd won the tournament. In a sense, he kind of had.

FULL NAME:	DATE OF BIRTH:	PLACE OF BIRTH:	NATIONAL TEAM:	CAPS / GOALS:
Davor Šuker	*January 1, 1968*	*Osijek, Croatia*	*Yugoslavia, 1990–1991; Croatia, 1990–2002*	*2 / 1; 69 / 45*

PIA SUNDHAGE

HERE IS PERHAPS NO MORE PER- manent fixture in women's soccer than Pia Sundhage. Raised in Ulricehamn, a small Swedish town of 10,000 inhabitants about 60 miles east of Gothenburg, Sundhage joined the Swedish national team in 1975, at age 15. Sweden, owing to a progressive movement in the '60s and '70s that pushed an almost parodically Swedish dual agenda of gender equality and participation in recreational sports, was one of the earliest pioneers of modern women's soccer. By the time most other nations were just beginning to create their own women's programs, Sundhage was already a veteran. In 1984, she led Sweden to victory in the first-ever women's Euros. In '89, she became the first woman to score an international goal at Wembley. By the inaugural Women's World Cup in 1991, Sundhage was 31 and had been playing football full-time for over 15 years. She sported a serious looking mullet and an aura of grizzled authority, and she made women's soccer in 1991 feel like a fact rather than an idea.

Sundhage retired shortly after the 1996 Olympics. Rather than fading into the background, she refashioned herself into one of the most important coaches of modern football. Most fans in the US know her from her four years with the USWNT, where she coached the American women to two Olympic gold medals and a World Cup final, strumming her guitar at every opportunity along the way.

The Swede has spent time at just about every major powerhouse of women's international football: one year in China, four years in the US, six years back in Sweden, three years and counting with Brazil. What the Lord giveth, he also taketh away. Sundhage led the US to two Olympic golds; she is also directly responsible for their lack of a medal in 2016, helming the Swedish team who took them out in the quarterfinals. Rarely has a major tournament rolled around without Sundhage's fingerprints all over it.

If you've happened upon a choicy, revealing quote about a player or game in the past 15 years, Sundhage was probably the author. She is blunt and unabashed. And prone to spontaneous musical numbers. This is a woman who belted out Dylan when accepting her 2012 FIFA World Coach of the Year award. Caroline Seger, the Swedish midfielder, tells a story of Sundhage's first day with the national team. Sundhage stopped in the middle of introducing herself and started serenading the locker room. The US women used to cheer when she sang. The Swedes just stared blankly. It didn't seem to deter her; she plowed right on to the end of the song. Years earlier, Sundhage had walked into the USWNT locker room to find "no regrets" written on a chalkboard. She promptly crossed it out and scrawled "have fun" in its stead. This is Sundhage as she's always been: comfortable, assertive, eccentric, ebullient, and entirely immune to convention and outside judgment. Capable of instilling confidence without pressure. If women's soccer is the same way, it's because they've been following her lead for nearly 50 years.

FULL NAME:	DATE OF BIRTH:	PLACE OF BIRTH:	NATIONAL TEAM:	CAPS / GOALS:
Pia Mariane Sundhage	*February 13, 1960*	*Ulricehamn, Sweden*	*Sweden, 1975–96*	*146 / 71*

CARLOS VALDERRAMA

THE COLOMBIAN NATIONAL TEAM in 1990 was a Pablo Escobar–funded fever dream, swirling dirty money, ruthless cartel warfare, and huge quantities of cocaine into the already labyrinthine world of Latin American football. After a referee in the top Colombian league was murdered for a controversial decision in a league game in November of 1989, there had been calls to bar the country from the World Cup, but FIFA put only the most ginger of feet down, forcing the Colombians to suspend the rest of their league season. So there they were in Italy that summer, not the tournament's main event, but easily its most intriguing. They showed up to their first match in Bologna with statement-piece hair, an air of danger, and a nonchalance that boggled the mind when you considered the fact that this was their first time qualifying for the World Cup since 1962 and, of course, that the team was controlled by capricious, vengeful drug lords.

The Colombian centerpiece, both from an aesthetic and a logistical perspective, was undoubtedly captain Carlos Valderrama. Sporting a gravity-defying, humidity-spurning, principles of aerodynamics–rejecting blond afro, a dark Burt Reynolds mustache, and an ever-growing collection of beaded jewelry dangling from his neck and wrists, Valderrama looked, more than anything, like an *SNL* parody of a South American footballer. Already 29 at his debut World Cup, his nickname was, ironically enough, *el Pibe* (*the Kid*).

The Colombians played a style called *toque toque*. Similar in both name and method to the tiki-taka of Pep Guardiola's Barcelona, the players traveled up and down the pitch in complex, kaleidoscopic triangles, dominating possession and mesmerizing opponents with short, perpetual motion-passing patterns. But whereas tiki-taka is a modernist version, a kind of warp speed, mechanistic take on the idea, the Colombian toque is a swinging, rhythmic, remarkably unharried affair. Football as Ultimate Frisbee. When you set it to samba music, they pass on the downbeat.

Valderrama functioned as the team's metronome. Once described by journalist Tim Vickery as "a player who always had the ball, and never had the ball," he lacked pace but apparently had no need for it, jogging languidly around the pitch with masterful touch and perfect cadence, serenely picking up teammates' passes and redirecting them with casual, metrical precision.

Valderrama's crowning achievement in the 1990 World Cup came in Colombia's final group-stage fixture. Despite 88 minutes of ball domination against an already knock-out stage–qualified West Germany, Colombia found themselves down 1–0 to a strike from German winger Pierre Littbarski. The Colombians needed at least a draw to go through. As the game ticks into stoppage time, they regain possession. Dribbling up the center of the pitch, Luis Fajardo hands the ball off to Valderrama, who is standing still, just waiting for it at the edge of the center circle. He spins around not one but two German players, leaving them on the ground beside him, zips the ball to Freddy Rincón, who one-touches it to Fajardo, who in turn pinballs it straight back to Valderrama. Ambling into space, Valderrama spots Rincón sprinting forward on the right and sends him a gorgeous through pass that rolls right to his feet at the 18-yard line. Rincón gently knocks it straight through the legs of the West German keeper, and Colombia is into the round of 16. It is disgustingly, wonderfully blasé. Such was the magic of el Pibe.

Four days later against Cameroon, the other side of Colombia's nonchalance is put on display when Roger Milla cherry-picks a dillydallying Colombian keeper René Higuita—he of the flowing renaissance curls and the trade-marked scorpion kick, an objectively ridiculous move, in which he would clear the ball by launching himself into a handstand to kick the ball away with his heels (you won't regret YouTubing it)—and propels Cameroon past Colombia into the quarterfinals.

Valderrama had subsequent triumphs—beating Argentina 5–0 in a 1993 World Cup qualifying game (a victory so famous in Colombia it is simply referred to as *el 5–0*), becoming a pioneering player in the newly formed MLS, and leading Colombia's qualification into the next two World Cups—but in memory, he remains in Italia 90. Hair flying, bracelets jangling, exuding a preternatural, almost laughable calm in the center of a world of chaos.

FULL NAME:	DATE OF BIRTH:	PLACE OF BIRTH:	NATIONAL TEAM:	CAPS / GOALS:
Carlos Alberto Valderrama Palacio	*September 2, 1961*	*Santa Marta, Colombia*	*Colombia, 1985–98*	*111 / 11*

MARCO
VAN BASTEN

ARCO VAN BASTEN WAS NINE years and 231 days old when Johan Cruyff debuted the Cruyff Turn at the 1974 World Cup. For the next 18 days, the Dutch team was in full control, rewriting the rules of the game as they went along. The world watched in a daze as these orange-clad footballing poets stood poised on the precipice of becoming the next great footballing power. Marco van Basten was nine years and 249 days old when West Germany, heavy on defense and dream-crushing, stopped the Dutch dead in their tracks in the World Cup final.

Despite completely reinventing football, the highs of '74 dissolved quickly into a puddle of disappointment and anticlimax. A sans-Cruyff Dutch side in 1978 gave up two goals in extra time to lose another tight World Cup final to Argentina. They slumped out of the group stage at the 1980 Euros. In the winter of 1981, they humiliatingly failed to qualify for the '82 World Cup. Total Football was the flavor of the decade, but the Netherlands were on the decline.

Van Basten grew up in the world of Total Football, making his Ajax debut in the spring of 1982 as a 16-year-old substitute, symbolically replacing the mighty Cruyff himself. And you can see its track marks in his almost cold clinicality, his seriousness, the copious notes he was reported to keep (feints mastered, performances analyzed, tactics logged). But as a player, Van Basten was much more of a traditional striker than a total footballer, his great skill not awareness or movement, but an astounding, gymnastic ability to score from anywhere, via any means. Aerial volleys, headers, curling left-footed strikes. His bicycle kick against Den Bosch in '86 will jolt your heart into your mouth: Van Basten on the full stretch, three feet in the air and fully upside down, reversing the ball to send it spinning into the top corner. The Den Bosch players just stand there staring, mouths agape as Van Basten clambers up off the ground to sedately celebrate the accomplishment. When Van Basten left Ajax for AC Milan the following year, he walked away with three league titles, three Dutch Cups, one European Golden Shoe, 129 goals in 133 league appearances, and a growing reputation as the most talented striker in Europe.

At Euro 1988, thanks in large part to a Van Basten hat trick against England in the group stage, the Netherlands propelled themselves into the semifinals—the country's first tournament since 1980—face to face once again with nemesis West Germany. At 1–1 in the 88th minute, Van Basten slides in past the last defender to score the game-winning goal. Had that been his final contribution for the tournament, that would have been enough. Reveling in their revenge, nine million Dutch people took to the streets that night, the largest public celebration since Liberation. But then, nine minutes into the second half of the final against the USSR, midfielder Arnold Mühren sends a rather poor cross over to Van Basten on the right edge of the penalty area. It's too high, has too much spin, sits in the air for too long, and tumbles too close to the goal line. Every other player in the world would have sent it back into the box and hoped that a teammate was there to drive it home. Not Van Basten. He takes the ball on the volley and sends it curving right past the Russian keeper into the top corner at what is, upon first, second, and third watch, an impossibly acute angle. His leg seems to extend telescopically behind his body, bending the ball away from him as he twists in the opposite direction. The more you see, the less you understand the physics of how it's done. Netherlands manager Rinus Michels staggers onto the pitch, his hands covering his eyes in disbelief. You almost forget that the goal has essentially sealed the Euro win for the Dutch team, because the achievement pales in comparison to the sheer improbability of the goal itself.

After the heartbreak of 1974, the Dutch had enveloped their national team in a protective myth of glorious defeat. They were somehow too good, too attractive, too moral, doomed to be always the bridesmaid, never the bride. They returned to underachievement two years after the Euro win, losing, yet again, to West Germany. Van Basten suffered a series of injuries in the early '90s and was retired by 1995, just 12 years into his career, becoming the most accomplished what-if player of all time. But with that game, with that goal—with every goal, really—he made you believe that the Dutch were on the precipice of something greater than glorious defeat.

FULL NAME:	DATE OF BIRTH:	PLACE OF BIRTH:	NATIONAL TEAM:	CAPS / GOALS:
Marcel van Basten	*October 31, 1964*	*Utrecht, Netherlands*	*Netherlands, 1983–92*	*58 / 24*

ABBY WAMBACH

N 1998, JUST THREE YEARS INTO their existence, the women's soccer team at the University of Florida found themselves in the final game of the NCAA championships, facing off against dynastic favorites North Carolina. Up 1–0 in the second half, the Gators huddled for their final TV time-out. Stepping into the circle, their coach opened her mouth to make one last rallying speech to inspire the young team over the line. Before she could get out any sound, a wild-eyed 18-year-old Abby Wambach burst into the middle and bellowed, "We are not fucking losing to these bitches." And that was all there was to say really, so the coach just nodded and sent the players back onto the field, where they clinched their first-ever national title.

Part human, part battering ram: That was Wambach from the very start. She turned up at the USWNT training camp in 2001, a loud, assertive, perennially unintimidated 21-year-old rookie in a sea of seasoned veterans. If the '99ers represented the old school of understated determination and self-effacing teamwork, Wambach was something else entirely. She didn't just want to win; she wanted to dominate, roaring at full volume as she propelled herself headfirst into every huddle, every attack, every set piece fray. Julie Foudy bought her a shirt that read, "Help I'm talking and I can't shut up." The old guard eventually fell away, and Wambach vigorously seized the reins, making herself so synonymous with women's soccer in the US over the next decade that simply uttering her name would conjure images of last-minute headers and Olympic gold games in the minds of even the least sport-inclined of citizens. A goalscoring terminator, she bludgeoned her way up and down the field, racking up more international goals than any other person in the history of the sport had managed before: 184 to be precise. Nearly half of them scored with her head.

To say that Wambach was dominant or tough or powerful would be to undersell what was, at its heart, a—slightly terrifying—monomaniacal physical commitment to the game. In a World Cup qualifier against Mexico in 2010, Wambach collided with a Mexican defender in stoppage time and split her head open on the other player's teeth. Refusing to be subbed off for the two final minutes, Wambach dropped to the side of the pitch with blood pouring down the side of her face and tapped her foot impatiently as a bewildered medic stapled the gash back together. Then she got up and finished the game.

With 184 goals, you've got a lot of highlights to choose from, but the one everyone most likes to relive is Wambach's 122nd-minute header in the quarterfinals of the 2011 World Cup. It's the last minute of extra-time stoppage time, Brazil is up 2–1, and the US is staring down the barrel of the worst World Cup result in the team's history. Streaming forward on the left flank for a last-ditch counterattack, Megan Rapinoe launches an arching final prayer cross from 45 yards out. There are seconds left in the game; she doesn't even look up beforehand to see if anyone will be there to receive it. When she does finally look up, there is Wambach, like a heat-seeking missile, rising above the keeper and the Brazilian defense to slam it home. In some ways, this should be Rapinoe's moment: The goal doesn't exist without her astonishing cross. But the glory belongs entirely to Wambach, who had spent the final half hour of the game running with one finger brandished in the air, bombarding her teammates with the reminder that all they needed was one chance. When the chance finally came, Wambach was there, because she was always there, explosive, unbeatable, built entirely—like all great American institutions— on intimidation, persistence, unwavering self-belief, and undeterrable brute force.

FULL NAME:	DATE OF BIRTH:	PLACE OF BIRTH:	NATIONAL TEAM:	CAPS / GOALS:
Mary Abigail Wambach	*June 2, 1980*	*Rochester, New York, United States*	*United States, 2001–15*	*255 / 184*

GEORGE WEAH

IN JANUARY 2018, GEORGE WEAH was sworn in as president of Liberia. Only hindsight will reveal whether or not this was a good idea. But there is perhaps no greater testament to nor easier quantification of Weah's legacy as a footballer than the 60 percent of Liberians who voted him into office against the vice presidential incumbent in the winter of 2017.

Weah grew up in Clara Town, an intensely poor neighborhood of 75,000 people built on a marsh on the western edge of Monrovia, Liberia's capital city. It is a dense, crowded area, shanties with tin roofs pressed up against dilapidated one-story buildings, the streets strewn with trash, barefoot kids splashing through standing water left by the torrential downpours for which the city is famous. Showing a precocious gift for football, Weah quickly graduated from the dusty field where the Clara Town kids gathered to play. He started locally in Monrovia, playing for two of the best-named teams in the sport—the Young Survivors and the Invincible Eleven—before moving to Cameroon at 21 to play for Tonnerre Yaoundé. Within a year, Weah had caught the attention of Arsène Wenger, then manager of AS Monaco. Impressed by what he saw and not wasting any time, Wenger brought him straight over to the principality.

Weah spent eight years in the French top tier, first with Monaco, then with PSG, winning three Coupes de France and one league title along the way. By the time he arrived at AC Milan in 1995, he was well established as one of the most entertaining players in Europe. With immense imagination and the technique to back it up, Weah played a style of football that was exciting and unpredictable. He was famous for the kind of solo wonder goals that had you up out of your chair, one hand clutched to the forearm of the person next to you, one hand holding your jaw to make sure it didn't slip off, like the one he scored against Verona in September 1996. He runs the ball up the entire length of the field, vaulting over diving defenders like they are obstacles in a video game he's already beaten, arriving unscathed at the other end to smoothly launch the ball past the outstretched fingers of a hapless Verona keeper. Serie A, thanks to Italia 90 and newly negotiated international broadcasting rights, was having a moment, and Weah was right at the center of it. You tuned in to watch him dance.

But while most of the world was tuning in to watch Weah from the comfort and safety of mid-'90s tech bubble–induced prosperity, Liberia was waging a bloody, decade-long civil war. In a national period defined by violent ethnic warfare, casualty-heavy political coups, and indescribable suffering, Weah's significance cannot be overstated. He was a uniting presence, to the point that rebel soldiers would agree to put down their guns and pause their street-fighting to watch him play. Though ethnically Kru like most of the Clara Town population, Weah, both by talent and by physical distance, transcended the confines of Liberia's internal conflict. He was their light in the storm, projecting a vision of Liberia to the rest of the world—as well as to Liberians themselves—that was dynamic, skilled, successful, sophisticated, and totally untainted by civil war. The entire country exalted and adored him in equal measure.

Realizing the importance of football in a country like Liberia, Weah lifted the Liberian national team—perennial underdogs of African football—onto his own shoulders, funding and coaching the team himself. Their nickname, the Lone Stars, so-called after the single star on Liberia's US-inspired flag, could just as easily have been a reference to Weah, the team's own lone star. In 2002, edging into his late 30s and nearing retirement, Weah led the Lone Stars, who had never managed roughly anything in their 50 years of existence, on an incredible World Cup qualification run. The entire country stopped in its tracks to support them. Liberia didn't manage to qualify, losing to Ghana in their penultimate fixture and ceding their spot to Nigeria by a single point. But Weah had shown them what they could do, what they could be. And that's not something you easily forget. "Today, we all wear the jersey of Liberia, and the victory belongs to the people," Weah promised in his inaugural address.

FULL NAME:	DATE OF BIRTH:	PLACE OF BIRTH:	NATIONAL TEAM:	CAPS / GOALS:
George Tawlon Manneh Oppong Ousman Weah	October 1, 1966	Monrovia, Liberia	Liberia, 1986–2002	75 / 18

SUN WEN

HE US WORLD CUP VICTORY IN 1999 plays such an outsized role in the history of women's soccer that it's sometimes possible to forget that there was another team on the field that day. That rather than dominance, the victory, decided by a single penalty miss after a scoreless 120 minutes, was the product of a bit of good fortune and (as any Chinese fan is quick to remind you) a fair amount of creative rule interpretation on the part of Briana Scurry, who leapt off her line well before a Liu Ying penalty was struck. History is, of course, not written by the vanquished.

The USWNT's ascendancy in 1999, though told as a one-protagonist affair—the US women in the spotlight and the rest of the nations prancing around behind them in supporting roles—is in reality the story of two nations. It is the culmination of a decade-long face-off between East and West, each repeatedly staring into their own reflection over the course of those first 10 years of modern women's soccer and finding themselves face to face with the other. The US announced themselves at the inaugural World Cup in 1991, but they did it in Guangzhou; gazing down at them from the stands were 60,000 Chinese fans, for whom the World Cup was their triumph as much as America's. In 1995, China and the US were exact mirror images; after drawing 3–3 in the opening game of the group stage, they lost 1–0 in symmetrical semifinals, the US conceding in the first 10 minutes, China in the last. The following year saw the US and China go head-to-head for Olympic gold, dueling aggressively to take the reins as the best team in the world. It was a tight game; the US won with a second-half goal by Tiffeny Milbrett. The 1999 final then was not an encore, but a grand finale 10 years in the making. And this time, China, who had just cruised 5–0 past a strong Norwegian team in the semis, had the slight edge.

The best player at the 1999 World Cup was neither Mia Hamm nor Sissi, but Sun Wen, the Chinese captain.

She was small, quick, and agile, with an impressive knack for slipping in behind frustrated defenders and unleashing precise, unhesitating shots before the camera has even managed to locate her. Wen has seven goals for the tournament, tied with Sissi for the Golden Boot. Afterwards, she will also receive the Golden Ball, and will be named FIFA Female Player of the Century along with Michelle Akers. Though lacking the media gloss of some of her fellow stars, she was widely agreed to be the most talented female striker in the world.

As she steps up to take the final penalty for China, the commentators introduce her as "the greatest goalscorer." Wen sends her ball coasting comfortably into the net, but Brandi Chastain steps up after her, and the rest is, quite literally, history. As the American women celebrate in the foreground, you can just make out the Chinese women in the very top corner of the screen, sprawled on the ground near the center circle in exhausted, devastated defeat.

After 1999, the two countries' paths diverged. The US women—although they didn't win another World Cup for 16 years—stayed within touching distance of the top, never coming below third in the tournaments that followed. China, however, failed to make it past the quarterfinals in any subsequent World Cup, their supremacy in Asian football increasingly challenged by Japan and North Korea until it disappeared completely. Journalists returned to writing think-pieces about why China's national ethos wasn't suited to soccer, and new rivalries emerged. The lone Chinese player in a sea of other, more trophied nationalities, Sun Wen's presence in the pantheon of greats has become somewhat of an archeological artifact, the last remaining vestige of a once-great Chinese team. If history is, in fact, written by the victors, second-bests tend to be erased from its pages. Rarely do we remember the Steve Wozniaks. But there she stands, a stalwart reminder of exactly how close China came to claiming the throne.

FULL NAME:	DATE OF BIRTH:	PLACE OF BIRTH:	NATIONAL TEAM:	CAPS / GOALS:
Sun Wen	April 6, 1973	Shanghai, China	China, 1990–2006	163 / 106

XAVI

XCEPTING PERHAPS JOHAN CRUYFF, never has a player been more wholeheartedly devoted to a single footballing philosophy than Xavier Hernández Creus. Asked once to describe his approach to the game, he stated unblinkingly, "I pass and I move, I help you, I look for you. I stop, I raise my head, I look, and, above all, I open up the pitch." And that was it. This was Xavi. The living, breathing, quick-passing embodiment of Spanish tiki-taka.

In the final years of the 20th century, as the world was just beginning to turn away from the rougher, more physical football that had dominated the game in the '80s and '90s, Barcelona's youth academy was quietly churning out an entire generation of small, technically expert passing specialists. They were schooled in a kind of modified version of Total Football, which Cruyff had introduced in the academy at the beginning of his reign as Barcelona coach, and had been kept in place by the procession of Dutch managers who succeeded him. Outside the thick stone farmhouse walls of the academy, La Masia, possession was still mostly considered a byproduct—something that had happened when you did other things right. Inside those walls, it was everything. This produced a diverse roster of possession-obsessives who played a style dubbed *tiki-taka*, after the constant, almost mechanical way they moved the ball around the pitch. At the center of that movement was Xavi, a compact midfielder from the Catalan city of Terrassa, north of Barcelona. At first, fans called him *Parabrisas*, or *Windshield Wiper*, for his disposition towards sideways passes; when they realized what their windshield wiper was capable of, they adjusted the name somewhat, changing it to *Maki: Machine*.

In a sense, Xavi's job in the new possession-based system was very simple. To quote Pep Guardiola, who took over as Barcelona manager in 2008 and turned tiki-taka from ideology to gospel, Xavi had only two tasks: Get the ball, pass the ball—most often to his fellow diminutive teammate, Andrés Iniesta. But in sport, as in life, the simpler the task, the more difficult to complete it—and the more moving to see it performed perfectly. When Xavi did his job well, he could make entire games feel like they had been pre-choreographed. He'd check over his shoulders obsessively, eyes bugging cartoonishly out of his head from the effort of constantly mapping and remapping the composition of the pitch in his mind, determined as he was to control every game purely with positioning and vision and unnervingly immaculate passes. Teammate Dani Alves described Xavi as "playing in the future." He sent balls not to where you were, but to where you would be. That, in essence, is the basic principle of tiki-taka. There was no one better at it or more committed to it than Xavi, who would go entire games without missing a pass.

Eager to replicate Barcelona's success, the Spanish national team quickly followed suit, adopting Pep's tiki-taka and ensuring its place as the defining style of 21st-century Spanish football thus far. After almost 90 years with only one trophy to their name (that 1964 Euro win), Spain won the 2008 Euros, the 2010 World Cup, and the 2012 Euros in quick succession. Xavi doesn't feature very prominently on any of those scoresheets—he did not score any game-winning goals. But, as at Barcelona, you only had to tune in for a few seconds to understand that he was the very essence of the Spanish national team. All balls flowed through him.

FULL NAME:	DATE OF BIRTH:	PLACE OF BIRTH:	NATIONAL TEAM:	CAPS / GOALS:
Xavier Hernández Creus	*January 25, 1980*	*Terrassa, Catalonia, Spain*	*Spain, 2000–14*	*133 / 13*

LEV YASHIN

N OCTOBER OF 1941, LEV YASHIN turned 12 years old. Four months earlier, the German army had breached the borders of the Soviet Union and begun their long march inwards. By October, they were 50 miles outside of Moscow and advancing rapidly. Just in time for his birthday, Lev Yashin and his family, along with thousands of their neighbors, were evacuated hurriedly out of the capital city and relocated to a small city on the Volga River, 500 miles east of Moscow. Lev was sent to work in a military weapons factory as an apprentice engineer. When the war finally ended four years later, the Yashins returned to Moscow, and Lev went to work with his father at a local metalworks factory. On weekends, he played for the factory's football team. At 18, Lev grew tired of factory work and joined the army. But when his goalkeeping talent was spotted during a pick-up game with his platoon, Lev was sent straight back to Moscow, new assignment in hand.

There is a poem by the famous Russian poet, Yevgeny Yevtushenko, which begins, "Now here's a revolution in football/The goalkeeper comes rushing off his line." The Russians know better than anyone: Behind every great revolution is a great leader. This particular revolution was ushered in by one humble factory-worker-turned-soldier-turned-national-goalkeeper, a young man with the face of a 1930s hitman. They called him *the Black Spider*. Black, because that was the color he wore, head to foot, no matter what team he was playing for; spider, because eight arms were the only possible explanation for how he managed to reach all those balls. At an imposing 6'3", dressed in all black, with that nickname, that face, and his thick Russian accent, Lev Yashin could have been a world-class Bond villain. And indeed, his dark, towering presence at the other end of the field often struck fear in the hearts of advancing opponents. But while Yashin's reach and reflexes were immediately intimidating, what struck people the most was his bravery.

Yashin was the first goalkeeper who was consistently willing to come out of goal to block crosses, launching himself through defenders and opponents to punch the ball away. He'd dive through spiked feet and throw himself onto approaching balls. Sometimes, he'd even run outside of his area to head away long passes propelled towards strikers charging at him, full speed ahead. Rather than sit back and wait for shots to be fired at him, Yashin chose to go to them, shouting instructions at his defenders, jumping into the action, and directing play from the penalty box.

When Russia hosted the World Cup in 2018, Yashin's face was plastered on every street corner. His status in Russia is near-mythical. This is partly because Yashin lifted the Russian team to heights they had never been—and have never reached again. The Soviets won gold at the 1956 Melbourne Olympics and won the Euros (then the European Nations' Cup) in 1960; they made the quarters of the 1958 and 1962 World Cups and the semis in England in 1966. Wins all propelled in large part by Yashin's stalwart refusal to concede goals.

But it's also because of what he symbolized. In the late '50s and '60s when Yashin played, the memory of World War II still burned vividly in the minds of those who had experienced it. Here was this man who, as a child, had been forced out of his home by an invading army. Now he was the quintessential last defender, rushing off his line while the world watched with bated breath. The soldier who wouldn't turn away and give up the fight, even after everyone else had, throwing himself in the way to prevent his country from being breached again.

FULL NAME:	DATE OF BIRTH:	PLACE OF BIRTH:	NATIONAL TEAM:	CAPS / GOALS:
Lev Ivanovich Yashin	*October 22, 1929*	*Moscow, USSR*	*Soviet Union, 1954–70*	*74 / –*

ZICO

BRAZIL 1982. A TEAM RECALLED with such nostalgia, such longing, like a summer fling that ended at the peak of its thrill, sealed forever in an amber of golden reverence. Each player was an artist, and together they formed a free-flowing, inventive ensemble, filling the field with nutmegs, back heels, rabonas, and the delight of creation. It was fantasy football in its truest sense, bringing to life the kind of enchanting, flamboyant approach to the game that for most people had previously only existed in their imaginations. The world was sliding into the gray conservatism of the Reagan era, but there before our eyes was Brazil in their glorious Technicolor.

If Sócrates, with his medical degree, his politics, and his perfectly measured through balls, was the brain of the team, Zico was the heartbeat. He possessed a combination of speed, touch, and creativity the likes of which had not been seen in many years. The Brazilian fans, reminded of another great man to wear the number 10, graced him with a fitting nickname: *the White Pelé.* As if on a one-man style mission, he would whirl towards goal, spinning around defenders, lifting the ball gently over outstretched legs, sending it lofting cheekily over unexpectant heads. One assumes that in Brazilian elementary schools, the concepts "around, through, and over," are taught with a video of Zico's international highlights.

His feathery free kicks—tantalizingly slow, lightly arching, impossible to block as they crested gracefully into the top left corner—were a sight to behold. His bicycle kick goal against New Zealand in the group stage is an exclamation point in sporting form. And it marks the start of a run of eight consecutive goals that Zico either scored or was directly involved in. Zico, Sócrates, Falcão, and Cerezo were the golden midfield of the golden team. There was this feeling in the air when they played, like they were unstoppable. Like it was perhaps not even humanly possible to stop something that godly and perfect. Global fans who couldn't have even found Brazil on a large-print, labeled map of South America were suddenly waving yellow and green flags, cheering for the Seleção. The swagger, the fearlessness, the finesse. It was everywhere. You just wanted to open your mouth and drink it in.

And then along came Italy. With the ironically named physical force that was Claudio Gentile marking Zico so closely that he had torn a six-inch hole in the side of his shirt by the end of the first half and striker Paolo Rossi exploiting Brazil's defensive gaps to score on the counterattack at every opportunity, the Brazilian carnival came abruptly crashing down. As quickly as it had begun, the fun was over; they were canonized alongside Hungary 1954 and Netherlands 1974 as the greatest team to not live up to its potential, and the world put the jogo bonito on the shelf in favor of a more pragmatic style of play.

It's not clear that Zico ever truly recovered from the 3–2 defeat to Italy. He moved to Udinese in Serie A the following fall, and while his spectacular goals quickly made him a fan favorite, his two years in Italy were punctuated by clashes with officials, beef with management, and tax evasion, as if he were on some kind of personal reparations mission to force the country to pay for their crimes. By 1985, he was back in Brazil, but a knee injury kept him mostly on the bench in Mexico in 1986, and by 1990, the golden midfield was gone and it was too late. When Zico talks about 1982, which he does often, with varying levels of bitterness, the loss at the hands of Italy isn't a personal failing. It's a global affront to good taste and common decency, as if it were not simply gauche, but actively offensive to play football less attractively. In all fairness to Zico, after seeing him in action, you're not quite sure he's wrong.

FULL NAME:	DATE OF BIRTH:	PLACE OF BIRTH:	NATIONAL TEAM:	CAPS / GOALS:
Arthur Antunes Coimbra	*March 3, 1953*	*Rio de Janeiro, Rio de Janeiro, Brazil*	*Brazil, 1976–86*	*71 / 48*

ZINÉDINE ZIDANE

JULY 12, 1998. TWO DAYS OUT FROM the 209th anniversary of the Storming of the Bastille. France, the host of the tournament, has just won the World Cup for the first time in 70 years of competition. Frenchmen, French-women, and little French children flood the streets, millions of them, pouring onto the Champs-Elysées, Paris's most famous avenue. They sing, they shout, they cry. There are flags waving, horns honking, fireworks going off left and right. It is a cacophonous mélange of noise and euphoria and patriotic fervor. It's difficult to make out specific words over the cracks of the fireworks and the blares of the car horns and the roar of one million people pouring their hearts out at once, but if you focus in, you can hear a sustained chant rumbling through the crowd: "Zidane Président." At the top of the avenue is the Arc de Triomphe, that most iconic of French monuments, dedicated to those who fought for France in the revolution and Napoleonic Wars. Projected onto the Arc's left facade are the unmistakable features of the team's central midfielder, Zinédine Zidane. He has just become the face of a nation.

Zidane, the son of Algerian immigrants, was raised in La Castellane, a small, crowded housing estate on the outskirts of Marseille. Often described as a labyrinth of concrete, La Castellane cuts a menacing figure, its blank white towers jutting up against the Massif des Calanques outside the city. The official term for the neighborhood, showcasing that quintessentially French knack for understatement, is a *quartier sensible*—a sensitive quarter. Zidane, his parents, and his four older siblings lived in an apartment so small the family could not all sit down to eat at once. Compared to many of their neighbors, the Zidane family was relatively well-off.

Zidane was a quiet kid—serious, a little anxious, conscientious, and eager to please. He played soccer in the long, skinny paving-stone courtyard outside of his building. There were no wings, so he learned to play down the middle; there were no rules, so he learned to protect the ball by keeping it at his feet. Eventually, people started to take note of the reserved, hardworking youth with the power to stop any ball dead in front of him and spin it exactly where he wanted it to go. At 14, Zidane left home to play professionally, moving first to Cannes, 100 miles down the coast, and then to Bordeaux, on the other side of the country. It was at Bordeaux that Zidane was christened *Zizou*, the nickname that would soon be on the tongues of the entire nation.

After a rocky start to the 1998 tournament saw him suspended two games for stomping on the ankle of a Saudi player during the group stage, Zidane came back to make history, scoring two nearly identical headers in the final against Brazil, propelling France to victory. The following year, 312 little Zinédines were born in France. They went crazy for Zidane, bestowing upon him the pure, unconditional love of a country for its favorite son. Because that's what Zizou was. The personification of France, not as it had been or as it hoped to be, but as it was. The Algerian kid with the French nickname. The poor, working-class boy who had made it out of the *quartier sensible*. The man who was calm, cool, and composed, but prone to the occasional violent outburst to remind you where he was from and exactly how much he was willing to take. Of course, the country loved him because he led them to World Cup glory and because he could hurtle and spin across the pitch as if the ball were glued to his feet. But more than that, they loved Zidane because they looked up at him and saw themselves.

Eight years later, France found itself back in the finals at the World Cup, this time against Italy. In the 110th minute, with the game drawn even at 1–1, Zidane, provoked by a comment from Italian defender Marco Materazzi, took one step forward, then turned around and headbutted Materazzi square in the chest. He was immediately sent off with a red card—only the fifth player in the history of the tournament to receive a red in a final. The game went into penalties and Italy beat France by one, their best penalty-taker sitting alone in the locker room, 250 yards away. This was Zidane's last professional match.

That evening, Paris went quiet for a moment in disbelief. The world waited, anticipating an eruption of anger from French fans to match Zidane's own fateful eruption. Yet, slowly but surely, they poured out of their houses, flooding the streets of Paris once again, waving their tricolored flags, singing, shouting, crying, and chanting "Zizou, Zizou." To love is to forgive.

FULL NAME:	DATE OF BIRTH:	PLACE OF BIRTH:	NATIONAL TEAM:	CAPS / GOALS:
Zinédine Yazid Zidane	*June 23, 1972*	*Marseille, France*	*France, 1994–2006*	*108 / 31*

ACKNOWLEDGMENTS

THE AUTHORS WOULD LIKE TO THANK:

The rest of the Men in Blazers Team. If Everton played as hard as them, the club would be Dynastic. Jonathan Williamson is the single greatest, as are Jordan Dalmedo, Jonah Buchanan, and the mighty, mighty Scott Debson. John Johnson, our Andrew Lloyd Webber.

ROGER BENNETT WOULD LIKE TO THANK:

The team at Chronicle. I have long revered Chronicle Books, and it is a joy to work with them on a project at long last. Thanks to Mark Tauber for launching the project, and Pamela Geismar and Eva Avery for leading it. We are indebted to the whole squad who worked on this book: Paul Kepple on design, Cecilia Santini as copyeditor and managing editor, Miles Doyle who edited, Michelle Triant the publicist, Liz Anderson the marketer, production manager Yuhong Guo, and the magical editorial director, Cara Bedick. Thanks to Malena Giordano for fact-checking. As always, indebted to agents Steve Herz and David Larabell.

Thanks above all to Nate Kitch. Our partner in this project. His aesthetic, creativity, passion, and patience are at Ballon d'Or levels. If Nate's Manchester United were half as talented as he is, they would be serial title-winners once again.

Big Love to my family: Samson, Ber, Zion, Ozzie, and Vanessa. And our dogs, Tony Hibbert and Martin Scorsese.

MIRANDA DAVIS WOULD LIKE TO THANK:

Or rather apologize to her family, friends, and Instagram followers for the endless complaints about the finite number of synonyms for *kick* in the English language. Special thanks to Ruthie, Best Davis and co-zine editor extraordinaire, who bore that burden (and many others) with an indulgence and willingness to help found only in sisters. Thank you to all the MIB boys for making it a pleasure to come to work every day, with a particular nod to Jonah, who fields an uncountable number of questions, concerns, and deranged football takes from me on a daily basis. To Eva, Cecilia, and Pamela, whose patience and attention to detail have heaved us over the finish line.

Last (but never least), thank you to Rog, who is an infinitely more generous, kind, and supportive boss than he has any right to be, and who included me in this project primarily on the basis of blind faith and a couple of funny emails I sent in 2019. An act of trust I hope I have repaid in kind.

SOURCES

Page 9: *In the words of that great poet-philosopher:* Jürgen Klopp. "Jürgen Klopp's Message to Supporters," Liverpool Football Club, March 13, 2020. https://www.liverpoolfc.com/news/first-team/390397-jurgen-klopp-message-to-supporters.

Page 11: *a part-time coach and hand-me-down kits:* Alexander Abnos. "Start of Something Big," *Sports Illustrated.* https://www.si.com/longform/soccer-goals/goal4.html.

Page 11: *Even US Soccer officials:* Glenn Crooks. "The Silent Trigger: The '91ers," *Our Game Magazine,* June 7, 2015. https://www.ourgamemag.com/2015/06/07/the-silent-trigger-the-91ers.

Page 12: *she wrote:* David Goldblatt. *The Games: A Global History of the Olympics* (New York: W. W. Norton, 2018), 123.

Page 16: *playing on one-and-a-half legs:* Daniel Storey. "Portrait of an icon: Roberto Baggio," *Footabll365,* November 4, 2015. https://www.football365.com/news/profile-of-an-icon-roberto-baggio.

Page 16: *The angels sing in his legs:* "World Cup Countdown: 6 Weeks to Go – Roberto Baggio & the Elusive Daemon of Genius," *Sports Illustrated,* May 13, 2018. https://www.si.com/soccer/2018/05/13/world-cup-countdown-6-weeks-go-roberto-baggio-elusive-daemon-genius.

Page 16: *Only those who have the courage:* Steve Slater. "Penalties Will Put World Cup Players on the Spot," *Reuters,* May 26, 2010. https://www.reuters.com/article/uk-soccer-world-penalties/penalties-will-put-world-cup-players-on-the-spot-idUKTRE64Q00C20100527.

Page 19: *salmon leaping up a waterfall:* Associated Press. "Gordon Banks, Goalkeeper Who Made a Famous Save, Is Dead at 81," *New York Times,* February 13, 2019. https://www.nytimes.com/2019/02/13/obituaries/gordon-banks-dead.html.

Page 24: *even negotiated their win bonus:* David Goldblatt. *The Ball Is Round: A Global History of Soccer* (New York: Riverhead Books, 2006).

Page 32: *Nearly all the core members:* Aidan Williams. "The Golden Ages of the Soviet National Team," *These Football Times,* July 26, 2017. https://thesefootballtimes.co/2017/07/26/red-army-the-golden-ages-of-the-soviet-national-team.

Page 36: *I have always held:* Andrew Shankweiler. *What Makes Us: Vero.* ESPN, 2015.

Page 40: *Listen, boss:* Adam Hurrey. "Gianluigi Buffon: 40 Reasons to Love the Juve, Italy Legend at Age 40," ESPN, January 28, 2018. https://www.espn.com/soccer/blog/espn-fc-united/68/post/3359993/gianluigi-buffon-turns-40-reasons-to-love-juventus-italy-goalkeeping-legend.

Page 43: *When the seagulls:* Simon Midgley. "When the Seagulls Follow the Trawler, It Is Because They Think Sardines Will Be Thrown into the Sea," *Independent,* April 1, 1995. https://www.independent.co.uk/news/uk/when-seagulls-follow-trawler-it-because-they-think-sardines-will-be-thrown-sea-1613641.html3.

Page 43: *Yeah, right:* Nick Moore. "Year Zero: The Making of Eric Cantona (Leeds/Manchester United 1992/93)," *FourFourTwo,* May 17, 2017. https://www.fourfourtwo.com/us/features/year-zero-making-eric-cantona-leedsmanchester-united-199293.

Page 47: *surveying the wreckage:* Harry Gregg. "I found Bobby Charlton and Dennis Viollet in a pool of water . . . I thought that they must be dead," *Daily Mail,* February 4, 2008. https://www.dailymail.co.uk/sport/football/article-512100/I-Bobby-Charlton-Dennis-Viollet-pool-water---I-thought-dead.html.

Page 48: *coined by captain:* "Icon: Brandi Chastain," Radio Free Soccer. https://radiofreesoccer.com/icon-brandi-chastain.

Page 51: *I don't go through life:* David Winner. *Brilliant Orange: The Neurotic Genius of Dutch Soccer* (New York: Harry N. Abrams, 2008).

Page 51: *the proudest memory:* Matt Davis and Richard Winton. "A Dutch Icon," BBC Sport, March 24, 2016. https://www.bbc.com/sport/live/35716471/page/2.

Page 52: *Keegan was quicker:* John Brewin. "Greatest Managers, No. 4: Bob Paisley," ESPN, August 8, 2013. https://www.espn.ph/football/news/story/_/id/1511253/bob-paisley.

Page 55: *When Real discovered:* Carl Worswick. "The Ball and the Gun," *The Blizzard* no. 7, December 2012.

Page 55: *the entire orchestra:* Ben Lyttleton. "Alfredo Di Stefano, the Foundation on Which Real Madrid's Success Stands," *Sports Illustrated,* July 7, 2014. https://www.si.com/soccer/2014/07/07/alfredo-di-stefano-real-madrid-dies-legacy.

Page 55: *In the words of Arrigo Sacchi:* Simon Talbot. "Alfredo Di Stefano: Icon," *FourFourTwo,* July 7, 2014. https://www.fourfourtwo.com/us/features/alfredo-di-stefano-icon.

Page 56: *A Los Angeles Times profile:* Grahame L. Jones. "Mexico's Rising Star," *Los Angeles Times,* June 27, 2004. https://www.latimes.com/archives/la-xpm-2004-jun-27-sp-nuwusa27-story.html.

Page 59: *Drogba—who was nowhere near:* Carl Anka. "Noughty Boys: Didier Drogba was the 'clutch' centre-forward who united a nation," BBC, April 2, 2019. https://www.bbc.co.uk/bbcthree/article/4ce7b135-2c8c-421f-8168-b31726ea3a46.

Page 60: *address his teammates:* Andy Brassell. "Remembering Eusebio," ESPN, January 4, 2014. https://www.espn.com/soccer/blog/name/93/post/1841023/headline.

Page 63: *On Sunday mornings:* Paul Cocozza. "Arsenal Enjoy Fleeting Moment," *The Guardian,* May 3, 2004. https://www.theguardian.com/football/2004/may/04/newsstory.sport6.

Page 64: *One eve-of-finals training injury:* Rob Smyth. "The Forgotten Story of Just Fontaine's 13-Goal World Cup," *The Guardian,* January 12, 2012. https://www.theguardian.com/sport/blog/2012/jan/12/just-fontaine-13-goals-world-cup.

Page 64: *I found myself with nothing:* Simon Burton. "The Joy of Six: Tales from the Boot Room," *The Guardian,* February 8, 2013. https://www.theguardian.com/sport/blog/2013/feb/08/the-joy-of-six-football-boots.

Page 64: *He claimed he could:* "The World Cup's Hat-Trick Kings," FIFA, July 6, 2014. https://www.fifa.com/tournaments/mens/worldcup/2014brazil/news/the-world-cup-s-hat-trick-kings-2399906.

Page 64: *I like to think:* Simon Burton. "The Joy of Six: Tales from the Boot Room," *The Guardian,* February 8, 2013. https://www.theguardian.com/sport/blog/2013/feb/08/the-joy-of-six-football-boots.

Page 67: *so called for his resemblance:* Amy Lawrence. "Cafu Born to Win," *The Guardian,* May 21, 2005. https://www.theguardian.com/football/2005/may/22/sport.comment2.

Page 68: *Described by his biographer:* Ruy Castro. *Garrincha: The Triumph and Tragedy of Brazil's Forgotten Footballing Hero* (New York: Yellow Jersey Press, 2004).

Page 68: *the greatest three minutes:* Paul Simpson. "World Cup Icons: 17-Year-Old Pele Makes Brazil's Own Psychologist Look Silly (1958)," *FourFourTwo,* June 19, 2019. https://www.fourfourtwo.com/features/world-cup-icons-17-year-old-pele-makes-brazils-own-psychologist-look-silly-1958.

Page 72: *the second poorest:* A.D. Horne. "Debts Paid, Romania Says," *Washington Post*, April 14, 1989.

Page 72: *ahead of only Albania:* Alison Smale. "Albania: Third World Misery in Europe," Associated Press, April 13, 1991. https://apnews.com/article/348de950d335c40a2e76db6a9ab18fa8.

Page 72: *the scores of their league matches:* Rob Gloster. "Awfully Tough to Beat a Ceausescu Team," *Los Angeles Times*, April 1, 1990. https://www.latimes.com/archives/la-xpm-1990-04-01-sp-883-story.html.

Page 76: *plucking dirt:* Molly McElwee. "Ada Hegerberg Exclusive Interview: 'I went through sadness, anger, incomprehension,'" *The Telegraph*, April 23, 2020. https://www.telegraph.co.uk/football/2020/04/23/ada-hegerberg-exclusive-interview-went-sadness-anger-incomprehension.

Page 79: *worse than any player:* Grahame L. Jones. "U.S. 'Sword' Still Has Three Edges," *Los Angeles Times*, May 31, 1995. https://www.latimes.com/archives/la-xpm-1995-05-31-sp-7817-story.html.

Page 79: *You can't draw better:* Jere Longman. "SOCCER; Losing Is Never an Option," *New York Times*, September 30, 2003. https://www.nytimes.com/2003/09/30/sports/soccer-losing-is-never-an-option.html.

Page 83: *Zlatan doesn't do auditions:* "Zlatan Ibrahimović: The 20 Most Ridiculous Things He Has Ever Said," *The Telegraph*, February 27, 2017. https://www.telegraph.co.uk/football/2016/01/29/zlatan-ibrahimovic-the-20-most-ridiculous-things-he-has-ever-sai/zlatan-doesnt-do-auditions.

Page 83: *We are Zweden:* Zlatan Ibrahimović. Twitter, November 13, 2017. https://twitter.com/ibra_official/status/930202878588936192?lang=en.

Page 87: *the most emphatic display:* Robin Bairner. "Sir Alex Ferguson: Manchester United History & Managerial Career Profiled," *Goal*, August 1, 2019. https://www.goal.com/en-us/news/sir-alex-ferguson-manchester-united-history-managerial/1oeahji6r8eu6189gihl5qfu3y.

Page 87: *Cork first:* Amy O'Connor. "This 'Cork First, Ireland Second' Cocktail Is the Ultimate Display of Cork Pride," *The Daily Edge*, March 7, 2017. https://www.dailyedge.ie/cork-first-ireland-second-3275816-Mar2017.

Page 87: *We could have watered it:* Barry Glendenning. "World Cup Moments: Roy Keane Tells McCarthy to 'stick it up your b*****ks,'" *Irish Times*, March 24, 2018. https://www.irishtimes.com/sport/soccer/international/world-cup-moments-roy-keane-tells-mccarthy-to-stick-it-up-your-b-ks-1.3480613.

Page 91: *He put French football:* James Eastham. "Tribute to Raymond Kopa, Ballon d'Or Winner and France's First Great Player," *When Saturday Comes*, March 8, 2017. https://www.wsc.co.uk/stories/13713-tribute-to-raymond-kopa-ballon-d-or-winner-and-france-s-first-great-player.

Page 91: *the greatest collective individualist:* Sid Lowe. "Farewell to Raymond Kopa, the Magic Man Who Helped Elevate Real Madrid," ESPN, March 3, 2017. https://www.espn.co.uk/football/spanish-primera-division/15/blog/post/3073923/raymond-kopa-was-an-innovator-who-formed-key-part-of-best-attack-ever-at-real-madrid.

Page 91: *he told the press:* Associated Press. "Raymond Kopa, the 'Napoleon' of Soccer, Dies at 85," *New York Times*, March 3, 2017. https://www.nytimes.com/2017/03/03/sports/soccer/raymond-kopa-dead-real-madrid-star.html.

Page 95: *Cruyff admitted:* Planet Football. "15 Quotes on Michael Laudrup's Genius: 'He saw things that nobody else saw,'" *Planet Football*, August 30, 2019. https://www.planetfootball.com/quick-reads/15-of-the-best-quotes-on-michael-laudrup-he-saw-things-that-nobody-else-saw.

Page 96: *Lilly remarked:* "espnW Names Wilton's Kristine Lilly as the 36th Greatest Athlete of the Last 40 Years," *The Hour*, May 4, 2012. https://www.thehour.com/wilton/article/espnW-names-Wilton-s-Kristine-Lilly-as-the-36th-8142550.php.

Page 100: *a brief profile:* Philip Hersh. "Tiny Swede Is a Titanic Scorer," *Chicago Tribune*, September 20, 2003. https://www.chicagotribune.com/news/ct-xpm-2003-09-20-0309200227-story.html.

Page 103: *a challenge to coach:* Sam Borden. "Pia Sundhage of Sweden Is a Coach at Home on the Move," *New York Times*, June 9, 2015. https://www.nytimes.com/2015/06/10/sports/soccer/for-pia-sundhage-swedens-itinerant-coach-its-old-home-week.html.

Page 104: *Maradona himself said:* Martyn Herman. "How Maradona's 'Hand of God' Quote Went Round the World," Reuters, November 25, 2020. https://www.reuters.com/article/soccer-argentina-maradona-reuters/how-maradonas-hand-of-god-quote-went-round-the-world-idUSKBN2853CL.

Page 108: *he petulantly declared:* "I Am an Idol and Should Be Treated Like One, Says Lothar Matthaeus," *The Guardian*, November 8, 2009. https://www.theguardian.com/football/2009/nov/08/lothar-matthaeus-germany-football-idol.

Page 111: *When Stan gets the ball:* Jonathan Molyneux-Carter. "Rewind to 1964: Stanley Matthews' FA Cup Record, Aged 49, with Stoke," ESPN, March 7, 2017. https://www.espn.com/soccer/english-fa-cup/0/blog/post/3076923/rewind-to-1964-stanley-matthews-fa-cup-record-aged-49-with-stoke.

Page 112: *Vittorio Pozzo swore*: Damian Mannion. "Superstar Giuseppe Meazza: Italy's World Cup Winner with a Stadium Named After Him and a Love of Scoring Goals and Brothels," *talkSport*, September 18, 2018. https://talksport.com/football/387103/giuseppe-meazza-was-italys-world-cup-winner-who-had-a-love-of-scoring-goals-and-sleeping-in-brothels.

Page 116: *I don't really care:* Tim Stillman. "Vivianne Miedema Reacts to Victory Over Brighton," *Arseblog News*, September 29, 2019. https://arseblog.news/2019/09/vivianne-miedema-reacts-to-victory-over-brighton.

Page 120: *First, she goes around:* Martin Rogers, "Meet the USA's Best Friend and Biggest Threat on Japanese World Cup Team," *USA Today*, July 4, 2015. https://www.usatoday.com/story/sports/soccer/2015/07/04/world-cup-final-usa-japan-aya-miyama/29716849.

Page 123: *proclaimed succinctly:* Leonard Solms. "Meet Portia Modise, Africa's Highest Goalscorer and Defiant Gay Icon," ESPN, June 28, 2021. https://www.espn.com/soccer/south-africa-rsaw/story/4417448/meet-portia-modiseafricas-highest-goalscorer-and-defiant-gay-icon.

Page 124: *Pelé called Moore . . . Sir Alex Ferguson called him:* Anthony Sealey. "Legends: Bobby Moore," *Total Football Magazine*, October 30, 2011. https://www.totalfootballmag.com/features/legends/legends-bobby-moore.

Page 124: *George Best once proclaimed:* Tony Parsons. "Bobby Moore: His Incredible Life Story," *GQ Magazine*, January 12, 2017. https://www.gq-magazine.co.uk/article/bobby-moore-wife-tina-england.

Page 127: *she had replied:* Carolina Morace. "No Longer a Man's Game," *The Players Tribune*, February 11, 2017. https://www.theplayerstribune.com/articles/carolina-morace-womens-soccer.

Page 127: *Morace pontificated:* Frances Kennedy. "Letter from Rome: Morace Takes on the Men," *Independent*, June 27, 1999. https://www.independent.co.uk/sport/letter-from-rome-morace-takes-on-the-men-1102974.html.

Page 131: *Müller proclaimed:* Mark Lovell. "Lewandowski Reaches 100 Bayern Goals, But Muller Still Out Front," ESPN, March 12, 2017. https://www.espn.com/soccer/club/bayern-munich/132/blog/post/3080642/where-does-robert-lewandowski-sit-in-bayern-munich-history.

Page 131: *His motto:* "Gerd Müller, Supreme Striker at Bayern Munich Who Was Also a Record-Breaking Goal-Scorer for West Germany – Obituary," *The Telegraph*, August 15, 2021. https://www.telegraph.co.uk/obituaries/2021/08/15/gerd-muller-supreme-german-striker-bayern-munich-also-record.

Page 131: *In Müller's words:* Vineet Basu. "Unspectacular, Unpredictable, Unstoppable: Gerd 'de Bomber' Mueller," *Sportskeeda*, December 27, 2012. khttps://www.sportskeeda.com/football/unspectacular-unpredictable-unstoppable-gerd-der-bomber-mueller.

Page 135: *wrote the* New York Times: Paddy Agnew. "Nakata, 21, Lifts Perugia and Ranks 5th on League Scoring Chart: Italy's Japanese Soccer Sensation," *New York Times*, November 30, 1998. https://www.nytimes.com/1998/11/30/sports/IHT-nakata-21-lifts-perugia-and-ranks-5th-on-league-scoring-chart.html.

Page 136: *Bruno Bini proclaimed:* Julie Lévy-Marchal. "Louisa Necib, itinéraire d'une enfant de la balle," *20 Sport*, June 29, 2011. https://www.20minutes.fr/sport/750209-20110629-louisa-necib-itineraire-enfant-balle.

Page 140: *Get me to the hospital:* Hilary Mitchell. "Why We Should All Be More Like Legendary Lesbian Football Player and All-Around Badass Lily Parr," *Pink News*, February 14, 2021. https://www.pinknews.co.uk/2021/02/14/lily-parr-lesbian-footballer-football-lgbt-history-month.

Page 140: *a local newspaper declared:* Amy Lofthouse. "LGBT+ History Month: Lily Parr – Trailblazer with a 'Kick Like a Mule,'" BBC Sport, February 5, 2021. https://www.bbc.com/sport/football/55884099.

Page 144: *In the words of Henry Kissinger:* Henry Kissinger. "Pele: The Phenomenon," *Time*, June 14, 1999. http://content.time.com/time/subscriber/article/0,33009,991264,00.html.

Page 147: *I'm a well-educated person:* Dan Roan. "UEFA President Michel Platini Will Not Return £16,000 Watch," BBC Sport, September 19, 2014. https://www.bbc.com/sport/football/29285817.

Page 147: *When I was a kid:* John Brewin. "All-Time Top 20: No. 18 Michel Platini," ESPN, April 7, 2014. https://www.espn.com/soccer/blog/name/93/post/1845136/headline.

Page 148: la Republicca *noted:* Sammie Frimpong. "The Sad Case of Saadi: Meet Muammar Gaddafi's Footballing Son," *Goal*, March 8, 2014. https://www.goal.com/en-gh/news/4375/comment/2014/03/08/4670408/the-sad-case-of-saadi-meet-muammar-gaddafis-footballing-son.

Page 151: *the BBC wrote:* "Obituary: Ferenc Puskás," BBC Sport, November 17, 2006. http://news.bbc.co.uk/sport2/hi/football/1035447.stm.

Page 151: *Syd Owen noted:* Richard Jolly. "Tactical Trends for the 2018 World Cup," ESPN July 14, 2014. https://www.espn.co.uk/football/blog/name/67/post/1948199/headline.

Page 155: *a little finagling:* Wendie Renard. "Life at the End of the World," *The Players' Tribune*, January 17, 2019. https://www.theplayerstribune.com/articles/wendie-renard-life-at-the-end-of-the-world.

Page 155: *the* New York Times *once described her:* Christopher Clarey. "For Wendie Renard and France, Another Misstep and Another Win," *New York Times*, June 17, 2019. https://www.nytimes.com/2019/06/17/sports/womens-world-cup-france-wendie-renard.html.

Page 156: *she once explained:* Luke McLaughlin. "1993: Hege Riise," UEFA, July 4, 1993. https://www.uefa.com/womenseuro/news/011b-0e1087d9e72a-015c6b967136-1000--1993-hege-riise.

Page 159: *He's not a man:* Rob Smyth. "Ronaldo at 40: Il Fenomeno's Legacy as Greatest Ever No9, Despite Dodgy Knees," *The Guardian*, September 17, 2016. https://www.theguardian.com/football/blog/2016/sep/17/ronaldo-40-birthday-brazil-greatest-ever-striker.

Page 160: *Brian Phillips once wrote:* Brian Phillips. "Confessions of a Failed Ronaldo Fan," ESPN, August 16, 2018. https://www.espn.com/espn/feature/story/_/id/24340372/cristiano-ronaldo-probably-most-gifted-athlete-history-world-why-hard-complicated-writes-brian-phillips.

Page 160: *Ronaldo once ascribed:* Tony Manfred. "Cristiano Ronaldo on Why People Hate Him: 'I am handsome, rich, and a great player,'" *Business Insider*, September 15, 2011. https://www.businessinsider.com/cristiano-ronaldo-real-madrid-2011-9.

Page 163: *In this condition:* Thomas Rogers. "Man in the News; from Disgrace to Hero," *New York Times*, July 12, 1982. https://www.nytimes.com/1982/07/12/sports/man-in-the-news-from-disgrace-to-hero.html.

Page 168: *big blond Viking:* Jere Longman. "World Cup '98: Strength in the Mouth of the Goal; the Assertive Schmeichel Gives Denmark Advantage," *New York Times*, July 3, 1998. https://www.nytimes.com/1998/07/03/sports/world-cup-98-strength-mouth-goal-assertive-schmeichel-gives-denmark-advantage.html.

Page 172: *she asked incredulously:* Kristina Rutherford. "The Evolution of Christine Sinclair," *Sportsnet*. https://www.sportsnet.ca/soccer/big-read-the-evolution-of-christine-sinclair.

Page 172: *Sinclair was photographed:* Ken MacQueen. "A Bronze Medal Comeback for Canada's Soccer Women," *Maclean's*, August 9, 2012. https://www.macleans.ca/society/a-bronze-medal-comeback-for-canadas-soccer-women/.

Page 172: *The first thing he did:* Stuart James. "John Herdman: The English Coach Out to Transform Canadian Football," *The Athletic*, February 27, 2021. https://theathletic.com/2413906/2021/02/28/john-herdman-the-english-coach-out-to-transform-canadian-football.

Page 175: *Alfred Polgar once wrote:* Jonathan Wilson. *Inverting the Pyramid: The History of Soccer Tactics* (New York: Bold Type Books, 2018), 58.

Page 179: *So declared striker:* Patrick Kingsley and Bim Adewunmi. "Why Women's Football in England Is a Whole New Ball Game," *The Guardian*, June 21, 2011. https://www.theguardian.com/football/2011/jun/21/england-womens-football-transformed.

Page 179: *the answer was:* Anna Kessel. "England's Hot Shot," *The Guardian*, September 2, 2007. https://www.theguardian.com/sport/2007/sep/02/football.newsstory1.

Page 180: *I am an anti-athlete:* Brian Glanville. "Sócrates Obituary," *The Guardian*, December 4, 2011. https://www.theguardian.com/football/2011/dec/04/socrates.

Page 180: *Pelé once remarked:* Brian Glanville. "Sócrates Obituary," *The Guardian*, December 4, 2011. https://www.theguardian.com/football/2011/dec/04/socrates.

Page 183: *Solo stepped onto:* Molly Langmuir. "The Audacity of Hope Solo," *Elle*, June 11, 2019. https://www.elle.com/culture/a27891036/hope-solo-soccer-fifa-womens-world-cup.

Page 183: *Solo called the Swedes:* "Hope Solo Explains 'Cowards' Comments on Swedish Television," *Sports Illustrated*, October 14, 2016. https://www.si.com/soccer/2016/10/14/hope-solo-sweden-olympics-cowards-explanation.

Page 184: *Stoichkov is a predator:* Simon Talbot. "The Incredible Adventures of Romario and Stoichkov in Barcelona," *FourFourTwo*, May 7, 2019. https://www.fourfourtwo.com/us/features/romario-hristo-stoichkov-barcelona-johan-cruyff-manchester-united.

Page 184: *God is Bulgarian:* William Gildea. "Bulgaria's Nasty Boy Plays Nice," *Washington Post*, July 12, 1994. https://www.washingtonpost.com/archive/sports/1994/07/12/bulgarias-nasty-boy-plays-nice/ce400387-c6fb-44ff-bd6d-7e813e41bde0.

Page 184: *There are only two Christs:* "World Cup Countdown: 6 Weeks to Go – Hristo Stoichkov Inspires Bulgaria to the Brink of Glory," *Sports Illustrated*, May 11, 2018. https://www.si.com/soccer/2018/05/11/world-cup-countdown-6-weeks-go-hristo-stoichkov-inspires-bulgaria-brink-glory.

Page 191: *tells a story:* Sam Borden. "Pia Sundhage of Sweden Is a Coach at Home on the Move," *New York Times*, June 9, 2015. https://www.nytimes.com/2015/06/10/sports/soccer/for-pia-sundhage-swedens-itinerant-coach-its-old-home-week.html.

Page 192: *described by journalist:* Aidan Williams. "Carlos Valderrama and the Moment I Fell in Love with Colombian Football," *These Football Times*, December 8, 2020. https://thesefootballtimes.co/2020/08/12/carlos-valderrama-and-the-moment-i-fell-in-love-with-colombian-football.

Page 196: *We are not fucking losing:* Kate Fagan. "After the Storm," ESPN, October 8, 2014. http://www.espn.com/espn/feature/story/_/id/11655083/us-women-soccer-star-abby-wambach-lives-extreme.

Page 199: *Weah promised:* "Excerpts from the New President's Inaugural Address on 22 January 2018," United Nations Peacekeeping, March 30, 2018. https://peacekeeping.un.org/en/excerpts-new-presidents-inaugural-address-22-january-2018-his-excellency-mr-george-manneh-weah.

Page 203: *I pass and I move:* Planet Football. "10 Xavi Quotes to Explain His Football Philosophy: 'Combine, Pass, Play,'" *Planet Football*, November 9, 2021. https://www.planetfootball.com/quick-reads/x-xavi-quotes-to-explain-his-football-philosophy-combine-pass-play.

Page 203: *Dani Alves described:* Sid Lowe. "Xavi Hernández, the Football Romantic Set to Make Champions League History," *The Guardian*, September 30, 2014. https://www.theguardian.com/football/blog/2014/sep/30/xavi-hernandez-champions-league-record.

Page 208: *Zidane was christened* Zizou: Patrick Fort and Jean Philippe. *Zidane* (London: Ebury Press, 2018).

Page 208: *312 little Zinédines:* Jean Le Bail. "Comment les Zinedine et Bixente ont peuplé les maternités après la Coupe du monde 1998," *L'Équipe*, October 30, 2015. https://www.lequipe.fr/Football/Actualites/Comment-les-zinedine-et-bixente-ont-peuple-les-maternites-apres-la-coupe-du-monde-1998/601098.

PHOTOGRAPHY CREDITS

Cover illustrations are based on photographs from the following sources:

Mia Hamm: REUTERS / Alamy Stock Photo

Diego Maradona: dpa picture alliance archive / Alamy Stock Photo

Marta: IMAGO / Ulmer

Lionel Messi: REUTERS / Alamy Stock Photo

Pelé: Action Plus Sports Images / Alamy Stock Photo

Background cover image:

Miro Novak / Alamy Stock Photo

Illustrations are based on photographs from the following sources.

Michelle Akers: John T Greilick / AP / Shutterstock

José Andrade: Public Domain via Wikimedia Commons

Nadine Angerer: IMAGO / Xinhua

Roberto Baggio: Allstar Picture Library Ltd / Alamy

Gordon Banks: Roger Bamber / *Daily Mail* / Shutterstock

Franco Baresi: Offside Sports Photography

Gabriel Batistuta: Offside Sports Photography

Franz Beckenbauer: *L'Équipe* / Offside Sports Photography

Kyle Beckerman: BPI / Shutterstock

David Beckham: Mark Leech / Offside Sports Photography

George Best: *Daily Mail* / Shutterstock

Oleg Blokhin: SPUTNIK / Alamy

Zbigniew Boniek: Colorsport / Shutterstock

Vero Boquete: Francesco Scaccianoce / LiveMedia / Shutterstock

Lucy Bronze: Dave Shopland / BPI / Shutterstock

Gianluigi Buffon: Kerim Okten / EPA / Shutterstock

Eric Cantona: Colorsport / Shutterstock

John Charles: John Varley / Varley Picture Agency / Offside Sports Photography

Bobby Charlton: Gerry Cranham / Offside Sports Photography

Brandi Chastain: REUTERS / Alamy

Johan Cruyff: Bert Verhoeff / Anefo Collection / Dutch National Archives

Kenny Dalglish: Jim Duxbury / ANL / Shutterstock

Alfredo Di Stéfano: *L'Équipe* / Offside Sports Photography

Maribel Domínguez: IMAGO / epd

Didier Drogba: Back Page Images / Shutterstock

Eusébio: Trinity Mirror / Mirrorpix / Alamy

Julie Fleeting: Colorsport / Shutterstock

Just Fontaine: *L'Équipe* / Offside Sports Photography

Formiga: Armando Franca / AP / Shutterstock

Garrincha: *L'Équipe* / Global Photo / Offside Sports Photography

Paul Gascoigne, first image: *L'Équipe* / Offside Sports Photography; second image: Mark Leech / Offside Sports Photography

Gheorghe Hagi: Douglas C Pizac / AP / Shutterstock

Mia Hamm: Chris O'Meara / AP / Shutterstock

Ada Hegerberg: Balazs Czagany / EPA-EFE / Shutterstock

April Heinrichs: Gary Hershorn / REUTERS / Alamy

Thierry Henry: Back Page Images / Shutterstock

Zlatan Ibrahimović: Colorsport / Shutterstock

Nwankwo Kanu: IMAGO / Bildbyran

Roy Keane: Mark Leech / Offside Sports Photography

Sam Kerr: AP / Shutterstock

Raymond Kopa: AGIP / Bridgeman Images

Stephanie Labbé: CHINE NOUVELLE / SIPA / Shutterstock

Michael Laudrup: IMAGO / Magic

Kristine Lilly: Back Page Images / Shutterstock

Gary Lineker: Colorsport / Shutterstock

Hanna Ljungberg: Pablo Martinez Monsivais / AP / Shutterstock

Carli Lloyd: Martin Meissner / AP / Shutterstock

Diego Maradona: Carlo Fumagalli / AP / Shutterstock

Marta: Sipa / Shutterstock

Lothar Matthäus: Colorsport / Shutterstock

Stanley Matthews: *L'Équipe* / Offside Sports Photography

Guiseppe Meazza: Archivi Farabola / Offside Sports Photography

Lionel Messi: Sebastiao Moreira / EPA / Shutterstock

Vivianne Miedema: Gavin Ellis / TGS Photo / Shutterstock

Roger Milla: Public Domain via Wikimedia Commons

Aya Miyama: Martin Meissner / AP / Shutterstock

Portia Modise: WENN Rights Ltd / Alamy

Bobby Moore: Gerry Cranham / Offside Sports Photography

Carolina Morace: Colorsport / Shutterstock

Alex Morgan: Charlotte Wilson / Offside Sports Photography

Gerd Müller: Witters / Offside Sports Photography

Nadia Nadim: IMAGO / Panoramic

Hidetoshi Nakata: Back Page Images / Shutterstock

Louisa Nécib: Jonathan Larsen / Diadem Images / Alamy

Perpetua Nkwocha: Ahmad Yusni / EPA / Shutterstock

Lily Parr: Courtesy of the Lizzy Ashcroft Collection

Christie Pearce Rampone: Julie Jacobson / AP / Shutterstock

Pelé: Claude Parnall / Evening News / Shutterstock

Michel Platini: Peter Robinson / PA Images / Alamy

Birgit Prinz: Rolf Vennenbernd / dpa Picture Alliance Archive / Alamy

Ferenc Puskás: R Fortune / *Daily Mail* / Shutterstock

Megan Rapinoe: Francisco Seco / AP / Shutterstock

Wendie Renard: Efrem Lukatsky / AP / Shutterstock

Hege Riise: Thomas Kienzle / AP / Shutterstock

Ronaldo: Itsuo Inouye / AP / Shutterstock

Cristiano Ronaldo: Pedro Fiuza / NurPhoto / Shutterstock

Paolo Rossi: AP / Shutterstock

Hugo Sánchez: Offside Sports Photography

Homare Sawa: Kai Pfaffenbach / REUTERS / Alamy

Peter Schmeichel: Colorsport / Shutterstock

Briana Scurry: Nick Ut / AP / Shutterstock

Christine Sinclair: Gavin Ellis / TGSPHOTO / Shutterstock

Matthias Sindelar: *L'Équipe* / Offside Sports Photography

Sissi: REUTERS / Alamy

Kelly Smith: WENN Rights Ltd / Alamy

Sócrates: Wolfgang Rattay / REUTERS / Alamy

Hope Solo: Eugenio Savio / AP / Shutterstock

Hristo Stoichkov: Tony Marshall / PA Images / Alamy

Luis Suárez: Touring Club Italiano / Marka / UIG / Bridgeman Images

Davor Šuker: Luca Bruno / AP / Shutterstock

Pia Sundhage: Dan Hansson / SvD / SCANPIX / TT News Agency / Alamy

Carlos Valderrama: Mark Leech / Offside Sports Photography

Marco van Basten: Colorsport / Shutterstock

Abby Wambach: Martin Meissner / AP / Shutterstock

George Weah: *L'Équipe* / Offside Sports Photography

Sun Wen: John Buckle / PA Images / Alamy

Xavi: Giuliano Bevilacqua / Shutterstock

Lev Yashin: *Daily Mail* / Shutterstock

Zico: John Varley / Varley Picture Agency / Offside Sports Photography

Zinédine Zidane: Jerry Lampen / REUTERS / Alamy

ABOUT THE AUTHORS AND ILLUSTRATOR

THE AUTHORS are part of the team behind Men in Blazers, a platform committed to growing the game we love, football, in the nation we adore, the United States of America. Ardent believers that "Soccer is America's Sport of the Future . . . as it has been since 1972." Find our podcasts and television show via our Twitter and Instagram at @meninblazers. Courage.

NATE KITCH is an award-winning illustrator, artist, and maverick based in Oxford in the UK. He creates collaged works for various publications all over the world. Often drawn to the abstract and textural, he is inspired by chess, jazz, and absurdism, which all pour into the melting pot that is his own mind, where he spends many days occupied. Find Nate's work at natekitch.com and @natekitch on Instagram and Twitter.

ROGER BENNETT

Nathan Congleton

MICHAEL DAVIES

MIRANDA DAVIS

Chloe Edwards

NATE KITCH